STORYTELLING
AND
SPIRITUALITY
IN
JUDAISM

Storytelling and Spirituality in Judaism

YITZHAK BUXBAUM

A JASON ARONSON BOOK

ROWMAN & LITTLEFIELD PUBLISHERS, INC.
Lanham • Boulder • New York • Toronto • Oxford

A JASON ARONSON BOOK

ROWMAN & LITTLEFIELD PUBLISHERS, INC.

Published in the United States of America
by Rowman & Littlefield Publishers, Inc.
A wholly owned subsidary of The Rowman & Littlefield Publishing Group, Inc.
4501 Forbes Boulevard, Suite 200, Lanham, Maryland 20706
www.rowmanlittlefield.com

PO Box 317
Oxford
OX2 9RU, UK

British Library Cataloguing in Publication Information Available

Library of Congress Cataloging-in-Publication Data

Buxbaum, Yitzhak.
 Storytelling and spirituality in Judaism / by Yitzhak Buxbaum.
  p.   cm.
 Includes bibliographical references and index.
 ISBN 0-7657-6166-1 (cloth : alk. paper) — ISBN 1-56821-173-2 (pbk. : alk.
paper)
 1. Hasidim—Legends—History and criticism.   2. Parables, Hasidic—
History and criticism.   3. Legends, Jewish— History and criticism.
 4. Spiritual life—Judaism.   5. Storytelling—Religious aspects—Judaism.
 I. Title.
 BM532.B85   1994
 296.1'9—dc20   94-6122

Printed in the United States of America

℗™ The paper used in this publication meets the minimum requirements of American
National Standard for Information Sciences—Permanence of Paper for Printed Library
Materials, ANSI/NISO Z39.48-1992.

Contents

PART II HASIDIC TEACHING
ABOUT THE METHODS AND PRACTICES
OF STORYTELLING

How to Learn, Tell, and Listen

Dedication
and
Acknowledgments

I would like to express my deepest appreciation to my wonderful mother and friend, Jeanette Buxbaum, for reading the manuscript and providing suggestions and help regarding language, grammar and style. During the preparation of this book, on the 29th day of the month of Nissan, the year 5754–April 10, 1994–my beloved mother, of beautiful soul, passed away. I dedicate this book to her blessed memory that shall shine before my eyes every moment of my life. I would like to thank Professor Samuel Dresner and my friend and fellow Jewish storyteller, Justin Lewis of Toronto, Canada, for reading the manuscript and offering suggestions about both form and content. I am particularly grateful to Justin for advising me to put the story of The Sigh and the Sneer, which I had relegated to an endnote, into the text; it became the major part of an added chapter, Chapter 4. I would also like to gratefully acknowledge the gracious assistance I received at the Hebrew Union College Library in New York City, from Dr. Philip Miller, Head Librarian, and Mr. Henry Resnick, library assistant.

Introduction:
Storytelling and Spirituality

Storytelling has always been a prime vehicle for communicating spirituality. Some of the greatest Jewish teachers were expert storytellers. Then, as time passed, events in their own lives also became stories. Judaism is largely based on and communicated through tales. The Torah has two parts: instruction about commandments, and stories. "In the beginning . . . ," it starts, as if the Holy One, blessed be He, was an elder with a long white beard, who sat us on His knee and began: "Once upon a time." In recent centuries, Hasidism revived sacred storytelling and the sacred story—especially tales about tzaddikim, the hasidic holy men.

The purpose of this book is to elevate stories and storytelling in people's esteem, so they will understand their holiness and appreciate them at their full worth. There are those who enjoy stories and storytelling but in the back of their minds think, "After all, they're only stories." But in the same way that the Western Wall of the Temple is not just a wall, a mere pile of stones, neither are the stories of the Torah or of the tzaddikim "just stories."

Holy stories are the light of the world. When we understand that, when both tellers and listeners know they are engaged in sacred activity, we will hold stories and storytelling more dear. The teller will tell with the tongue of faith, the listeners will hear with ears of faith, and the circle of holiness will be closed.

STORYTELLING REVIVAL AND RELIGIOUS REVIVAL

In recent years storytelling has made a tremendous comeback. Increasing numbers of people have been attracted to this ancient art form that was long overshadowed by more powerful modern arts and entertainments. What accounts for this renewed popularity? Part of the answer is that while storytelling has the immediacy and liveliness of the theater, its having only one performer makes it much more affordable and accessible, with people easily relating to its modest and simple format. Storytelling's charm can be compared to that of folksinging. Although folksinging cannot compete with the sophistication of large orchestras or the dynamism of popular music, what it does have is authenticity. Storytelling also shares that kind of appeal. It certainly cannot match TV, movies, or the theater in scale, variety, or complexity. But it does have an earthy and homely charm that takes us back to a simpler and truer time. It is both authentic and intimate. As part of this modern renewal of interest in storytelling, Jewish storytelling also has experienced a revival.

At the same time as this storytelling revival has taken place, there has been a Jewish religious revival in America. The point where these two streams in the Jewish current merge is in religious storytelling. The new Jewish storytellers, professionals and amateurs, regularly tell hasidic and other religious tales. But as with many other things, newcomers can easily imagine they are discoverers. Columbus and the Europeans "discovered" America, but the Indians had always been here. Similarly, although newcomers enchanted by Jewish storytelling might think they have landed on virgin territory, that is hardly the case. Stories and storytelling have always been important in Judaism, particularly in Hasidism.

FROM STORIES TO STORYTELLING

Over the last generation, interest in hasidic stories has grown tremendously, spurred by the writings of Martin Buber and Elie Wiesel among others. Many people are attracted by the extraordinary figures of the hasidic rebbes and have learned to appreciate the profound wisdom of hasidic tales. But there is also much to learn from the hasidic spiritual practice of story*telling* that can enhance and enrich contemporary Judaism.

Most people are familiar with hasidic tales from books, but oral storytelling *preceded* and was the original source for most written collections— in Hebrew, Yiddish, and later English. Today also a vibrant culture of oral storytelling flourishes among hasidim. There are many thousands of stories floating around, passed from mouth to ear, from rebbes to hasidim and from parents to children. Some have appeared in print, others have not. Every so often a new written collection is published, drawn from this pool of oral tales. There is no question that if the hasidic custom of widespread participation in telling and listening to stories is adopted by the larger Jewish community, storytelling can contribute considerably to the current renewal of Judaism in America.

I have always loved hasidic stories. The spiritual wisdom they contain nourishes my soul like nothing else, and they regularly provide me with much of my religious inspiration. Over the years I developed the habit of repeating to family and friends hasidic tales that were meaningful to me and enlivened me. Gradually, I began to tell longer stories and tried to communicate my love for Judaism to others through storytelling. Finally, I became a *maggid*, a religious storyteller, and tell hasidic tales, usually in Jewish settings.

I am constantly studying Hasidism and reading hasidic stories, and in recent years I have discovered that there are many hasidic teachings and stories *about* storytelling. There is a "mini-theology" of storytelling. Just as there is a theology of prayer—for example, what it is, why we pray, how prayer "works"—so is there a theology of storytelling. The rebbes asked and answered the questions: What is the place of storytelling among spiritual practices? Why do stories captivate and charm us? How should they be told and listened to? What are their effects? That they reflected on storytelling this way undoubtedly shows its importance in Hasidism. Their teachings have fascinated me because of my own intense involvement with stories and storytelling, and as my research progressed and my knowledge grew, I realized that others would be interested in learning about this subject too.

That is why I have written this book. I hope it will increase people's appreciation of hasidic stories when they become aware of their living, oral context; inspire those who have a taste for hasidic stories to begin storytelling; and encourage those already involved to broaden their activity and deepen their spiritual relation to their storytelling. Because in Judaism storytelling and spirituality are intertwined.

I

STORYTELLING IN HASIDISM

History and Development
of Hasidic Storytelling

1

What Made Hasidic Storytelling Different?

STORYTELLING FROM BIBLICAL TO PRE-HASIDIC TIMES

It is not my purpose in this book to write a history of Jewish storytelling. My main interest and focus is on hasidic storytelling. But it is valuable to at least glance at what preceded in order to appreciate the innovations that made hasidic storytelling different.

The ancient history of Jewish storytelling is shrouded in obscurity. Only a few meager details in the Torah cast any light on the subject. One of them is in connection with Passover.

The Story of the Exodus

From the earliest times, Jewish parents passed on Jewish stories and traditions to their children, particularly on the occasions of festivals and ceremonies. Today also at the Passover *seder*, when the child ritually asks the meaning of the unusual ceremony, his parent answers by recounting the story of the Exodus. When the Torah commands the Passover sacrifice, it says: "And when your children ask you, 'What do you mean by this service?' you shall reply: 'It is the sacrifice of the Lord's passover, for He passed over the houses of the children of Israel in Egypt, when He slew the Egyptians but spared our houses'" (Exodus 12:26). When the Torah commands eating *matzot*, unleavened bread, it says: "And you shall tell (*v'higad'ta*) your son on that day, 'It is because of what the Lord did for me when I came out

of Egypt'" (Exodus 13:8). From such verses the rabbis derived the obligation on Passover to relate the story of the Exodus, a telling (*haggadah*) whose
form was finally fixed and written down in the *Haggadah* (the text of the
ritual storytelling).

Gehazi and Elisha

In biblical times there must have been expert storytellers who specialized in recounting the legends of Israel, but we know little about such
people. Perhaps sacred storytelling was usually the responsibility not of a
guild of storytellers[1] but of a guild of "sons (disciples) of the prophets." In
one of the few places where the Torah records a storytelling event, we find
Gehazi, the disciple and personal attendant of the prophet Elisha, telling
stories about his master to the king of Israel. "Now the king was talking
with Gehazi, the servant of the man of God, saying: 'Please tell me all the
great things that Elisha has done'" (2 Kings 8:1-6). While Gehazi was telling the king how Elisha had brought back to life a sick boy who had died,
the boy arrived, with his mother, who verified the story to the king. It is
only to be expected that the prophets' closest followers would pass on
stories about them, and therefore that the king would ask Gehazi about
Elisha, for who would know more stories about his great deeds than his
disciple and personal attendant?

Throughout the Ages

Jewish religious books contain a tremendous number of stories—which
were undoubtedly originally oral—from every century and every place where
Jews have dwelt, a fact that provides evidence of the enduring popularity
of storytelling among Jews. Both religious teachers and ordinary people
have engaged in storytelling, and from the earliest times folk preachers,
called *maggidim* (singular, *maggid*), have specialized in using stories and
parables in their sermons.[2] The Talmud and *Midrash* are full of folktales,
fables, and parables told by the rabbis and also of stories about the rabbis
themselves. Throughout the ages, storytelling has been an integral part of
Jewish religious life, but with Hasidism it finally came into its own.

STORYTELLING IN HASIDISM

Hasidism is the radical pietistic reform movement that transformed Eastern European Jewish life in the eighteenth and nineteenth centuries. Its

founder, Rabbi Israel Baal Shem Tov (also called the "Besht"), paved the way to a Judaism more joyous, mystical, popular, and communal and brought masses of simple people back to an active religious involvement. One of the ways he attracted them was by storytelling. Later, during his lifetime and after his death, many stories were told about him.

As Hasidism developed and grew, numerous communities were formed, centered around charismatic holy men, called rebbes or tzaddikim. The first few generations of the movement saw the emergence of so many leaders of great spiritual power that the phenomenon has few parallels in religious history. These perfected men, the tzaddikim, were the models for their devoted followers—their hasidim—and also for others of their own and later generations. Tales were told about their wondrous piety, their goodness, humility, and wisdom, and the miracles they did for those who believed in them. Storytelling about the deeds of one's rebbe and other tzaddikim became an essential part of hasidic life. But there were also countless tales about ordinary people who, in moments of holiness, had performed great deeds. And all these various tales had more purposes than can be listed: inspiring faith and reinforcing trust in God, arousing repentance, and teaching values and good practices.

But what made hasidic storytelling different? For Jews have always told religious stories. The answer is that only Hasidism vigorously encouraged storytelling, moving it from the periphery to the center of Judaism. Rebbes praised it as a *mitzvah* (divine commandment) and a spiritual practice; they reflected on it deeply and taught about its significance. This was all new; there was and is nothing like it outside Hasidism. Not only did rebbes often tell stories, they instructed their hasidim to do likewise. As a result, telling and listening to tales became popular as never before and were enthusiastically embraced by masses of ordinary hasidim. This revival of religious storytelling played a major role in the rapid growth of the hasidic movement. Thus, at the same time that storytelling promoted Hasidism, Hasidism promoted storytelling.

Note to the Reader

With a few exceptions, all the rabbis mentioned in this book were or are hasidic rebbes (or occasionally, hasidim).

2

Hasidic Praise of Stories and Storytelling

THE BAAL SHEM TOV: STORYTELLING AND THE DIVINE CHARIOT

Rabbi Israel Baal Shem Tov, the founder of Hasidism, held storytelling in the highest esteem. He said: "Whoever tells stories praising the tzaddikim is as if engaged in the mystic study of the Divine Chariot (*Maaseh Merkavah*)."[1]

Rabbi Menahem Mendel of Rimanov explained: "The stories of the tzaddikim are *Maaseh Merkavah* because the tzaddikim *are* the Chariot."[2]

Since the tzaddikim are themselves the "chariot," the vehicle of Godliness in this world, telling stories about them is equivalent to engaging in the mystic study of the Divine Chariot.

To explain this more fully: The prophet Ezekiel saw an amazing vision of the divine vehicle borne by angels—a chariot moved by four strange hybrid creatures—on which was enthroned the fiery Majesty of the Lord.[3] The part of Jewish mysticism that explores the mystic secrets of Ezekiel's prophetic vision is called *Maaseh Merkavah*, the Account of the Divine Chariot. The rabbis considered it the deepest wisdom. The Talmud states that Rabban Yohanan ben Zakkai knew every branch of the Torah, "both great and small," and explains that "great" refers to the Account of the Divine Chariot and "small" to legal discussions, like those of Abaye and Rava, which comprise the major portion of the Talmud.[4] But in the *Midrash* (rabbinic biblical exegesis), the rabbis say of the Patriarchs Abraham, Isaac, and Jacob, who represent all the perfected tzaddikim: "The Fathers—they indeed are

9

the Chariot [the vehicle of God's will on earth]."[5] The Baal Shem Tov made use of a second meaning of *maaseh* ("account") as "story" and of the teaching that the tzaddikim are the *merkavah*, the Chariot, and said that studying the lives of the tzaddikim by telling stories about them is equivalent to studying *Maaseh Merkavah*, the most sublime, mystical part of the Torah.[6]

But the Baal Shem Tov's comparison of *Maaseh Merkavah* to storytelling about tzaddikim is not merely based on word play and superficial. The angelic creatures that move the heavenly Chariot in Ezekiel's vision represent different aspects of divine service. According to the Kabbalah, the tzaddikim are the earthly counterparts of the angels and serve as God's Chariot on earth, just like the angels in heaven. Therefore, while mystics study Ezekiel's vision to learn the secrets of divine service as performed by angels, a person learns how that divine service is performed on earth from storytelling about tzaddikim.

THE MAGGID OF MEZRITCH: PRAISE

The Besht's great disciple and successor as leader of the hasidic movement, Rabbi Dov Ber, the Maggid of Mezritch, taught something similar. He quoted Psalm 113:1, "Give praise, O servants of the Lord, give praise to the name of the Lord," and read the Hebrew as "Giving praise to the servants of the Lord is equivalent to giving praise to the Lord." Praising the tzaddikim by telling stories about them is like praising God.[7] Since praise of God is a form of prayer, the Maggid equated storytelling about tzaddikim to prayer, just as the Besht had equated it to Torah study, these being the two most important spiritual practices in Judaism. Storytelling is, of course, not a substitute for Torah study or prayer, but—according to the Besht and the Maggid—its value and potency as a spiritual practice matches theirs.

INSPIRATION AND IMITATION

If the Besht and the Maggid of Mezritch valued storytelling so highly, what is its excellence? The answer is that storytelling has a unique ability to inspire those who hear about the noble qualities of the tzaddikim and the way they served God with devotion and self-sacrifice. But admiration must always lead to imitation. Rabbi Nahman of Bratzlav, the Baal Shem Tov's great-grandson, who loved stories and was famous as a storyteller, said:

Stories of the tzaddikim inspire a person, awakening his heart and setting it on fire, arousing him to turn to God with an intense and overpowering craving. Some great and awesome tzaddikim have said that their arousal to God was through stories of the tzaddikim, that set their hearts on fire for God, until they began to exert themselves in His service and merited what they merited; happy are they.[8]

Elsewhere, Rabbi Nahman explains why a person's heart is aroused when hearing stories of the deeds of tzaddikim:

Telling stories is very great, for the stories of tzaddikim awaken the heart and kindle the inner fires of love for God with intense desire. Because when one tells the stories of a tzaddik, the eternal impression created by his service of God is aroused, and its vibration awakens the heart to God, blessed be He, with powerful longing and yearning.[9]

Rabbi Nahman himself was turned to God through stories. Rabbi Nathan of Nemirov,[10] his foremost disciple, reports:

I heard this from the Rebbe's own lips, when he revealed the lesson on the importance of telling stories about tzaddikim.... The Rebbe said, "I myself was greatly motivated to serve God through stories of tzaddikim. Many great tzaddikim used to visit the home of my holy parents. We lived in Medzibuz, which had also been the home of the Baal Shem Tov. Many would come and visit the Baal Shem Tov's grave, and they would mostly stay at my father's house. It was from them that I heard many stories of tzaddikim, and this moved me toward God." It was through this that the Rebbe attained the great things that he did.[11]

Rabbi Menahem Mendel, the Kotzker Rebbe, said that he became a hasid because of a certain old man who told stories of the holy tzaddikim. He said, "He told and I listened."[12]

Rabbi Nahman and the Kotzker were two of the fieriest rebbes of all, actually burning up for God. To think that two such holy flames were lit by storytelling!

Rabbi Elimelech of Lizensk had regular daily sessions of storytelling. Between *Minhah* and *Maariv*, the afternoon and evening prayer services, he told stories of tzaddikim in simple language, and everyone present took inspiration from the stories and learned lessons for his own conduct.[13] Rabbi Elimelech said: "It is a good sign for a person if when he hears stories praising the virtuous deeds of the tzaddikim and their sincere and holy service of God, blessed be He, his heart becomes aroused and inflamed with hope that he too might serve God sincerely. This is a sign that God is with him."[14]

Rabbeinu Bahya[15] wrote:

A person is obliged to examine the lives of the tzaddikim and speak about their virtue. And doing so is better than eating honey, for eating much honey is not good, but however much one examines the glory of the tzaddikim it is always good and benefits the mind. There is no doubt that whoever constantly praises the tzaddikim only does so because of his own pure character and good nature, for everyone praises his own kind and those whose traits he aspires to share. . . . Therefore, praising them is sweeter to him than honey. . . .[16]

The Story Is Greater

A thought that explains the greatness of stories: The rabbis teach that "the *maaseh* (one who instigates or inspires a deed) is greater than the one who did the deed."[17] For example, someone who collects charity and inspires others to give is even greater than the one who gives the charity. But understanding *maaseh* according to its other meaning, "story," we can read the Hebrew: "The story of the deed is greater than the doer"—because the story will inspire many others to imitate his action.

SACRED ACTIVITY

The holy Seer of Lublin told how he once passed by a *Beit Midrash* and saw a supernal light coming from it. He thought, "Certainly, there are great scholars inside, studying the Torah in holiness." But when he entered, he saw two ordinary hasidim, not studying Torah but sitting and conversing with each other. The rebbe asked them, "Friends, what are you talking about?" The hasidim answered, "We are talking about the deeds of the tzaddikim." When he heard that, the Seer was very moved, for he realized that the great light he had seen was caused by their telling stories of the tzaddikim.

Afterward he said that this made clear to him the meaning of the verse, "Then they that feared the Lord spake one with the other: and the Lord hearkened and heard, and a book of remembrance was written before Him, for them that feared the Lord, and that thought upon His name" (Malachi 3:16). He said that speaking about the tzaddikim brings a revelation of the light of the Divine Presence—that is the light he had seen—and is good both for the tzaddikim themselves—those "that feared the Lord"—and for those who tell and hear the stories—"that thought upon His name."[18]

Why is telling stories about them good for those tzaddikim who are in the other world? Hasidim say that it is because they are elevated in heaven when people in this world are aroused to serve God from their examples.

GOD LOVES STORIES

The Lubliner, applying the words of Malachi to storytelling about tzaddikim, said that it causes a revelation of the *Shechinah* (Divine Presence) and God's light. Elsewhere, the same verse is used similarly but more directly: that when Jews sit and tell holy stories, God, so to speak, comes and listens, as it says: "and the Lord hearkened and heard."[19] We can add that God also loves to *tell* stories, for did He not come down on Mount Sinai and tell Moses all the stories of the Torah?[20]

RABBI ISRAEL OF RIZHIN

Just as Rabbi Nahman of Bratzlav, the Besht's great-grandson, was famous for his storytelling, so was his younger contemporary, Rabbi Israel of Rizhin, the great-grandson of the Maggid of Mezritch. He did not teach Torah at his Sabbath table, as did most of the other rebbes; instead, he influenced his hasidim primarily through personal contact with each individual. Every day he devoted a large amount of time to receiving visitors; after listening carefully to their troubles and questions, he answered each visitor with a wise comment or by telling a parable or story that had a lesson attached.[21]

Rabbi Israel of Rizhin esteemed storytelling so highly that he sometimes told stories before the morning prayers as a preparation and inspiration for praying. His involvement was so intense, however, that he could get carried away. One morning, surrounded by his hasidim, he began telling stories of the tzaddikim with such enthusiasm that he lost all track of time; he went on for so long that the hour of prayer passed. He suddenly stopped in the middle and said: "The time for prayer has already passed and I didn't pray. But, essentially, what is the difference between telling stories about tzaddikim and praying? Prayer is in the category of 'Praise the Lord!' while telling stories is in the category, 'Praise the servants of the Lord!' In the Book of Psalms, David, the sweet singer of Israel, sometimes puts 'Praise the Lord!' before 'Praise the servants of the Lord!' but other times he puts them in the reverse order, indicating that they are equal.[22] This teaches us," concluded the rebbe, "that telling stories of the tzaddikim is the same as praying."[23]

The Rizhiner was willing to delay the prayers for storytelling, which not only was a holy activity but set a person's heart on fire and made him yearn to pray. He could tell stories for hours, and in this instance became so enthused and engrossed in the telling that he forgot the time and forgot to pray! When he realized what he had done, he explained his lapse by using a teaching of his great-grandfather, the Maggid of Mezritch (quoted previously) that praising the tzaddikim in stories is equivalent to praising God.

RABBI AARON OF KARLIN

Rabbi Aaron of Karlin gave his hasidim a daily order of divine service that included many spiritual practices. But he once said to them:

> The most important thing in one's daily service of God is the very innermost point of one's heart. What is that "point"?—faith and devotion.[24] If a person has that innermost point, everything else will be good, including his praying and studying. How does one acquire that point? One reaches it through stories.[25]

Sometimes elderly hasidim took it upon themselves to influence younger people and, as had happened with Rabbi Nahman of Bratzlav and the Kotzker, draw them to Hasidism. Rabbi Aaron of Karlin obviously had a keen appreciation of storytelling. The following, about one of his elderly hasidim, illustrates how storytelling can inspire and activate that "innermost point."

One of the most prominent veteran hasidim of Rabbi Aaron of Karlin was Rabbi Aaron Asher. He had reached old age, but was still vigorous, and always preferred the company of the young men, in order to draw them to Torah and Hasidism. He would sit with them at one table and quicken them with pungent hasidic sayings and gripping tales of tzaddikim. . . . He was like an ever-flowing fountain of hasidic tales and would talk about wondrous events, from which he drew up precious pearls—religious lessons that had practical consequences—that set his listeners on fire and excited their emotions. At the end of a story he always raised his voice in a song. His voice, suffused with a special grace and profound feeling, was so sweet to the ears of those who heard it that everyone sitting there was overwhelmed and irresistibly drawn in to join him. Their singing soon became powerful and passionate, and before long they all began dancing, holding hands, arms linked, until the tide of their fervor swelled so they were actually near expiry.[26]

THE ULTIMATE COMPLIMENT

Why did the Besht, the Maggid, and the other rebbes praise, glorify, and extol storytelling, saying that telling stories about tzaddikim was like studying Maaseh Merkavah and praising God? Undoubtedly their reason was that they knew its profound spiritual value and wanted as much as possible to encourage hasidim to engage in storytelling. And the hasidim complied heartily. Indeed, they gave storytelling that final compliment of piety: While the Torah says that God keeps the Sabbath, and the rabbis of the Talmud added that He studies Torah and prays, the hasidim claimed that—He loves storytelling about tzaddikim.

3

The First Hasidic Storyteller: The Baal Shem Tov

THE HIDDEN TZADDIKIM

The place of storytelling in Hasidism goes all the way back to its founder, Rabbi Israel Baal Shem Tov. The Baal Shem Tov, who said that telling stories of the tzaddikim was like engaging in the mystic study of the Divine Chariot, was himself a remarkable storyteller. In his earlier days, the Besht was part of a movement of what were called "hidden tzaddikim," mystics who concealed their piety and worked as manual laborers or traveled around as wandering mendicants. They mingled with the common people and sought to strengthen their faith and deepen their involvement with Judaism.

According to hasidic tradition the hidden tzaddikim pioneered a novel way of attracting the common people to religion: through recounting the narratives of the Torah and the *Aggadah* (tales and parables of the Talmud and *Midrash*).[1] For ten years the Besht wandered about from one place to another, alone or as a leader of a group of hidden tzaddikim, to draw people to God by storytelling. They told stories about the religious qualities treasured by the Jewish people, stories that taught the awe of heaven and refinement of character.[2] The Besht particularly emphasized stories about love for fellow Jews.[3] It seems that his youthful participation in this storytelling proselytism contributed to his lifelong involvement in and appreciation of storytelling. It also helps explain why he compared it to mysticism: The mystics of the movement of the hidden tzaddikim were kabbalists, as was the Besht. Sometimes they engaged in their mystic studies and meditations, at other times they told stories about the pious heroes of the Torah, Talmud, and later periods to their unlearned comrades. Either way they were serving God and directing themselves to the same spiritual reality. Undoubtedly this storytelling proselytizing by the hidden tzaddikim paved the way for the hasidic variety, which played such a vital role in the expansion of the hasidic movement.

EVEN SIMPLE FOLK

Another aspect of the Besht's teaching about the equivalence of storytelling and mystic study and meditation is the way it encouraged simple folk by equating their divine service to that of the greatest mystics. While only the most serious and learned intellectuals could study the Kabbalah, even simple people could tell stories. Since storytelling is oral, even illiterate people can participate. The Baal Shem Tov had a profound appreciation of the divine service of simple Jews. He taught that the fervent prayers and Psalms of illiterate people of simple faith gave God as much pleasure as the Torah study of the scholars. The common folk might not be able to study Torah—since they did not understand Hebrew—but they could at least recite the Hebrew prayers and Psalms with devotion and fervor, even without understanding the meaning of what they were saying. In a similar fashion, the Besht taught that their divine service of storytelling was equal to the divine service not only of talmudic scholars but of kabbalists. They certainly could not match the great kabbalists' studies and meditations on Ezekiel's Divine Chariot, but they could tell tales of the tzaddikim, which had equal spiritual worth and gave God immense pleasure.

CHILDREN

The Besht's storytelling was not only for adults but for children, who often joined the crowds listening to him tell stories.[4] When as a young man he became a leader of the hidden tzaddikim, he initiated a program of fortifying Judaism among the common people by providing education for children, even those in isolated villages. He himself did this kind of work, serving for a period of time as an assistant *melamed* (primary school teacher). The Besht told the children, who of course are most receptive to storytelling, stories fitting their level of understanding, such as the beautiful stories of the Five Books of Moses, the tales of the Patriarchs and Matriarchs, of Moses, of how God gave the Torah to the Jewish people on Mount Sinai, the tales of the prophets, and of the sages of the Talmud.[5] He must have received some of his early training as a storyteller from his days as an assistant *melamed.*

THE "BAAL SHEM TOV JEW"

For religion to reach the common people it must be presented in a popular way, and stories do just that.[6] There is a hasidic concept of a "Baal Shem Tov Jew" who, although a simple person, has the spiritual capacity to be a vessel for holiness and can be inspired by tales, melodies, and miracles.[7] Even today, when the general level of education is much higher than in former times, most people have little interest in religious "philosophy," but they can be inspired by stories. However, it should not be thought that storytelling is only for those who are less intelligent! Sometimes certain dry scholars and intellectuals, who are not attracted by stories, attempt to disparage them by saying they are only for the simple-minded. But many of the greatest Torah scholars have had a deep appreciation of stories and storytelling.

IRRESISTIBLE CHARM

A hasidic tale shows how the Besht's storytelling attracted not only ordinary workingpeople but also rabbis and the religious elite. The Besht and other hasidic rebbes exerted their spiritual influence and elevated their followers in many ways: Some people were elevated by Torah teaching, others by hearing the rebbe's fervent praying or singing, and still others by seeing his ecstatic dancing. The Besht once said: "Some people can only be lifted up by storytelling."[8] Perhaps the following story illustrates that saying.

One summer the Baal Shem Tov visited the city of Sharogrod, where Rabbi Jacob Joseph was the rabbi. Rabbi Jacob Joseph did not know the Besht and had never seen him. Although he had heard that he was a great tzaddik and miracle worker, he did not give these reports any credence and did not believe in him. The Baal Shem Tov, however, desired to attract him and make him a disciple.

Arriving in the early hours of the morning, when people were leading their animals to pasture, the Besht stopped in the middle of the street and climbed down from his wagon. When a man passed by leading his cow with a rope, the Besht motioned to him with his hand to come over, and when he did he began telling him a story. Before long the man had entirely forgotten where he was going and why and stood fastened to the spot, next to his cow, listening to the Besht weave his enchanting tale.

Before long someone else passed by, and catching a few snatches of a story, he too drifted over to listen to what the Besht was saying. Soon, another of the passersby stopped, then a few more; they all stood there spellbound within the charmed circle created by the magic sound of his voice. The number of people around the Baal Shem Tov grew larger and larger, until he had attracted almost everyone in the town. A large crowd surrounded him, listening with fascination to his delightful tales that were suffused with love of God. Among them also stood the *shammos* (caretaker) of the synagogue.

During the summer, Rabbi Jacob Joseph prayed at eight o'clock in the morning, and the *shammos*, who had the key, opened the door every day at 6:30. That day the rabbi came to the synagogue and saw that it was still closed. Being by nature an irritable person, this infuriated him. The *shammos*, meanwhile, was listening to the Baal Shem Tov with the others, some of whom were standing with their tallis and *tefillin* (prayer shawl and phylacteries) bags under their arms. They had been on their way to the synagogue and had completely forgotten where they were going. However, just then the Baal Shem Tov signaled to the *shammos*, motioning with his hand as if opening a door with a key, and he suddenly remembered about the synagogue! He ran as fast as his legs could carry him and, when he arrived there out of breath, found the rabbi standing outside, alone and fuming. Not only was the synagogue locked, but the men who came every day for the morning prayers were not there! The *shammos* explained that a visitor to the town was standing in the street telling stories, and everybody was listening to him. The rabbi was greatly incensed by this, but it did him no good, and he had to pray alone.

After praying, the rabbi ordered the *shammos* to bring the storytelling visitor to him. He would have him given stripes for preventing the congregation from praying together! Meanwhile, the Baal Shem Tov had finished his storytelling and returned to the inn where he was staying. The *shammos* went looking for him and when he found him conveyed the rabbi's order that he come to him at once. The Besht went immediately, and when he arrived, the rabbi, who was still furious, said to him, "Are you the one who stopped the community from praying as a congregation?" "I am the one, master," the Baal Shem Tov replied humbly, "but I beg the rabbi not to be angry at me, and allow me to tell him a story." Rabbi Jacob Joseph said, "Go ahead."

The Besht told him a story, and the rabbi was so moved by it that he calmed down. He also began to talk to the Baal Shem Tov respectfully, addressing him as "sir." The Besht, on the other hand, stopped calling him "rabbi" and "master" and began to speak to him as an equal, addressing him also as "sir." Then the Baal Shem Tov said to him, "If you would like, I'll tell you another story." The rabbi nodded and said, "Please do." When he finished that story, the Baal Shem Tov asked him if he would like to hear still another. When he said yes, the Besht said to him, "Listen closely.

"I was once driving a wagon with three horses—one dark brown, one chestnut, and one white—and they were not able to neigh. A peasant called out to me from his wagon, 'Slacken the reins!' I slackened the reins, and once again the horses were able to neigh.—Do you understand what I am saying?" asked the Besht. "I understand, master," said Rabbi Jacob Joseph humbly.

At that point, Rabbi Jacob Joseph began to converse with the Baal Shem Tov, and during their conversation he attached himself to him—as disciple to master—with all his heart and soul. Then the Besht said to him, "I still haven't prayed, and I want to go now and do so." While he went to the synagogue to pray alone, Rabbi Jacob Joseph went home and showed him great honor by having a fine meal prepared for him. After the meal the two of them went out for a walk and all the people of the town accompanied them, and saw that the Baal Shem Tov had attracted their rabbi to him. From then on, Rabbi Jacob Joseph became one of the foremost disciples of the Baal Shem Tov.[9]

In this story we see how the Besht would stand in the street and attract a crowd of simple working people by his magical storytelling. He also was able to charm Rabbi Jacob Joseph, who became one of his greatest disciples and authored the books that brought the Besht's teachings out into the world. Rabbi Jacob Joseph was certainly a great intellectual, yet the stories won him over also. He began addressing the Besht harshly and condescendingly, but after hearing one story, he addressed him as an equal, and after two more stories, as his master. He was notoriously irritable, but his rage subsided under the soothing sweetness of the Besht's tales. Note that the Besht had no qualms about delaying the prayers by his storytelling. While he was telling his stories, the men on their way to the synagogue, including the *shammos*, stood there with their tallis and *tefillin* bags under their arms. The tales were so sweet that, like the first man with his cow, they forgot where they were and where they were going. We had seen something like this earlier, with Rabbi Israel of Rizhin delaying the morning prayers to tell stories and becoming so absorbed in them that he forgot to pray. This motif undoubtedly indicates the great importance of storytelling. The tales the Besht told to charm the crowd and then the rabbi were not like the short parable story at the end, where he instructed Rabbi Jacob Joseph about his religious practice. (In the next chapter we will see an example of the former type.) However, the meaning of that final parable touches the heart of the Besht's message and teaching. The body's animal powers, represented by the horses, must be reined in and directed to do the will of the soul, whose purpose is to serve God. But if they are controlled too strictly—if "the horses cannot even neigh" —a person becomes tense and angry; all joy is suppressed. And there can be no true divine service without joy. Rabbi Jacob Joseph had gone astray. His strictness with himself made him strict with others, and he was always angry and sad, for how can an angry person be happy? The essence of the Besht's way in Judaism was to serve God with joy: That is why he had a place for singing and dancing, and also for storytelling.

Among the many different occupations he engaged in when he was a hidden tzaddik, the Besht was a wagon driver and he acquired expert knowledge about horses. Like many great storytellers and parabolists, he was also an acute observer of the world around him and learned lessons about divine service from many everyday occurrences. The story he told the rabbi came from those earlier days when he was still learning how to drive a wagon and handle the horses. But from the peasant's cry to slacken the reins, he had also learned an invaluable lesson about serving God.

The Besht not only praised storytelling but was himself a master storyteller. Finally, his life became the subject of innumerable stories, and even, as shown here, a story about storytelling.

4

The Besht's Stories

As the Baal Shem Tov stood on the street attracting passersby into the charmed circle of his storytelling, he was also drawing them into the new world of Hasidism. One version of the story about how the Besht made Rabbi Jacob Joseph of Polnoye (earlier of Sharogrod) his disciple by storytelling contains one of the tales he told to the crowd.

THE SIGH AND THE SNEER

The Besht said: "In a certain town there lived a poor man, with a wife and many children, who earned a hard living as a porter. He knew how to recite the prayers, although he did not know the meaning of the Hebrew words. Every morning he rose before sunrise, ran to the synagogue, quickly said the prayers, and then rushed off to a day of back-breaking labor to earn enough for a dry crust of bread for his hungry children. In the evening, after work, he always went to the synagogue to pray but was usually late to arrive. His prayers were often disjointed and incomplete, and, exhausted by his labors, he would doze off standing or sitting. Then he returned home, physically broken and crushed, only to be pained by the sight of his family's hardships and suffering.

"In the same neighborhood, there lived a young scholar whose Torah study was his livelihood; he received a regular stipend that freed him from any financial worries. When he came to the synagogue in the morning, he

23

prayed slowly, as was proper, with full concentration, then sat down for his regular morning session of in-depth Talmud study. Afterward, he went home for a meal and later returned to study more Torah with an untroubled mind. He was always early for the afternoon and evening prayers, which he recited carefully and slowly.

"Every day, after the evening prayers, the porter and the young Torah scholar met on the street as they walked home. The porter, who trudged along bent over, let out a deep sigh when he saw his neighbor the Torah scholar. He thought to himself how his neighbor spent his day under the yoke of study of the holy Torah, while his day was spent bent under the yoke of heavy burdens. How he wished he could pray and study Torah like his neighbor, like a Jew should!

"Meanwhile, the young Torah scholar, who walked erect with an arrogant bearing and a feeling of his own dignity, cast a dismissive glance at the porter. On his lips was a contemptuous smile, as he thought of the abyss that separated him from his ignorant neighbor—as if to say, 'What have I in common with you?'

"Days, weeks, months, and years passed, until both the porter and the scholar left this world. When the Torah scholar appeared before the Heavenly Court, he came before the bench with head held high and confident steps. 'Heavenly judges!' he exclaimed, 'I learned much Torah, I prayed with concentration, I was careful to do all the mitzvot, the light as well as the heavy!' The judges were satisfied with his deeds and about to pronounce a favorable judgment, when at the last moment an angel approached and asked for their attention. Without speaking further, he put on one side of the scale of judgment all the oversized and heavy Talmud books that the Torah scholar had studied and the large siddur (prayer book) from which he prayed. On the other side of the scale he placed only the contemptuous smile that used to pass over his lips as he looked at his porter neighbor—and it outweighed the other scale.

"After him the porter appeared before the Heavenly Court, with bent head and trembling knees. He approached the bench and in a quavering voice said, 'Righteous judges! I am ashamed to come before you. I was not able to learn Torah and did not pray as I should have—my prayers were often confused and incomplete. Almost all my time every day was spent carrying burdens to support my wife and children. . . .' But even before he could finish speaking, an angel came and put on the scale the sigh he emitted when he saw his Torah scholar neighbor—at not being able to study and serve God as he did—and that sigh weighed down the scale to the side of good."[1]

SELECTING THE RIGHT STORIES

In order for the Besht's storytelling to accomplish its purpose, he required the appropriate stories, for part of any religious storyteller's art is selecting stories that fit his listeners' spiritual needs and reach them where they are. This story of The Sigh and the Sneer spoke directly to the Besht's audience of ordinary townspeople—farmers, shopkeepers, tailors, and shoemakers— who encountered him on the street. The Baal Shem Tov admired the uncomplicated religiosity of simple workingpeople and understood that although their actions might not always meet the high standards of the scholars, their hearts burned with humble devotion and piety. He sympathized with them in a way exactly opposite to the arrogant scholar's sneering contempt for the porter, and he communicated his warm attitude through this story and others.

A story's effect depends on the combined charm of the tale and the teller and on the bond the teller forms with his audience. This story has a holy sweetness and was channeled through a holy vessel—the gracious and incomparable Baal Shem Tov. He won the people's hearts for himself and for Hasidism by his personality, his sympathy, his storytelling, and by the kind of stories he told them: stories with grace that communicated hasidic devotion and, often, praise and compassion for common people.

5

The Besht's Use
of Secular Tales[1]

THE TALE OF THE WIFE'S TEST

Not all the Baal Shem Tov's tales were standard religious stories about tzaddikim and pious simple people. In discussing the first verses in the Book of Lamentations and the destruction of the ancient Temple in Jerusalem, Rabbi Jacob Joseph of Polnoye records a different kind of story he heard from his master[2]:

A Jewish merchant was once on a ship at sea when a terrible storm arose and threatened the lives of everyone on board. The merchant stood and prayed to be saved in the merit of his chaste wife (that God should save him not because he is worthy but because she is, since she is pure and chaste, and he is important to her). A gentile merchant who overheard this expressed his astonishment that he prayed to be saved in his wife's merit. When the man answered that she was worthy of such praise, the gentile replied, "You may think her chaste, but I'm sure that I can seduce her. What token do you want for my success?" The Jew said, "She has an expensive ring on her hand. If you bring it, I'll know that you seduced her." They agreed that whoever lost the bet would give all his merchandise to the other.

After the ship arrived safely in port, the husband stayed away from home. The gentile went to seduce the wife but was not even able to get near her. He visited her several times, claiming to have a secret message from her husband, but she would have nothing to do with him. Finally, he

27

bribed her maid to steal the ring and succeeded in obtaining it. He brought it to her husband, who had to give him all his merchandise. The husband then returned home empty-handed. He not only had lost all his merchandise from the trip, but believed his wife to be unfaithful.

When the woman heard that her husband had returned, she dressed up and went out of the house to greet him lovingly. But he paid no attention to her. She was confused, not knowing why his love and affection seemed to have disappeared. He went inside with her but was cold to her, showing no feeling toward her at all.

Finally, he decided to test her a second time: He sent her from his house and put her on a ship that had no captain, just a single sailor, who was actually the husband, who had disguised his dress and speech. The "sailor" made advances to her, but she sternly repulsed him and pushed him away. He then refused to give her anything to eat or drink. After sailing on the ship for several days without food or even water, she was forced to plead with the sailor to give her something to eat and drink to keep her alive. "If you kiss me," he replied, "I'll give it to you." She was forced to comply. Later he demanded that she sleep with him, and under duress she yielded.

Afterward, when they sailed near a coast, she jumped from the ship and swam ashore. When searching for food, she saw two fruit trees. A person who ate the fruit from one of them became leprous; a leprous person who ate fruit from the other was cured. She took fruit from the second tree in her bag. When she came to the king's palace, disguised as a man, and the king, who had leprosy, needed that cure, she provided it and was rewarded with great wealth.

She then returned home to her husband and angrily complained about what he had done to her, sending her from his house in a ship with a single, vile sailor, whom she was forced to kiss and sleep with, because she was starving. Her husband inwardly rejoiced at her extreme anger, which proved her chastity. After that, when he investigated, he discovered that the gentile had lied about her and had stolen her ring. Once this was revealed, he punished the man, etc.

THE TALE'S INTERPRETATION

At the end of the story, Rabbi Jacob Joseph continues with the Baal Shem Tov's explanation of the tale:

This story applies to everything that has happened and will happen in the world, from the destruction of the Temple, until the coming of the Messiah, soon and in our time. My master, the Baal Shem Tov, made a soul-ascent to heaven and saw that the archangel Michael, the great intercessor for Israel, argued on Israel's behalf that even their contemptible sins were really virtues, since they were all done to obtain money to arrange a marriage for their daughter with a Torah scholar, or to give charity and so on. The "chaste wife" is the *Shechinah* [the Divine Presence in this world], according to the secret of "a woman of valor is the crown of her husband." Samael [*samech-mem-alef-lamed*; Satan][3] became jealous and said, "Now the Jewish people have the Temple and sacrifices [and obey You], but if You want to test them, destroy the Temple and I'll seduce them, so to speak, etc." By means of the maid, he stole the ring. These are the lots for the two goats, one for God, the other for Azazel [another name for the Satan; Leviticus 16:5f.]; and because of sin, the left side won and the Temple was destroyed. . . . He sent her away in a boat. God, blessed be He, so to speak, disguised Himself within the name Sa'el [*samech-alef-lamed*; removing from Samael the letter *mem*, which stands for *mavet*, death, leaves Sa'el, whose *gematria* (numerical equivalent) is *Havaya-Adonai* (the Lord God)]. This is the secret of the wife's confession [about being forced to succumb to the sexual demands of the sailor], which represents the complaint of the *Shechinah* [i.e., the Congregation of Israel] against God, blessed be He, that She was forced [by the suffering of the exile], etc. Afterward, it was revealed that She had been falsely accused. Then, "a slaughter by God in Bozrah" [Isaiah 34:6], etc.[4]

The Baal Shem Tov heard the angelic intercessor for Israel, Michael, justifying the Jewish people's sins by claiming that their intentions were pure. In a similar way, the story of The Wife's Test justifies the sins of the Jewish people by suggesting that they were forced into them by the terrible suffering of the exile. This effective "argument" restores Israel into God's good graces and will speed the redemption. According to the traditional Jewish view, the Satan (the "Adversary") is an angel of God who performs God's will to test people. Although we cannot discuss fully the Baal Shem Tov's deep kabbalistic understanding of this story, its bold mystic teaching and application is that God has disguised Himself or one aspect of Himself, so to speak, as Satan, and when the sufferings of the exile cause the Jewish people to submit to the temptations of their evil inclinations and they are seduced to sin, they are really only seduced by their disguised "Husband." In their hearts they remain pure. Thus, in the story, the wife was compelled to sin by being starved by her own husband, and when she "sinned" it was really with him.

CONTROVERSIAL STORYTELLING

The Besht's prolific traditional storytelling was strange to the more staid establishment rabbis of his time. Their reaction to a nontraditional story such as this would have been even more extreme. Although it begins rather piously and tamely with the Jewish merchant praying that he be saved from shipwreck in the merit of his wife's chastity, the story quickly takes a different turn when he accepts the gentile's bet about seducing his wife. This is not a simple religious story praising the piety and good deeds of rabbis or laypeople. It is essentially secular and even risqué. The husband acts outrageously and offensively by Jewish religious standards by testing and betting on his wife's virtue in resisting a gentile seducer. Even the application would have provoked controversy: It is one thing to hint at God's connection with the Satan, but to openly present God masked in satanic disguise would probably have been too much for most rabbis, even today. Furthermore, there would be an obvious danger in telling such a story to religiously and intellectually immature disciples, who might misunderstand and misuse it to justify sinning. Considering the nature, not only of the story but of its application, it is possible that the Besht told this tale exclusively to elite disciples, not to ordinary people or to outsiders.

DEEPER MEANINGS OF SECULAR TALES

The Baal Shem Tov's religious use of the tale of The Wife's Test is certainly surprising and it is even more surprising to realize that he did not create the story. It is a widespread, ancient, and popular European folktale found, among other places, in Giovanni Boccaccio's *Decameron*![5] Thus, the Besht appropriated this secular tale—and probably others—for religious purposes. Perhaps not all his "secular" stories were as potentially shocking as this one. But why did he choose to express deep, mystical concepts by means of such a story? Perhaps he wondered at the attraction these tales held for

Jews and gentiles alike and asked himself what their inner meaning was. Today also psychologists and others analyze folk and fairy tales for their deeper meanings. Clearly the Baal Shem Tov preceded them. Appreciating the attractive power of these profane tales, the Besht attempted to elevate them and other worldly speech into the realm of the sacred by revealing their hidden spiritual meanings. He taught: "The leader of the generation is able to raise up the speech and stories of the people of his generation by linking the material to the spiritual."[6] The Baal Shem Tov similarly appropriated gentile melodies and transformed them into holy songs, for example, by singing a profane love song to the Shechinah, God's "female" presence. This bold practice parallels his use of risqué secular stories. (In a later chapter I will discuss how the Besht's great-grandson, Rabbi Nahman of Bratzlav, continued and advanced the Besht's radical path in storytelling.)

The Baal Shem Tov obviously sought to give storytelling its widest scope. But as would be expected, not everyone concurred with his judgment.

CONDEMNATION AND PRAISE

Insofar as the Baal Shem Tov's use of secular stories became known, his storytelling must have aroused consternation among more conservative religious figures. In a book written during the Besht's lifetime, Rabbi Moshe, son of Rabbi Jacob of Satinov, protested against an unnamed storytelling preacher, perhaps the Besht:

> Now newcomers interested in money have arrived on the scene, and have turned the word of God to shame. One windbag "preaches" by telling people stories, parables and jokes. And they do not say to themselves, "These are all frivolous things, and cannot help remove obstacles before me, that I should walk the straight path that is upright in God's eyes."[7]

Some scholars believe that these "newcomers" are the Besht's hasidim, and that the "preacher," who claims to have the holy spirit ("wind"), is the Baal Shem Tov.[8] While this Rabbi Moshe may have been shocked and scandalized by the Besht's use of secular stories, the Besht's grandson, Rabbi Moshe Hayim Ephraim of Sudilkov, wrote praising the Besht's ability to serve God even with "non-religious" stories.

I myself saw and heard my master and grandfather, may he rest in
Eden, his memory for a blessing for the World-to-Come, speak about
non-religious matters and tell stories and with his holy and pure wisdom use them to serve God. . . . His exalted spiritual level gave him
an extraordinary ability to "be wise," even with "outside matters"–
non-religious affairs and stories–for he could clothe his pure wisdom in them and serve God with them."[9]

This comment refers not only to storytelling but also to everyday
speech, for the Besht served God even when conversing about seemingly
secular and worldly matters.

A SERVICE OF GOD

We see then that the Baal Shem Tov's storytelling flair carried him beyond
the bounds of the conventional story repertoire. He not only told traditional, edifying stories but boldly appropriated even risqué secular stories
for spiritual purposes and used them to clothe exalted mystical teachings.
And in either case, he not only taught others by means of stories but considered his storytelling an integral and essential part of his service of God.

6

The Besht's Storyteller Disciple

Not only was the Baal Shem Tov himself a master storyteller, but before
his death he specifically instructed one disciple to become a professional
storyteller and to tell stories—about him.

THE STORYTELLER AND THE BISHOP

Before his death, the Baal Shem Tov called all his disciples to him and told
each of them how to conduct himself and how to earn a living after his
passing. He further told some of them what would happen to them in the
course of time. One of the disciples, named Rabbi Jacob, was also the Besht's
personal attendant. The Baal Shem Tov called Rabbi Jacob to him and said,
"You shall travel to all the places where they know of me, and tell stories
about what you saw when you were with me, and that will be your livelihood." Unhappy at this unexpected and unusual commission, Rabbi Jacob
mildly protested, saying, "What will come from this? How will I be able to
support myself, wandering around telling stories?" "Don't worry," said the
Besht, "because you will actually become rich from this, God-willing."

When the Holy Ark of God (the Baal Shem Tov) was buried, and as-
cended to heaven, leaving the living bereft, the disciples obeyed all the
instructions he had given them. Rabbi Jacob traveled widely as a storyteller,
telling stories about his holy master, and he earned an abundant living.

Two and a half years after the Besht's death, Rabbi Jacob heard that
there was a wealthy man in Italy who paid a gold coin for each story that

he was told about the Baal Shem Tov. He was overjoyed at this news, because if he went to Italy and told the hundreds of stories he knew, he would earn enough money not to have to travel for a year or more. So he purchased a horse and coach, hired a servant to drive, and made preparations for the long journey. It took him seven months to reach his destination, because he spent time in each city he passed through, telling stories to earn money for his travel expenses.

When he finally arrived in the city where the wealthy man lived, he asked the townspeople about him, and they told him that he was fabulously wealthy and his estate like the court of a king. But he was also extremely pious, and studied Torah and prayed the whole day, leaving his business affairs in the hands of trusted administrators. On the Sabbath, at each of the three meals, he asked to be told tales of the Baal Shem Tov, and after the Sabbath he paid a gold coin for each new story that he had never heard. Rabbi Jacob inquired about the man's origins—where he was from, where he was born—and whether he had always lived there. They told him that he had arrived ten years earlier and bought the estate from the lord of the city, who was a minister in Rome. He settled down, and provided a livelihood for many Jews who now worked on the estate. He then had a synagogue built there, and the townspeople pray there morning and evening. On the Sabbath, most of them go to eat at his table.

Rabbi Jacob went to the mansion where the man resided and asked his servants to tell him that the personal attendant of the Baal Shem Tov has arrived, and he is ready to tell him many stories about the Besht, that he knows about firsthand, not through hearsay. One of the servants reported this to his master, who had him return the message that he should wait until the Sabbath, and then he can tell us the stories. Otherwise, the magnate ordered that a comfortable room be made available for Rabbi Jacob to stay in. So they provided him with a private, second story room, and that was where Rabbi Jacob stayed until the Sabbath.

When the townspeople heard that the visitor was a disciple of the Baal Shem Tov, and his personal attendant, they all gathered to hear his stories, because since the arrival of the magnate they had become accustomed to hearing tales of the Besht every Sabbath. When they were sitting at the Sabbath table, after having sung some traditional *zemirot* (Sabbath table hymns), the magnate asked Rabbi Jacob to tell them a story about the Besht.

But Rabbi Jacob suddenly and completely forgot everything he knew and could not recall even a single story! Desperately struggling to jar his memory, he tried every storyteller's device he knew: He tried to visualize the Baal Shem Tov's face, or the city of Medzibuz, or various close disciples of the Besht—anything that might help him remember. But nothing worked! He could not remember even one story, for, incredibly, he had forgotten everything that had ever happened to him. It was as if he had amnesia. Under the piercing gaze of all those at the table, he sat there struggling mightily to concentrate on anything that might lead him to remember a story of the Besht. He racked his brain to produce any detail connected with the Besht, but could not recall a thing; it was as if he had been born that very day. Understandably, Rabbi Jacob became confused as a result of all this. He was also terribly embarrassed, but his embarrassment did not help him. All the members of the magnate's household and the townspeople were indignant, suspecting him of having made the whole thing up. "This fellow came here pretending to be an intimate of the Besht," they said to each other, "but it's clear he's a fraud and a cheat. He probably never saw the Besht in his life!" The magnate himself, however, was calm and said to him, "We'll wait until tomorrow; perhaps you'll remember something then."

Rabbi Jacob cried that whole night, and tried to picture the faces of the Besht's disciples or anything else that might shake loose his memory. Nothing worked; he had completely forgotten even how to begin telling a story of the Baal Shem Tov. It was as if he had never met the Besht.

At the Sabbath morning meal, after synagogue, the magnate again asked him if he was able to remember a story. Not knowing what to answer, Rabbi Jacob said to him, "Believe me, that this is no simple matter; nothing like this has ever happened to me before." The magnate was still patient and said, "We'll wait until the third Sabbath meal, perhaps you'll remember then." But he did not remember anything at the third meal either, and he became despondent about it. By this time, moreover, all the people in the household were outraged and wanted to humiliate and disgrace him for mocking the magnate with his brazen lies about being the Besht's attendant and so on. All the townspeople were also furious and made nasty remarks about him in his hearing.

The righteous tzaddik, Rabbi Jacob, accepted all this humiliation and abuse with love and, in fact, was astonished by the whole episode. Although dejected and depressed, he tried his best to find some religious explanation that would make sense of these confusing events, and convince himself that it had to be this way. Perhaps the Baal Shem Tov was angry at him, that instead of traveling to places where the Besht was known, he had gone off to a foreign country where they were not worthy of hearing such stories. He had many other thoughts like this, as he tried to understand what was happening to him. But the truth was that none of these pious explanations satisfied him; and that astonished him even more.

Overcome with grief, he prayed to God the whole Sabbath day. On *Motza'ei Shabbat* (immediately after the Sabbath), the magnate sent for Rabbi Jacob again; perhaps he would have some little reminiscence of some sort to tell him. But he didn't. It also pained the tzaddik that people were constantly coming over to him and asking sarcastically, "Have you remembered something?" Rabbi Jacob went to his room and cried. After getting hold of himself he went out again, thinking, "Perhaps Heaven does not desire that I become rich or that stories of the Baal Shem Tov be told here. But one thing I am certain of, is that this is no accident, God-forbid." So he decided to return home.

The magnate, however, sent to him again, asking that he wait until Tuesday and then, if he still did not remember anything, he could travel home. Rabbi Jacob stayed until Tuesday, but remembered nothing, so he went to his host to bid him goodbye. After being given a generous donation, he went and sat in the coach to begin his journey home. But as they began driving away, he suddenly remembered an incredible story about the Baal Shem Tov! He immediately told the driver to turn around and go back; then he jumped out of the coach, rushed into the magnate's house, and sent one of the servants to tell him that he had remembered an amazing story. The magnate sent for him to come in, brought him into his own room, and said, "Please tell me the story." Rabbi Jacob began to tell the tale:

"Once, on a Sabbath before the Christian holiday of Easter, the Baal Shem Tov was very preoccupied, and paced back and forth in his house. Immediately after the third Sabbath meal he ordered the horses harnessed and took three disciples with him—myself included—and we sat in the coach and traveled all night. None of us knew where he was taking us. As always when the Baal Shem Tov traveled long distances by miraculous speed, he had the driver put down the reins and the horses went where they would, by divine guidance. Wherever they stopped would be the intended destination. At daybreak we arrived at a very large city, and the horses came to a stop in front of a large house whose doors and windows were all closed and shuttered. The Baal Shem Tov ordered me to knock on the door. An elderly Jewish woman came out and yelled at us, 'What are you doing here at this time! They'll slaughter you all! This is the day the Christians stab any Jew who dares to walk out the door of his house, because today is their holiday. They also cast lots, to select some Jew on whom to take vengeance for their Messiah, if they find no Jew in the streets. Woe to the man who is chosen! They drag him from his house and beat him viciously, until he collapses, broken and bloodied. Yesterday, they cast lots and the rabbi was selected, because the Christians know that the Jews are careful not to be on the streets today. Now, when one of the Christians sees that Polish Jews have come here, they'll lead you all like sheep to the slaughter, and it will bring a disaster on us too. So flee the city quickly, while you can!' That is what the old woman yelled at us, weeping and sighing, her hands on her head.

"But the Baal Shem Tov paid no attention at all to her warning. He immediately went into the house and up to the large second floor, and ordered that his things be brought in. Meanwhile, the old woman's husband and all the occupants of the house huddled in fear against the walls, and looked on, no one saying a word, because they were terrified. The old woman came into the house wailing and yelling, and argued with the Baal Shem Tov. He did not answer her, but just pulled back the curtain from one of the windows, and stood there looking out. The old woman continued to yell: 'Why are you removing the curtain?!' But he ignored her. The Besht peered out the window and saw that on the street, opposite the house, there was a large raised platform, with many steps leading up to it. A large crowd had gathered in front of it, waiting impatiently for the bishop to come and deliver his Easter sermon, because that would be the signal to begin the pogrom. After a short while, the sound of church bells rang out announcing the bishop's arrival.

"The Baal Shem Tov was standing by the window watching, when suddenly he called me, 'Jacob, go and tell the bishop to come to me quickly.' When the people in the house heard him say this they all gasped, and trembled in fright. Then they all began to yell at once, 'Are you insane? You're sending a Jew to certain death; they'll tear him limb from limb!' They cursed him bitterly, but he paid no attention to them, and shouted, 'Jacob, go quickly! Don't be afraid!' I knew who was sending me, and trusted that my rebbe knew what he was doing; so I went without fear into the street and up to the platform, and no one said a word to me!

"I said to the bishop, in Yiddish, 'The Baal Shem Tov is here and he wants you to come to him immediately.' 'I know of his arrival,' the bishop replied, 'Tell him that I'll come right after the sermon.' I returned to deliver the message. The people in the house, meanwhile, had seen through the slits in the shuttered windows that I had walked unhindered to the platform and spoken with the bishop. They were stunned and could hardly believe their eyes. They hastened to apologize to the rabbi, but he paid no attention, just as he had paid no attention to what they had said before. When I told him the bishop's answer, he shouted, 'Go back and tell him to come immediately, and not be a fool!' I went back to the platform, where the bishop had begun his sermon. I pulled at his robe and repeated the Besht's words. He then said to the people, 'Please wait for a short while and I'll return to you.' Then he followed me back to the Besht.

"As soon as we entered, the two of them went into another room and closed the door behind them. After two hours the Baal Shem Tov came out, ordered that the horses be harnessed, and we left there immediately. What happened with the bishop—I don't know. To this day I don't even know the name of the city where we were, and the Baal Shem Tov never told me. I haven't thought about this incident for a long time, but I remembered it just now, and how I was involved; it's ten years since it happened."

When Rabbi Jacob concluded his story, the magnate lifted his hands to heaven and praised God. Then he said to Rabbi Jacob, "I know that you're telling the truth, because as soon as I saw you I recognized you. But I kept quiet. Now I'll tell you the rest of the story—because I was the bishop. Although I was born a Jew, one way or another, I went astray and converted. My soul was confused, but the compassionate Baal Shem Tov rescued me. I have holy ancestors and they appeared in the Besht's visions and begged him to save me. The Besht then came to me in my dreams every night and told me to turn back from the path on which I had strayed. The night when you set out, I had promised him that I would flee the city before Easter, because in my yearly holiday sermon I always reviled the Jewish People, and incited the Christians, who did not need much prodding, to kill a Jew.

"However, when I woke up that morning, my pride and lust for power exerted a tremendous pull on me. I was torn between my promise to the Besht and my lower nature and was of two minds. The Baal Shem Tov had already arrived, but I didn't know what I wanted to do. Then I saw the enormous crowd that was gathering, and how when I took one step out of my house all the church bells began to chime, announcing my imminent arrival. My evil inclination would not allow me to abandon all this honor, and I went to deliver my sermon. When you came and called me, I wanted to give the sermon before my good inclination overpowered me. But when you called me the second time, I was transformed and became another man; then I went with you. When I was with him in the room, the Baal Shem Tov gave me a penance and I completely repented. I distributed half of my money to the poor, because I was very wealthy. I also gave one fourth to the king, so he would allow me to travel to another country, on some pretext that I fabricated.

"Then the Baal Shem Tov told me what I must do every year to repent for my sins, and said to me, 'The sign by which you will know that your sins have been forgiven and your transgressions atoned for, is if a man comes and tells you your story.' So as soon as I saw you I repented as much as I was capable. When I saw that you had forgotten all the stories you knew, I understood that it was because of me, that I had not yet fully repented. Then I prayed from the bottom of my heart, and my prayer succeeded, with the help of God, because you remembered the story. Now I know that—praise God—my sin is forgiven, and I have repented for everything—praise God. You no longer have to wear yourself out traveling about to tell stories, because I will give you gifts that will provide for you all the days of your life. May the merit of the Baal Shem Tov stand for both of us, that we succeed in serving our Creator, with all our hearts and souls, all the days of our life. Amen."[1]

STORYTELLING ELEMENTS IN THE TALE

The Baal Shem Tov was himself an exceptional storyteller, and before his death he told his disciple and attendant, Rabbi Jacob, to become a story-teller—and tell stories about him. This tale contains many elements that will bring a smile to the face of any professional storyteller: the travails of wandering, the doubts about being able to make a living from storytelling, the excitement on hearing of a wealthy man who pays a gold coin for every story—the storyteller's dream! But there is also the storyteller's nightmare—forgetting every story one ever knew! Total amnesia! Like any good story-teller, Rabbi Jacob tries various devices to jar loose his memory, such as visualizing the Besht's appearance, but nothing works. What does finally awaken his memory is the repentance of the magnate, the former bishop. The underlying thought here is that the ability of the storyteller to remember and bring forth a story depends on the spiritual receptivity of the listener. This is an idea of general significance, not limited to the exceptional circumstances of this incident: that people must have a repentant attitude and open hearts to invite a story. This relates to another concept found here: When Rabbi Jacob could not remember, one of his pious speculations was that perhaps his listeners were not worthy of hearing these holy stories. Once, after the Rabbi of Vyelushka told a certain story he had heard from his grandfather, Rabbi Ezekiel Shraga, the Rebbe of Shinova, "he described how his grandfather had looked around the room before telling it, to see if any unworthy person was present, for as it says in the holy books, it is not fitting to tell a story to a crude person who will not believe it."[2] In my own experience as a storyteller, I have occasionally wondered not at the worthiness of my audience but at the appropriateness of telling sacred stories in a secular setting, where they might not be appreciated. Another typical element that appears in this tale is a traditional hasidic setting for storytelling: at the Sabbath table. (I will discuss the subject of settings for storytelling further in the next chapter.)

This story contains the only reference I am aware of to a professional hasidic storyteller. Perhaps it also explains why that is the case—in describing the difficulty of making a living this way. Today also it is rare to find a wealthy person willing to pay a gold coin for a story! Are we worse off as a result? Probably.

The last storytelling concept in this tale is that a story can be "intended" for a particular person. Many storytellers have had the gratifying experience of hearing that a particular story they told came to someone at a crucial moment and helped, or even saved, the person. If a story comes to mind in the presence of a certain person, one can even consider it a divine hint that that story is intended for him or her.

Often during a *drashah* [sermon], the Maggid of Jerusalem, Rabbi Sholom Schwadron [one of the few remaining traditional *maggidim* of the old type] will introduce a seemingly unrelated thought or story by noting, "Rabbi Elya Lopian once instructed me that if I am speaking publicly and suddenly a thought or particular story comes to mind, it is a sign from heaven that it was meant to be delivered to this specific audience because it is what they needed to hear."[3]

Rabbi Nahman of Bratzlav, who was a master storyteller, said that by telling stories a tzaddik can "throw his voice" a long distance, so it is heard far away. Bratzlaver tradition explains one meaning of this to be that a story's message may not be heard immediately but only when it reaches the person for whom it is intended.[4] A story may be passed from one person to another before it arrives at its true destination; it can be sent out on its flight, like an arrow from a bow, and even after traveling a far distance, can strike its target. In the tale of The Storyteller and the Bishop, the Baal Shem Tov not only sent out a story, he even sent out the storyteller.

Storytelling in Hasidic Life[1]

THE BESHT AND HIS DISCIPLES

It was the custom of the Baal Shem Tov to gather his disciples, and sing with them songs and praises of God with great fervor, and tell them stories of the tzaddikim, which arouse faith and love of God. He also instructed his disciples, who followed after him, to gather and do likewise.[2] The Besht was an exceptional storyteller, who loved tales of tzaddikim[3]; it is fitting, therefore, that even in his own lifetime stories were told about him, for who was a greater tzaddik than he?[4] His disciples continued telling stories about the Besht after his death, particularly during Sabbath meals, especially the third (Shalosheudas), and also during the Melaveh Malkah feast after the Sabbath. Rabbi Yehiel Michal of Zlotchov, for example, did not say the Grace after the third Sabbath meal until he had first told a story about his master, the Baal Shem Tov.[5]

ESTABLISHING A CONNECTION

Rabbi Hayim of Chernovitz, a disciple of Rabbi Yehiel Michal of Zlotchov, was once very ill and lay in bed unconscious for three days. Suddenly he began to sweat profusely, and after that he recovered. "My soul was already in the upper world," he said, "and I saw, in heaven, the holy Baal Shem Tov, may his merit protect us, walking with his disciples. I asked, 'Who is that?' They told me, 'That is the holy Baal Shem Tov.' I went over to him

41

and beseeched him to bless me for a complete healing. 'What connection do I have with you?' he asked. 'Did you ever visit me, do I know you?'" [A rebbe can only bless and help someone who has formed a connection to him or has benefited him in some way.] Rabbi Hayim said, "My rebbe, your disciple, the Rebbe Reb Michal of Zlotchov, tells a story about you every *Shalosheudas*. Once it was very late and he had already washed his hands to say the Grace After Meals, but I reminded him that he'd not told a story about you, because I know that when my rebbe tells a story about you, you receive gratification in the World of Truth. By this merit, I beg to be healed." The Baal Shem Tov consented and put his hand on Rabbi Hayim's head. Just then he began to sweat. He slowly recovered, until finally he was completely healed.[6]

This story teaches that since a tzaddik receives gratification from stories told about him—because his ideals are kept alive in this world—the teller (or here, the one who reminds him) forms a connection with the tzaddik and receives his blessings in return.

Most tzaddikim consider it a *mitzvah* and also a *segulah*, a practice mystically potent to draw down blessings, to tell stories about the Baal Shem Tov on *Motza'ei Shabbat*.[7]

REBBES AND DISCIPLES: THE MAGGID OF MEZRITCH

Just as the Baal Shem Tov's disciples told stories about him, it became customary for hasidim to tell tales of the greatness and piety of their rebbe— during his lifetime or after—and of other tzaddikim of their own or earlier generations. A hasidic tale relates that when Rabbi Menahem Mendel of Vitebsk, a disciple of the Maggid of Mezritch who went to live in the Land of Israel, sat at table for the third Sabbath meal, an old man, a disciple of the Baal Shem Tov, always told stories praising his master. Once, the Maggid of Mezritch—who was already in the other world—appeared in Rabbi Menahem Mendel's dream and said, "Aren't you my disciple? Why don't you also tell stories in my praise?" And he did.[8]

THE ORAL TRADITION

From those days until today, there has been a vigorous tradition of oral storytelling among hasidim. Some few will also "specialize" in storytelling, one requirement for that position usually being a phenomenal memory that allows a person to remember a tremendous number of stories exactly. A Lubavitcher hasid told me that his elderly father, who had been a "semi-official" chief Lubavitch storyteller, could repeat a story fifty years later exactly as he had heard it.[9]

HASIDOT

Hasidot, hasidic women, also participate in storytelling. The previous Lubavitcher Rebbe, Rabbi Joseph Isaac Schneersohn, writes how when he was a boy, his father, the rebbe, asked his mother and the boy's grandmother, Rivka, to tell him stories of tzaddikim. Like any grandmother, she was happy to comply. Rabbi Joseph Isaac, who as a boy and later a man loved stories, reports that she was an expert storyteller: "My grandmother spent all that blessed Tuesday telling me stories, each of which was orderly and animated. One felt that she was reliving in her memory the time when she had heard the story. And I also experienced the events of the story because of the way she told it."[10]

One of the things she told him then was that when she was just thirteen she already knew many stories that she had heard from her mother, grandmother, and aunts. She used to regularly gather the little girls in her family and tell them the many stories she knew about the Baal Shem Tov, the Maggid of Mezritch, and the early Lubavitcher Rebbes. Her uncle, the Tzemah Tzedek, who was then Rebbe of Lubavitch, learned about this, called her to him, and asked her how she knew so many stories. When she told him, he was very pleased.[11]

Later, when she was a daughter-in-law of the Tzemah Tzedek, he assembled all of his daughters-in-law who were living in his house and asked them to arrange a gathering every Motza'ei Shabbat to tell a story of the Baal Shem Tov. So every Motza'ei Shabbat one of them went in to the Rebbe, he told her a story of the Baal Shem Tov, and then she went back and told it to all the others.[12]

SETTINGS

Thus, storytelling won an established place in the life of the earliest hasidim. Many rebbes instructed their hasidim that whenever a number of them were gathered together they should always tell each other stories of the tzaddikim.[13] But what are the typical settings of hasidic storytelling?

Sabbath

Storytelling became an integral part of Sabbath activities, particularly at Sabbath meals. Rabbi Mendel of Vishnitz, for example, instructed his hasidim to tell stories of tzaddikim at the table Sabbath night, in honor of the Sabbath.[14] At the third meal, eaten communally in the Beit Midrash (House of Torah Study) or shtibel (small and intimate synagogue/House of Study) when the Sabbath is waning, rebbes often "say Torah" and include a tale or more in their teaching. The association with the Sabbath enhances the sacred character of the storytelling. And the holy storytelling sanctifies the Sabbath. We are told that it was the custom of Rabbi Yerahmiel Moshe of Koznitz to tell stories during the third Sabbath meal "to draw down the extra light of the Sabbath."[15] Saturday night after Havdalah (the ritual that separates the holy Sabbath from profane time), at the Melaveh Malkah, a fourth communal meal held to "accompany" the departing Sabbath, hasidim sometimes gather at the rebbe's table or at a private home just to hear tales of tzaddikim.[16] Rabbi Shalom Shachna of Prohobitch (Rabbi Israel of Rizhin's father) even recommended preparing for the Sabbath by telling stories. He once said to his hasidim: "Telling tales of tzaddikim Thursday night has a special potency, so that you will have a good Shabbos. And if you tell stories about me, you will also have a good Shabbos."[17]

Festivals

Tales are often told at festival meals, as at Sabbath meals. Sometimes rebbes or others have a custom to always tell a particular tale at a certain festival: Rabbi Pinhas of Koretz always told a certain tale on Purim, Rabbi Isaac Meir of Ger told a certain tale on Passover, Rabbi Meir of Premishlan told a certain tale on Shavuot, and so on.[18] Perhaps inspired by the storytelling spirit of the Haggadah, Rabbi Israel of Vishnitz told many stories after the Passover seder.[19] Rabbi Mordechai of Hosyatin (a son of the Rizhiner) used to tell stories of tzaddikim on the third and seventh nights of Hanukkah.[20]

Yahrzeit

Another festive occasion with a significant role in hasidic storytelling is the yahrzeit or hillula of a famous tzaddik—the anniversary of his death and his ascension to heaven. On this day hasidim mark the annual elevation of his soul in heaven and, when they praise him on earth and his life inspires them to live well, they cause his soul to ascend even higher. A tzaddik's *yahrzeit* is commemorated by lighting a memorial candle in his honor, and his life is celebrated by enjoying liquor to hearty *l'hayims* ("To life!") and by singing and dancing. Sometimes there is also a festive meal. But most important at such a gathering are the tales that recall the tzaddik's pious and wondrous deeds.[21] By praising and glorifying the tzaddik, the participants establish a link with him. They cause his soul to be elevated in the upper world, and they too are spiritually elevated.[22] It is believed that the tzaddik also repays with kindness those who remember him, interceding for them in heaven.[23] A contemporary rebbe, the late Rabbi Yitzhak Isaac of Skolya, who was a descendant of the Baal Shem Tov, would tell stories about the Besht for hours on his *hillula*.[24]

Praising and telling stories of tzaddikim on their *yahrzeits* goes back at least to the Baal Shem Tov, who explained the custom this way:

> The reason children observe their parent's *yahrzeit*—the anniversary of their father or mother's death—is that that day each year their soul is judged if it will ascend higher in heaven, for before a soul can ascend further it must be judged on ever smaller matters and concerning any religious stringencies it did not fulfill. Therefore, the children fast and donate charity on the *yahrzeit*, on behalf of their father or mother, to help their souls ascend higher, because "a son can gain merit for his father" (*Sanhedrin* 104a).
>
> But if a soul [of a tzaddik] has already reached a state of perfection, so there is nothing else on which to judge it, it cannot ascend any higher, because a soul cannot ascend without first being judged. Therefore, such a soul can only ascend if its merits are mentioned in this world, that is, the good deeds the person did during his lifetime. This explains the verse: "Then they that feared the Lord spake one with the other: and the Lord hearkened and heard, and a book of remembrance was written before Him, for them that feared the Lord, and that thought upon His name" (Malachi 3:16). [The Besht reads this verse as: "Then they spake one with the other *about* those who feared the Lord. . . ."] "Then they . . . spake one with the other"—This refers to a person who speaks to his comrade about "those who feared the Lord [the tzaddikim]," mentioning the good deeds they did during their lifetimes. "And the Lord hearkened and heard, and a book of remembrance was written before Him, for them that feared the Lord"—When those who feared the Lord are mentioned before Him,

blessed be He, through stories told about their good deeds, they come to remembrance before Him, blessed be He. And because of this they ascend higher in heaven. "And [for those] that thought upon His name"—This refers to those who "spake one with the other" about the good deeds and pious ways of those who feared the Lord. They are called "those who think on His name"[25] because the tzaddikim, whom they are speaking about and telling stories about, are themselves the Divine Chariot[26] [therefore, thinking and speaking about them is like thinking and speaking about God].[27] Those who "think on His name" [by telling stories of the tzaddikim] are also remembered before God, blessed be He, because they caused the souls of the tzaddikim to ascend.[28]

Where and How

Hasidim may hold a *Melaveh Malkah* feast or a famous tzaddik's *yahrzeit* celebration in a *Beit Midrash* or *shtibel*, or in a private home. If the rebbe is present, he leads the storytelling; if not, an honored elder or a learned visitor may begin the evening with a tale, after which other storytellers usually join in. Good storytellers are respected and appreciated. Sometimes a rebbe has an appointed chief storyteller[29] or a particular hasid "owns" the honor of telling a story on a certain occasion.[30] One story recalls another, and the stories range from miraculous to humorous, from short anecdotes to lengthy tales. A number of stories may be about one tzaddik—certainly if the occasion is his *yahrzeit* feast—or there may be discussion about a particular subject, with tales told about a number of tzaddikim. During and after the tales there is often conversational byplay, with the rebbe or elderly hasid who is presiding commenting on the deeper or more obscure meanings of the tales. Questions are raised and alternative views discussed.

The hasid, Rabbi Israel HaLevi Rosenzweig, was the regular storyteller at the *Melaveh Malkahs* of two Jerusalem rebbes of the previous generation, the Bialer Rebbe and, later, Reb Arele Roth. His grandson writes:

As is well-known, my grandfather was a wonderful storyteller, a mouth that emits pearls. When he told stories of the tzaddikim, he was actually like an ever-flowing fountain. Every tale he narrated was infused with charm and the fear of heaven, and by his telling he implanted pure faith in God and faith in the tzaddikim in the hearts of the holy flock. Storytelling about tzaddikim was for him a form of worship and even though he was an awesome *matmid* [constantly and unceasingly studying Torah], he would [nevertheless interrupt his studying to] sit for hours at a festive meal celebrating the *yahrzeit* of a tzaddik or at a feast of the Messiah King David [*Melaveh Malkah*], telling tales of tzaddikim.[31]

Daily

Sometimes tales of tzaddikim were told daily in the *Beit Midrash*, between *Minhah* and *Maariv*, as was the custom of Rabbi Elimelech of Lizensk.[32] Elie Wiesel described his experiences as a boy accompanying his hasidic grandfather to the *Beit Midrash*:

I would listen to them as night fell—between the prayers of *Minhah* and *Maariv*—in the House of Study filled with flickering shadows of yellow candles. The elders spoke of the great masters as though they had known them personally. Each had a favorite rebbe and a legend he liked above all others. I came to feel that I was forever listening to the same story about the same rebbe. Only the names of the people and places changed. Motives, deeds, responses and outcomes hardly varied; just as there was always a person in need, there was always someone to lend him a hand.

About his grandfather, he wrote:

In his presence, the others in the House of Study kept respectfully silent. A fabulous storyteller, he knew how to captivate an audience. He would say [to me]: "Listen attentively, and remember above all that true tales are meant to be transmitted—to keep them to oneself is to betray them."[33]

Sometimes hasidim share tales of the tzaddikim at night after they are finished studying Torah. That was the custom in the *Beit Midrash* of the Shpoler Zeideh (Grandfather)[34] and in the *Beit Midrash* of the Tzemah Tzedek of Lubavitch.[35]

Informal

Storytelling does not always require a festive meal or a formal setting. Hasidim exchange tales casually at the *Beit Midrash* or in any social situation. A hasidic tale begins by relating that when the Holy Jew (Rabbi Jacob Isaac of Pshis'ha) and Rabbi David of Lelov were traveling once and stopped at an inn, they sat down together to talk about tzaddikim.[36] Tales can even be told to oneself. Rabbi Menahem Nahum of Stepinesht (a son of Rabbi Israel of Rizhin) used to say: "Do you think that a person has to tell a story or a teaching of a tzaddik to someone else? It is not so at all. Just as when you recite the Sh'ma [the "Hear O Israel"] it is between you and God, in the same way, when you tell a story about a tzaddik, it can be between you and yourself alone." Rabbi Menahem Nahum particularly recommended telling such stories to oneself (and before God) upon waking or right before sleep.[37]

TYPICAL SCENES

Hasidism has many distinctive features: the rebbe as the center of the community, fervent prayer, consecrated meals, holy singing and dancing. Certain typical scenes are readily associated with hasidic life, such as a rebbe densely surrounded by a crowd of hasidim at a farbrengen (gathering) or a Sabbath meal. Everyone knows the mass-produced paintings with the stereotypical scene of two dancing hasidim. But if I were to imagine another scene that equally represents hasidic life, my choice would be a small group of hasidim sitting in a dark Beit Midrash late at night, in the intimate tent of a candle's dancing light, and sharing holy stories.

8

An Established Place in Hasidism: The Mitzvah of Storytelling

TO TELL, TO LISTEN, AND TO ASK

According to hasidic teaching, it is a *mitzvah* (divine commandment) to tell and to listen to tales of the tzaddikim.

Telling

A hasid writes: "Therefore it is a very great and important *mitzvah* to tell stories praising the tzaddikim and their service of God, blessed be He, for people will see their example and do likewise. And the more one tells stories praising the tzaddikim . . . the more praiseworthy it is."[1]

Listening

Another hasidic author writes that just as it is a *mitzvah* to tell stories of the tzaddikim, it is a *mitzvah* to listen to them, particularly since not everyone is able to tell stories in a charming way that delights the ears of his listeners. If a person cannot tell stories, he can at least listen.[2]

Asking

How can one perform the *mitzvah* of telling without a listener, or the *mitzvah* of listening without a teller, since each needs the other? The answer is that a person must ask his friend, either to tell him a story or listen to one he would like to tell. Rebbes and hasidim who love stories regularly make such storytelling requests of others.[3]

THE *HAGGADAH*

The Torah's prime storytelling commandment is to tell the story of the Exodus from Egypt at the Passover *seder*. Presumably, this oral storytelling was anciently and originally spontaneous, but today it is performed through the recitation of the written *Haggadah* (which means "telling"). At the beginning of the Passover *Haggadah*, it says: "Even were we all wise and all understanding, and all sages knowledgeable in the Torah, it would still be a *mitzvah* for us to recount the story of the Exodus from Egypt; and the more fully one tells the story, the more praiseworthy it is." This statement that even sages are required to tell the Exodus story is then illustrated by the famous tale of the five rabbis, at the end of the first century C.E., storytelling throughout the night about the events of the Exodus.

Rabbi Eliezer, Rabbi Joshua, Rabbi Elazar ben Azaryah, Rabbi Akiba, and Rabbi Tarfon were reclining [at a Passover *seder*] in Bnei Brak [a city in Israel] and were telling the story of the Exodus from Egypt the whole night, until their students came and said, "Masters, the time for reciting the morning *Sh'ma* [Hear O Israel] has arrived!"

The rabbis were not only praiseworthy in reclining at the *seder* and fully relating the story of the Exodus, but were so engrossed in the telling that they had to be reminded of the duty to recite the *Sh'ma* in the morning before the set time. Presumably, they had passed beyond knowing the difference between night and day! This is the classic ancient rabbinic tale that conveys the power of storytelling.

The Tzemah Tzedek, Rabbi Menahem Mendel, the third rebbe in the Lubavitch (Habad) dynasty, connected the *Haggadah* to hasidic storytelling. He said that just as it is a *mitzvah* to tell the story of the Exodus from Egypt, so is it a *mitzvah* to tell stories of the "hasidic exodus," namely, the spiritual exodus from the bondage of worldly limitations and constraints.[4] He further stated that the telling itself accomplishes this purpose: "It is a *mitzvah* to tell a hasidic story, and by the telling itself one exits the 'Egypt' of worldly limitations."[5]

But even scholarly hasidim sometimes have to be reminded of the value of storytelling and that it is a *mitzvah* to tell stories, so he continued, quoting and interpreting the *Haggadah*: "'Even were we all wise, and all understanding, and all knowledgeable in the Torah'—that is, perfect Habad hasidim—'it would still be a *mitzvah* for us to recount the story'—we must still tell hasidic stories. And these stories will take us out of Egypt."[6]

The three words used in the *Haggadah*—*wise, understanding,* and *knowledgeable*—represent the qualities of Wisdom (*Hochmah*), Understanding (*Binah*), and Knowledge (*Daat*) that characterize the path of HaBaD Hasidism. So the rebbe said that even if a person is a perfect Habad hasid, thoroughly knowledgeable in the teachings and philosophy of Habad Hasidism, and might think himself exempt from storytelling, he must still tell hasidic stories, because it is *they* that have a unique power to take him out of spiritual exile.

A CANDLE IN THE DARK

The Tzemah Tzedek's statement that stories particularly have the power to take a person out of the darkness of spiritual exile is graphically illustrated by a custom in his *Beit Midrash*. When his hasidim studied there in the evening, each one sat with a candle in front of him. But after Torah study, they put out most of the candles and gathered around one or two to share stories of the tzaddikim.[7] Now of course when they studied separately each had to have a candle to illuminate his book, and when they gathered together to tell stories, they did not need all the candles. But I sense a symbolic meaning in this custom all the same.

I have always had a special attraction to my mental picture of a group of hasidim sitting around a candle late at night in a *Beit Midrash*, in an intimate tent of light, sharing stories of the holy tzaddikim. For me, the meaning of this scene is that even more than Torah study, storytelling provides light and inspiration when we are in spiritual darkness.[8] That is why the Tzemah Tzedek taught that although a person might know all of hasidic teaching, he must still tell stories, for during times of personal exile, of darkness and depression, it is the stories, even more than the teachings, that can inspire and renew him and illuminate his path, to lead him out of Egypt.[9]

CLEAVING TO THE SAGES
THROUGH STORYTELLING

Telling tales of the tzaddikim and their holy ways is part of the mitzvah of cleaving to God[10] by cleaving to the sages.[11] Hasidic teaching constantly urges a person to seek the holy company and healing contact of tzaddikim, who can inspire and lift him up. But when this is not possible, storytelling is the next best thing and can "keep one in holy company." It can even allow a person to associate, so to speak, with tzaddikim who are no longer in this world. People need spiritual mentors and teachers, but can they always find them or succeed in getting close to them?

Rabbi Nahman of Bratzlav wrote: "By [telling and listening to] stories of the tzaddikim, we merit coming close to them."[12] Tales of tzaddikim remind a person that there are others more spiritually advanced than he, who can teach and guide him; the tales arouse his desire to search for such a person and help the seeker recognize him or her when she appears. Tales of tzaddikim are also a prayer—expressing the longing for a spiritual guide and mentor—that God hears and fulfills. That is what Rabbi Nahman meant by writing that through storytelling about tzaddikim a person merits coming close to them. In addition, the benefit someone derives from a spiritual teacher depends to a great degree on his openness and readiness to receive. The more he recognizes and appreciates the virtues of his teacher, the closer he can come to him and the more he can gain from his teachings and company. Storytelling about tzaddikim cultivates a person's reverence for those more spiritually elevated; it trains him to seek them out and then to humbly receive and learn from them.

COMFORTING THE SPIRITUALLY ILL

A hasidic author used another concept to promote the recognition of storytelling as a mitzvah: He wrote that just as it is a mitzvah to visit a person who is physically ill and comfort him with conversation, so is it a mitzvah to visit a person spiritually ill and comfort him with conversation and stories about the tzaddikim—to praise and glorify them and their wondrous ways, to arouse in him a burning desire and longing to follow their example.[13]

A spiritually ill person can be started on the road to recovery by listening to holy stories. Rabbi Israel of Rizhin said that you can give a Jew life by telling stories.[14] Here is a tale illustrating these teachings:

Stories Can Cure Depression

A hasid who was close to the holy rabbi, Rabbi Pinhas of Koretz, the remembrance of a tzaddik and holy man for a blessing for the life of the World-to-Come, was very poor. He had three daughters to marry off but no money for dowries or wedding expenses. After considering what to do about his problem he decided to travel around collecting donations so he could marry off his eldest daughter.

One day at eveningtime he arrived at a certain village and went into the house of the Jewish innkeeper to lodge there for the night. Inside he saw a youth, the innkeeper's son, restlessly pacing back and forth in his room, like someone deranged, muttering to himself over and over, "God, if you created man, why did You create the evil inclination? And if You created the evil inclination, why did You create man?"

The hasid, who was standing in the room, heard all this and was amazed. When the youth noticed him there, he greeted him, and the guest began to converse with him, telling him various things about holy tzaddikim, and especially about his own holy rebbe, Rabbi Pinhas, the remembrance of a tzaddik for a blessing—what he had seen with his own eyes and what he had heard from others. This restored the soul of the troubled youth, who listened attentively.

At mealtime they both went into the dining room together—the youth and the guest—and ate together. The innkeeper and his family were pleased at this because they saw the good effect the guest's conversation had in calming their son's mind. Until then he had been extremely depressed and had not been eating properly, although they did not know the reason. Now he was acting like a normal person.

After the meal the youth took the hasid to his room, where there was an extra bed for a guest. The next day also he did not leave his side. The two of them sat together and conversed, with the hasid telling him inspiring stories of tzaddikim and what he had seen and heard. The youth delighted in these stories. The guest stayed there several days and the youth greatly enjoyed his company; all the time the man was with him his mind was calm and lucid. When the guest left, the innkeeper of course gave him a generous donation, but as soon as he had gone, the boy became depressed and confused again and began to act in a disturbed manner, talking to himself as before.

What was the reason for his strange behavior? It was the custom of this village innkeeper, every year during the month of *Elul*, before the days of *Selihot* (early morning penitential prayers), to go with his family to the nearest city, where he rented a place for them to stay for all the Days of Awe. After Yom Kippur he would return home to his village. This year also, before the Sabbath of *Selihot*, he had gone with his son and the rest of his family to their regular place in the city. Before dawn Sunday morning, the first day of *Selihot*, the *shammos* (synagogue attendant) went from house to house knocking on doors to wake people up to come to the early *Selihot* service, and he also woke up this innkeeper. The innkeeper got up and dressed to go to the synagogue. His son, however, did not hear the sound of the *shammos*'s knocking and continued to sleep. His father did not wake him either, thinking that he would come on his own. But when everyone was in the synagogue and wanted to begin, they saw that his son had not come, so he sent the *shammos* back to rouse him from bed.

When the father had gone off, with his son still sleeping, he had left the candle burning. When the youth woke up on his own, he saw that his father and mother had gone to the synagogue and there was no one in the house. He was alone, except for their young maid, who was also sleeping in the house. The boy got up, and his evil inclination started to incite him to go to the girl, because now he had his chance when no one was at home. After mulling it over briefly, he decided to do it, but before he could actually go, the *shammos* came and knocked on the window to wake him, saying that his father had sent him to tell him to come quickly because everyone was waiting for him, to start the prayers. As soon as the *shammos* came, his evil thought disappeared. He went with the *shammos* to say *Selihot* with the congregation, and no one knew what he had been about to do.

The innkeeper stayed in the town until after Yom Kippur, as usual, and then returned to his home in the village. Because of this incident, however, the boy became very disturbed. Look what he had done, before *Selihot* and Yom Kippur! He had not only had these lewd thoughts but had also had an erection and ejaculated unintentionally. Brooding over his evil intention and the sin he had almost committed, had the *shammos* not interrupted him, he became extremely agitated and frequently emitted deep sighs. He was plunged into a dark depression and was drowning in regrets and remorse. But he did not reveal to anyone the source of his misery. He just kept repeating over and over his complaint, "God, if You created man, why did You create the evil inclination? And if You created the evil inclination, why did You create man?" And no one knew what had happened to him or why he kept saying this.

When the hasid arrived at the inn and began to talk to him and tell him sweet stories about the tzaddikim, he calmed down and his troubled

mind was soothed; he became lucid and happy. But when the hasid left
and he was alone again, he at once reverted to his former condition.

When his father the innkeeper and his mother saw his relapse they
immediately sent someone to bring the guest back to their house. Then
the innkeeper asked him to stay with them through the winter to teach his
son Torah and talk with him. "Why do you want to wander around collecting donations during the cold winter months?" he said. "Stay here with
us, in comfort, and whatever you think you would have collected, I'll give
you." The hasid agreed to stay and they settled on a fee for his efforts. He
was there for the whole winter and was an excellent doctor for the boy's
illness. As Passover approached, however, the hasid wanted to return home
for the holiday, and the innkeeper could not dissuade him from leaving,
even though he well knew that when he did, his son would have a relapse
and would return to his sorry condition.

The hasid told the man that he wanted to take the boy with him to his
home in Koretz—where his rebbe, Rabbi Pinhas, lived—and the boy could
stay with him in his house, where he would watch over him. He assured
the father that he was very close to the holy rebbe, Rabbi Pinhas. He would
take the boy to the rebbe and promised that the rebbe would draw him
close, and his mental condition would certainly improve. The father readily
agreed, only asking that the hasid promise him to take care of the boy and
in every way treat him as if he were his own son. The boy also agreed, and
the two traveled together to Koretz.

When they arrived, the hasid immediately went to greet the rebbe, as
customary, while the boy stood at his side. Rabbi Pinhas, meanwhile, saw
with his holy spirit everything that had happened to the boy and how he
had sinned. He gave the hasid a weak greeting and hardly spoke to him,
unlike the way he usually greeted him—with warmth and affection, speaking with him at length. As for the boy, the rebbe did not greet him or even
look at him. After standing there for a few minutes, the hasid went home,
surprised at the cold treatment he had received, but he told the boy not to
be concerned, that the rebbe was doubtless distracted by something or
bothered by some trouble, and when they would go back in the next day
or two he would surely treat them warmly.

On the holy Sabbath, the hasid went with the boy to Rabbi Pinhas's
table for the Sabbath evening meal, and they sat among the guests, the boy
at his side. The rebbe began to teach Torah at the table, expounding on
what the Gemara (Sotah 36b) says about the verse, "and he [Joseph] entered the house [of his master, Potiphar] to take care of his business" [Gen-

esis 39:11]: "Rab said that he went to actually take care of business; Samuel said that he went in to have sex with Potiphar's wife, but the image of his father Jacob's face appeared before his eyes and he did not go through with it." Then the rebbe began to call out, "Samuel, why did you slander that righteous man, Joseph, shaming and humiliating him by revealing his transgression, when the Torah was concealing it?!" He shouted this a second and a third time, but no one sitting there knew why, since it had nothing to do with the weekly Torah portion for that Sabbath. But when the boy heard it, he felt that the rabbi's words were directed to him. Agitated and cast into an emotional turmoil, he fainted and fell to the floor. The hasid, sitting next to him, was stunned by this. He revived him and immediately took him back to his house, where he put him to bed to rest and relax. In the morning he asked him what had caused him to become ill and faint, but the boy did not reveal his secret and said that he did not know why; he just suddenly felt weak and fainted.

The hasid took the boy once again to the rebbe's table for the Sabbath morning meal, and the scene of the previous evening was repeated: The rabbi began shouting the same words concerning the talmudic teaching, about Joseph entering the house to take care of his business, and "Samuel, why did you slander the righteous Joseph? The Torah was covering up for him and you interpret that he went in to have sex?!" And he repeated this a second and a third time. No one sitting there knew why the rabbi was saying this—first on Sabbath evening and now again—but the boy became agitated and fainted this time too. With much effort they finally revived him, and the hasid took him home.

After the Sabbath, the hasid took the boy to Rabbi Pinhas, who now began to treat them both warmly, because the rebbe had seen with his holy spirit everything that had happened to the boy and how he had sinned and by his words of Torah at the table had brought him to repent completely before God, so that he fainted twice. The boy remained with the rebbe after Passover for several weeks and became attached to him with all his heart and soul. He wrote to his father saying he could not leave his holy rebbe, Rabbi Pinhas, and asked him if he could please move the family to Koretz—which the father did for the sake of his beloved son. And everything was done with the agreement of the holy rabbi, may the remembrance of a tzaddik and holy man be a blessing for the life of the World-to-Come.[15]

Rabbi Pinhas knew by the holy spirit what the boy had done, and his Torah teaching at the table was directed to him so he would repent and be healed. When the boy heard the rebbe's words, he realized that his secret was known, and fainted. But although the rebbe rebuked him so he would repent, he did not judge him harshly. Although the boy had intended to commit a sexual sin, and was prevented only by his father's sending the shammos to wake him, did not something similar—according to the rebbe— happen to the biblical hero Joseph, who had also intended to sin with Potiphar's wife, had he not been restrained by a vision of his father's face? Thus, not even Joseph, who was the traditional model of sexual purity and restraint, had been perfect! The rebbe also chided the talmudic sage Samuel for revealing Joseph's secret, when the Torah—only hinting at what had happened—concealed it. Rabbi Pinhas also handled the boy's situation in a way to conceal his shame from others.

Rabbi Pinhas showed himself a true spiritual master in his dealings with the boy, and as the rabbis say: He pushed him away with one hand and drew him close with the other. Initially stern, refusing to greet him, he acted warmly and drew him close only after he had caused the boy to fully repent.

In this story we see how tales of the tzaddikim can help heal a spiritually ill person, dispersing the clouds of depression that surround him and soothing his troubled mind. When the hasid visited the innkeeper, he temporarily healed the tormented boy with his stories. But one purpose of stories of tzaddikim is to lead to a yearning to visit holy people and gain the benefit of their company. The stories the hasid told the boy were simply first aid, until he could actually see the real spiritual doctor and be cured.

9

Drawing People to God through Storytelling

The Baal Shem Tov made numerous converts to Hasidism by his story-telling. In later times also, hasidim often recruited new members to the banner of Hasidism and to their various sects by telling stories of their rebbe and other tzaddikim. Sometimes, however, this happened not directly, by "storytelling proselytism," but indirectly, simply by people seeing the holy joy of the hasidim and overhearing their inspired telling of tales.

REPENTANCE FROM STORYTELLING

An old Sadagorer hasid, Reb Abraham Altshtader, once described to some younger comrades, who sat with him at a festive meal on Shavuot, how even traveling to their Rebbe (Rabbi Abraham Jacob of Sadagora, a son of Rabbi Israel of Rizhin) filled hasidim of former days with unparalleled joy. In those days before the railroad, they journeyed in a group by wagon in leisurely fashion, stopping awhile at inns along the way. The trip from Reb Abraham's town to Sadagora took about two weeks. When they stopped at an inn to eat and then drink some liquor as they talked about holy matters, their heavenly joy created a palpable aura that powerfully affected everyone near them. They exerted a magnetic attraction on all who happened to be present and often drew them into their joyful session. They went from one town and inn along the way to another, attracting people, like bees to honey. People who simply chanced to overhear their hasidic conversations and storytelling became attached to them and had their lives transformed, for they realized that all their worldly pleasures could never even begin to match the brimming and overflowing delight they saw among these hasidim.

In Reb Abraham's own words: "We didn't purify their soiled souls by immersing them in mikvehs (ritual baths) or by prescribing harsh penances and afflictions, but with a little liquor, a fountain of joy, and a flood of exalted words and stories of tzaddikim."

As Reb Abraham began to tell a story about an incident that occurred on one such journey, all the hasidim sitting at the table with him leaned forward to have a clear view of his face and gestures as he spoke.

"I can still see in my imagination," he said, "as if it were yesterday, an innkeeper who was utterly submerged in worldliness, as his face gave clear testimony. This was on Rosh Hodesh Sivan [the New Moon holiday, of the Hebrew month Sivan]. We were traveling to the Rebbe for Shavuot [in the early part of that month] and arranged a Rosh Hodesh feast in a small village near the town of Kolomaya. The innkeeper kept the liquor flowing, and not ordinary liquor either, for it tasted like the legendary wine stored in the grapes since the Six Days of Creation [to celebrate the Messiah's arrival]. It was ninety-five proof, yet he gave it to us without charge. It seemed he had a hasidic spark in him, and that was actually the case, as it later turned out. We were warmed up by the liquor, until our feast became a real 'session.'

"You should know, my friends," said Reb Abraham, "that you need divine assistance for a 'session' like that. Sometimes we gather and talk about the most exalted spiritual matters, yet the Adversary succeeds and we don't at all feel what we should feel: the warmth, the inspiration, the Divine Presence are missing. Our hearts lack something.

"Other times we are with hasidim who are not great intellectuals but simple believing souls. We sit and drink, and slowly there develops a conversation of a special, exalted sort. That is a real 'Garden of Eden session' that lasts through the night, and no one even notices when the sun comes up and morning arrives. No one can bear to separate from his comrades. In such a session everyone tangibly feels the influence of the Rebbe [who binds them together as fellow hasidim and infuses them with holy power].

"At that session on Rosh Hodesh Sivan in the village inn, such a conversation developed. A holy warmth spread through all our limbs and we all felt heavenly inspiration, as if a shaft of heavenly light had entered our hearts, just as when the Torah was given at Mount Sinai. Extraordinary things were said about tshuvah (repentance), about how our Rebbe viewed sinners and the true path he prescribed for their repentance, different from some other rabbis.

"The innkeeper, who from time to time brought more liquor into our room, became interested in what we were saying and the stories being told. He asked our permission to join us at the table and listen to our conversation. We immediately realized that the power of the Rebbe was at work, that the spirit of holiness was beginning to overpower the spirit of impurity and it was our task to help it, since 'when someone comes to purify himself, he is helped.'

"'Here is definite proof for what was stated before,' said one of our group, 'about the true hasidic attitude to sin and repentance. Listen to this story. In the city of Pinsk in Russia, an incident occurred, where a woman who had just given birth, and was sleeping in the same bed with her newborn daughter, smothered the baby to death while asleep. As everyone knows, when a terrible event like this happens to a woman, she considers herself a "murderer," requiring a profound repentance to atone for her sin.

"'In the morning, the unfortunate woman hurried to the rabbi of the city and asked him to prescribe a regimen of repentance for her terrible sin. To begin with, the rabbi burdened her spirit by explaining to her the grave punishment she deserved for the sin of "murder." Then he prescribed for her penance eighty-four fasts, every Tuesday and Thursday. After each fast she should sleep on a hard bed, and all the time she should keep praying to God, blessed be He, that He forgive her sin.

"'The tzaddik, Rabbi Levi Yitzhak, later of Berditchev, just happened to be in Pinsk at that time, and the poor woman went to him, gave him a *pitkah* (petition-note given to a rebbe), and with copious tears poured out her heart, telling him what had happened and the penance given her by the town rabbi, to atone for her grave sin.

"'"God-forbid! God-forbid!" cried the tzaddik, when he heard the heavy penance the rabbi imposed on her. "May God protect and save us! Don't fast and afflict your body for even a single day! *Tshuvah* means that a person repairs what he earlier damaged. Fasts and afflictions can in no way repair such an unintentional sin. The proper path of repentance for you is this: to eat and drink to cheer yourself up, to sleep well and do everything you can to be healthy and strong, joyful and happy, so that you will be able to repair what you've damaged by raising well the children you'll have in the future to replace the one that died."

"'*That*, my friends,' concluded the hasid telling the story, 'is the teaching of a true tzaddik!'

"'Something similar happened with our Rebbe [Rabbi Abraham Jacob]—may he live long!—in Sadagora,' called out another hasid, and he began to tell the tale.

"'Once, a Jew from Chernovitz, who was a well-known sinner, came to Sadagora and asked the Rebbe to teach him the path of tshuvah. He told the Rebbe that, being acutely ashamed of his doings, he had previously traveled to the Rabbi of Kolomaya, where no one knew him, and that the rabbi had told him he must wander in "exile" for three years and for all that time must not eat more than a dry crust of bread and drink a little water every day.

"'Our holy Tzaddik smiled and said, "That is not the way! True repentance must be 'equivalent' to the sin, meaning that a person should not repeat the same sin, even if a similar opportunity presents itself. If you are always hungry and thirsty, tired and afflicted, you won't have the strength to resist the temptation when it occurs during your wandering. Therefore, eat and drink as much as you need, in your own home, amongst your family. But earnestly commit yourself, with a pure heart and strong resolve, to sin no more. Another aspect of an 'equivalent' repentance, to atone for your sin, is that you must distribute in charity to the poor the same amount of money that you spent over the course of the last year in sinning. That will be a true repentance. God, blessed be He, does not need or want human sacrifices. That is why the prophet said, in His name, 'I have no pleasure in the death of him that dies . . . therefore, repent and live!'"'

"On that same occasion," continued Reb Abraham, describing the scene to his younger friends, "another story was also told by one of our group:

"Once, on erev Rosh HaShanah, during the penitential prayers that begin, 'Remember the covenant!' the tzaddik and famous lover of Israel, Rabbi Moshe Leib of Sassov, made the following strange argument to the Master of the World, in order to exculpate the Congregation of Israel. He argued: 'Dear Father, You need the sins of the Jews! In Your crown are set thirteen radiant jewels, that represent the Thirteen Attributes of Your Mercy [derived by the rabbis from the attributes enumerated in Exodus 34:6-7]. If the Jews completely ceased to sin, You would be missing certain jewels in Your crown, such as patience and forgiving sin and transgression! How would Your crown appear if those jewels were missing?'

"When the Tzaddik of Pshis'ha heard this story about the Sassover, he said, 'This clarifies something I always found difficult to understand. Why does it say in the Shemoneh Esreh prayer: "[God,] who desires tshuvah (repentance)"—that God wants people to do tshuvah; shouldn't it have said that He is appeased by tshuvah? The words of the Rebbe of Sassov make clear that when it says that God "wants" *tshuvah*, it means that He is pleased when a person does *tshuvah*, for then He can forgive him his sins and justly be called "a forgiving and pardoning King." [The blessing that God "wants" *tshuvah* is followed by the one that calls Him a forgiving and pardoning King.]

[After repeating this tale that had been told by another hasid, Reb Abraham continued:] "The innkeeper who was listening to all this suddenly left the room, his face white as plaster. It was clear to us that powerful feelings of repentance were surging up within him.

"We continued to celebrate for a while more in honor of *Rosh Hodesh* and the upcoming holiday of Shavuot. When we were about to resume our journey the next day, we said goodbye to the innkeeper and thanked him for his warm welcome and the admirable way he entertained us. 'Do me a favor,' he said to us, 'and remain here just a little longer.' Then he turned to me and said, 'I'm sure your friends will forgive me if I speak with you for a few minutes privately. I have to speak to you about an important matter.'

"When we went to another room, he said, 'The joy I see among you and the beautiful stories you've told have forever stolen from me my peace of soul. My Jewish spark has been kindled. I'm a transgressor! Do you hear me, my dear fellow Jew? I'm a terrible sinner! It's true that I've never skipped the morning prayers or putting on *tefillin*, but you see, my dear fellow Jew, the afternoon and evening prayers are something else altogether! In an inn even a tzaddik couldn't be careful about them! In an inn you can't fully observe all the details of the Sabbath either. I try as best as I can not to handle money on the Sabbath, but my oldest daughter has ceased being concerned about it. What can I do? To our sorrow, we are still in Exile. So I let every poor traveler who enters my inn eat and drink free of charge. Nevertheless, I am a Jew and will have to answer for my sinful behavior. No one lives forever in this world! But to increase my pain, since yesterday, when I listened to your conversations, the thought of *tshuvah* has not left me. So I beg you: Take me with you, to your Rebbe, who will tell me how to do *tshuvah*!'

"The innkeeper said all this in one breath, without giving me a chance to answer or to ask him to clarify some of the details. But I felt gratified that heaven had made me an agent to save a Jewish soul from ruin, and I told him that yes, he could travel with us, to the holy tzaddik. . . .

"To make a long story short, I'll tell you that this transgressor became a decent, upright person, a faithful hasid, who even attained certain exalted spiritual levels. . . . And such happenings were common enough in former days, when we traveled to the Rebbe. . . ."[1]

Reb Abraham's story depicts a group of hasidim sitting in a storytelling session discussing the hasidic attitude to repentance, with a number of the hasidim telling tales one after the other about different rebbes, their own and others, that relate to this theme. His story also shows the powerful effect of this storytelling on an outsider, causing him to repent.

Judaism teaches two paths to repentance: A person can repent with fear of God and holy sadness or with love of God and joy. As this story and its component tales make clear, Hasidism chose the latter path. The scene of "former days" described by Reb Abraham was in the late nineteenth century, and the world has undergone radical changes since then. Yet today also more than a few people are still attracted to the joy faith inspires and aroused to a sincere repentance by religious storytelling.

Opposition to and Defense of Hasidic Storytelling

10

Traditional Opposition to Storytelling: Stories versus Teaching

TWO-PART TORAH

The Torah is made up of two parts: commandments about what and what not to do, and stories. Similarly, the Talmud is composed of *Halachah* (religious law) and *Aggadah* (stories and parables). Although most people appreciate both aspects of the Torah in varying degrees, different personality types often have a natural inclination to one aspect or another: to practicality and order or to a more fluid, multifaceted, even mysterious, reality.

RASHI

But since early times, some religious scholars have tended to discount stories as being of lesser value than the legal parts of the Torah. The Torah begins with stories; indeed, the whole Book of Genesis is almost completely stories. Yet, in his comment on the first verse of Genesis, the great Torah commentator, Rashi, notes that the Torah could have begun with the first commandment, which is in the Book of Exodus, and asks: "Why were all these stories necessary?" While Rashi may have asked this question merely to elicit his answer (which has no relevance to stories or storytelling), and because he knew it was an issue for others, obviously such a question could occur only to scholars who were so totally engrossed in legal studies that they were perplexed by the prominence the Torah gave to stories. However, if Rashi's words are taken at face value, and not as a mere rhetorical device, it is actually disturbing to think that such a question could even be asked.

ONE-SIDEDNESS

One of Judaism's greatest strengths has always been its profound intellectuality. But, from the early hasidic point of view, the reverse side of that virtue was the unfortunate tendency of some Torah scholars to concentrate exclusively on study and books, neglecting other ways of serving God. There was also a tendency among scholars to narrow Torah to *Halachah* alone, treating *Aggadah*, with its stories and parables, as a poor relation. The opponents of Hasidism, the *misnagdim* (singular, *misnagid*), were usually less interested in *Aggadah*—although it is an integral part of the Talmud—than were the hasidim, and some of them even frowned on storytelling, considering it a waste of time that could be spent studying Torah.[1] But from its very beginnings, Hasidism opposed such one-sidedness.

THE HASIDIC VIEW ABOUT THE RELATION BETWEEN STORIES AND TEACHINGS

THE BAAL SHEM TOV

The Baal Shem Tov did not limit his divine service to Torah study. He taught that a religious person must be well rounded, serving God in many ways and bringing an awareness of His presence into all his doings. He not only emphasized *Aggadah* and Kabbalah, rather than the legal studies of Talmud and Codes, but was also an avid storyteller.

The Baal Shem Tov's religious ideal was not the proverbial scholar "imprisoned" in the *Beit Midrash*, who limits his study to the four *amot* (cubits) of *Halachah*. How could the Besht bring the Torah's light to others if he sat day and night in the study hall? So he traveled all over to bring Jews back to God and met people of all kinds: Jews and gentiles, lords and peasants, merchants and shepherds, mystics and common thieves. A typical image of the Besht, found in countless stories, is of him racing somewhere in his horse-drawn coach at magical speed to go on one adventure or another. He taught the path of divine joy, of serving God not only through study and prayer but through song, dance, and also storytelling. Although Torah study was in the marrow of his bones, he served God in many other ways too. This broad-minded attitude and approach aroused the ire of some scholars, whose whole world was Torah books and who felt that by even slightly deemphasizing study, the Besht was denigrating them.

Living Torah

While some scholars reduced life to an intellectual category, something known only through books, the Besht transformed Torah books into living realities. A famous story tells how he made a disciple out of the superscholar, the Maggid, Rabbi Dov Ber, of Mezritch. When the Mezritcher first visited him, the Besht said to him: "Do you know Kabbalah?" When Rabbi Dov Ber answered yes, the Besht handed him a kabbalistic book and asked him to interpret a passage. As he began, the Baal Shem Tov leaped up saying, "How can I sit while we are involved in Maaseh Merkavah, the mystic Account of the Divine Chariot!" The rabbi then interpreted the passage, but as soon as he finished, the Baal Shem Tov snatched the book from his hands, saying, "You don't know it at all!" As the Besht expounded it, the room filled with heavenly light and the rabbi actually saw all the angels mentioned in the text. Afterward, the Besht told him that what he had said was correct, but without life.[2]

When the Baal Shem Tov studied and expounded Maaseh Merkavah, its teachings pulsed with life and vitality. We previously discussed his saying that telling stories of the tzaddikim was like studying Maaseh Merkavah. Certainly when he told stories also, their scenes, heroes, and events came vividly alive.[3]

His zealous reaction in jumping up and standing when Rabbi Dov Ber was expounding Maaseh Merkavah shows just how exalted he intended the comparison of storytelling to Maaseh Merkavah to be.

Scholars and Disciples

The Baal Shem Tov's joyful hasidic way attracted the common people, but some of the scholars scoffed. Just as they considered hasidic singing and dancing frivolous, so did they think storytelling not something for serious religious people.

It should not be imagined that even all of the Besht's disciples easily accustomed themselves to taking stories seriously. Most of his inner circle were themselves great scholars, whom he had drawn from the traditional scholarly world; their ingrained training mitigated against an appreciation of storytelling.

The Besht might have needed to convince some of these disciples, who were accomplished scholars and kabbalists, to interrupt their studies and engage in storytelling about tzaddikim. Perhaps the Besht's saying "Whoever tells stories praising the tzaddikim is as if engaged in the mystic study of the Divine Chariot (*Maaseh Merkavah*)"[4] was designed to encourage not only illiterate simple people but his elite disciples as well.

A Parable about Stories and Parables

The Besht told his disciples a parable: "There was once a king," he said, "whose sons always ate with him at his table. Even though a king's table is laden with all the best foodstuffs and delicacies, they were so accustomed to this rich fare that they derived no special pleasure from it. One day their father, the king, said to them: 'My advice to you is to take large sacks and fill them with the leftovers, and hide them away. There will be occasions when you will have more enjoyment from the leftovers than from the full meals.' And that is what actually happened. Once during a wartime siege of the city, they brought out the stored leftovers and enjoyed them tremendously.

"The meaning of this," said the Besht, "is that you should carefully store away in your memory the little things you hear from me—I'm not speaking about Torah teachings, but about parables and stories—because there will be occasions when they will be of great benefit to you."[5]

Hearing the rich philosophical and mystical lessons of their master, the Baal Shem Tov—eating at the king's table—every day, his scholarly disciples might have overlooked the simpler and more homely stories and parables he used to illustrate his teachings. However, he told them by means of this parable to take care and store away these stories and parables, because there would be occasions when they would derive more benefit from them than from the most exalted teachings.

The application of this parable is not, however, fully clear, for what kind of "occasions" did he mean? What benefits would they have? Perhaps he meant when they were in low spirits ("under siege") and would be revived more by stories and parables than by philosophical teachings, or when they had to teach simple people, where stories and parables would be indispensable. Perhaps, like the king in the parable, the Besht did not spell out the details of his advice. The main point to note is that he directed his disciples to not overlook his stories and parables, for there would come times when they would derive invaluable benefits from them.

In a Dream

A hasidic tale relates: "After the passing of the Baal Shem Tov, the memory of a tzaddik and holy man for life, the band of his holy disciples gathered together to share the Torah they had heard from his holy lips, each one according to his understanding. That night the Besht appeared to them in their dreams and said, 'Why do you concentrate so much on my teachings, and not on my fear of heaven?'"[6]

From where does one learn about the Besht's devotion and piety, his love and fear of God? From the stories told about him.[7] It seems that the Besht had to urge his disciples to talk and tell tales about his life and deeds.

THE MAGGID OF MEZRITCH AND HIS DISCIPLES

Oral and Written Torah

The Maggid of Mezritch, one of the Besht's greatest disciples and his successor as head of the hasidic movement, came to share his master's appreciation of storytelling. As we have seen, the Maggid tried to instill this awareness in his own disciples by teaching that praising the tzaddikim is like praising God.[8]

The first Lubavitcher Rebbe, Rabbi Shneur Zalman of Liadi, who was one of the great disciples of the Maggid of Mezritch, said: "When we heard teaching from the Rebbe, we considered it to be like the Oral Torah. When we heard a story from him, we considered it to be like the Written Torah."[9]

Of course, the Oral Torah (the Talmud, which was originally oral) is the commentary on the Written Torah (Bible).

To Be a Torah

Another great disciple of the Maggid of Mezritch, Rabbi Leib Saras, said, in a now famous comment, that he did not visit the Maggid to hear Torah from him but to see the way he tied his shoes. The goal was not simply to learn Torah but to "become" a Torah.[10] This can be accomplished only by actually being with a holy person and carefully observing his ways. But when that is not possible, hearing stories about him is the next best thing.

Indeed, a tzaddik or *tzaddeket* is "full of stories," and everything he or she does easily becomes a story. Why? Because the actions of a holy person are not based on self-directed motives, as are the actions of most people, but are God-directed; therefore, their actions are often strikingly unusual and astonishing; each act, no matter how trivial, is memorable and has something to teach.

Sapphires

Still another of the Maggid's disciples, Rabbi Jacob Joseph of Ostraha, known as Rav Yiby, commented on a verse in Isaiah (54:11) where God comforts an afflicted Israel and promises: "I will lay thy foundations with sapphires (*sappirim*)": These are the stories (*sippurim*) of tzaddikim.[11]

Like other midrashic comments, this one expresses a full thought in a few words. Sapphires and other jewels are ordinarily used for personal ornamentation. Therefore, the prophet says that even the foundations of buildings will be of sapphires. The rebbe's first point is that tales of the tzaddikim are precious, like sapphires. The same comparison of tales to jewels is made elsewhere in the hasidic tradition.[12] But the rebbe's words go beyond that: His comment on the prophet's teaching means that whereas a person might think that stories of the tzaddikim are mere ornaments of the Torah, beautiful but nonessential, in fact they constitute its very foundation.

How so? According to hasidim, the fundamental importance of stories is that they inspire a person to actually practice and fulfill the teaching of the Torah and the teaching of the rebbes. That is why stories are the very "foundation."

THE WHOLE PERSON

One of the primary differences between straightforward teaching and stories is that while teaching tends to be general and universal, stories are able, and more likely, to focus on personality, and when they are about a tzaddik, to focus on his personal example. The Baal Shem Tov's hasidic approach gave greater prominence to developing the whole person. That is why the hasidim especially appreciated stories. The tzaddik was the model of the perfected person, and stories were the natural vehicle for portraying the ideal he represented. The *misnagdim*, on the other hand, concentrated almost entirely on legal studies. Their religious view focused on the Law and obeying the commandments. While the hasidim also studied the legal side of the Torah, and zealously adhered to the commandments, their focus on the charismatic personality of the tzaddik, the sect leader, greatly encouraged their passion for stories and storytelling.

STORIES ARE "SO REAL"

A contemporary hasidic storyteller, Rabbi Shlomo Carlebach, has said:
"The difference between a teaching and a story is that in the first we are asking to learn something we do not know. But in the story we are asking to be made holy, to be made new, like a child, like a tzaddik. We are saying, 'Please tell me! Let me know what I know.'"[13]

Another saying of Rabbi Carlebach graphically explains why stories are indispensable and teachings alone insufficient:
"Stories are so real. Imagine that the Torah quoted all of our father Abraham's teachings and told us nothing about him. We wouldn't remain as his children today! We need to hear that there was a Jew, Abraham, who actually opened his door to the poor. It's making it real. A story is the most real thing in the world."[14]

The teachings explain what to do; the stories show someone actually doing it.

RABBI ISRAEL OF VISHNITZ

If some of the Baal Shem Tov's own disciples undervalued stories and storytelling, so that he had to correct their attitude, it is easy to imagine the attitude of some of his opponents and of misnagdim in later generations. A story about Rabbi Israel of Vishnitz in the early years of his leadership—when a rebbe is prone to being treated with less awe by older and advanced hasidim—casts light on this subject.

Two distinguished hasidim, Rabbi Mordechai Hana and Rabbi Berish Orenstein, were sitting together during the intermediate days of Sukkot, in a regular study session of theirs, learning Reishit Hochmah (a book of exalted kabbalistic teachings about character development and ethics). And because the book is so awesomely pure and holy, their zeal and fervor were aroused. When they noticed that the time had arrived for the Rebbe to conduct his midday meal, they rose and went to his sukkah (booth).

They found the Rebbe sitting down, surrounded by hasidim. When they approached, they heard that he was telling a story about an innkeeper and horses and so on. After their spiritual elevation from studying *Reishit Hochmah*, this did not appeal to them and seemed like a waste of time. So they sat down at the far end of the *sukkah* and continued their animated discussion about divine service.

Suddenly the Rebbe gestured to them to come closer and said: "Let me tell you a story. A certain young hasid used to travel to the holy Rebbe of Ropshitz, the memory of a tzaddik for a blessing, and his custom was to stay with him for four full weeks. During that time he recorded in a notebook everything he saw there. Even when the Rebbe went to the chicken coop, he immediately followed him and recorded how he fed the chickens, and so with everything else the Rebbe did. At the end of the four weeks, when he returned home, he would get up very early every morning to study Torah before *davvening* (praying), and one of his regular study sessions was to review the notebook and learn some spiritual practice from every word and every act of the Rebbe."

As he concluded his story, the Rebbe of Vishnitz said: "Now that you understand that a person can learn how to serve God from every word or act of his rebbe, will you also begin recording?"

When Rabbi Berish told this story, he used to say that the Rebbe's words made an impression on him that he never forgot.[15]

The Rebbe gently rebuked his hasidim for not realizing that if he was telling stories, it was not an idle activity. He not only hinted to these hasidim, who were excited about the teachings of *Reishit Hochmah*, about the depth of stories and storytelling, but he did so with a story.

11

Scriptural Support
for Storytelling

When the hasidic rebbes looked for scriptural support for their high evaluation of stories and storytelling, they often turned to two sources from the *Midrash.*

RASHI'S QUESTION

One text, mentioned in the previous chapter, is the opening remark of the most famous Torah commentator, Rashi, on the first verse of the Torah: "In the beginning [God created the heaven and the earth]." Some religious scholars felt that the Torah was basically a book of commandments. Why then did it begin with stories? Almost the whole Book of Genesis and the beginning of the Book of Exodus are stories. This had to be explained. Rashi, who took his comment from the *Midrash,* says:

> The Torah could have begun with the verse (in Exodus 12:2) "This month shall be unto you [the beginning of months; it shall be the first month of the year to you]" –which is the first *mitzvah* that Israel was commanded [indicating the month that should initiate the calendar]. Why did it start with "In the beginning"? The reason is that "He hath declared to His people the power of His works [in giving them the heritage of the nations–the Land of Israel]" (Psalm 111:6).

Rashi meant that the stories in Genesis showed that God created the whole world; He was its owner and it was He who gave the Land of Israel to the Jewish people.

The Hasidic Interpretation

The hasidic rebbes were more interested in Rashi's question and his observation—that the whole first section of the Torah is stories—than in his answer (which, as mentioned earlier, is not relevant to stories or storytelling). Rashi's question is referred to again and again in hasidic sources that discuss storytelling and was interpreted in different ways. Here are three examples.

Rabbi Israel of Rizhin's Book Endorsements

The Tzemah Tzedek (the third rebbe in the Lubavitcher [Habad] dynasty) once sent a distinguished hasid of his, the *gaon*, Rabbi Yitzhak Isaac HaLevi Epstein of Homiliya, to Rabbi Israel of Rizhin, in connection with a community matter. Trained as a Habad hasid, Rabbi Yitzhak was very interested in the ways and customs of Rizhiner hasidim and their rebbe, Rabbi Israel, and he observed everything carefully.[1]

When people first arrived at the Rizhiner's court[1] and came to exchange greetings with the rebbe, and also when they came later on to deliver their *kvittels* (petition notes) to be read before him, the procedure was that one of the rebbe's prominent hasidim, whom he appointed to be an intermediary between him and the hasidim—and called the *mekurav*—would stand at the rebbe's right, while the main attendant stood at his left.

One of the visitors then in Rizhin was a rabbi and well-known scholar from Bukovina, who was one of the rebbe's foremost hasidim. He had brought with him a book of talmudic interpretations he had written, in order to ask for the rebbe's endorsement. Another, ordinary hasid, who over a period of years had collected stories of tzaddikim and hasidim, also brought his book with him to ask for an endorsement.

When the rebbe was receiving people, both these visitors—the rabbi and the hasid—were standing with their books in their hands. According to the rebbe's instruction, the *mekurav* took their books from them and read aloud to the rebbe from a few places in the rabbi's book and then some stories from the compiler's book. After sitting absorbed in a religious mood for a while, Rabbi Israel began to speak about the great value of tales of the tzaddikim and of the strong impression they make in the palaces of the tzaddikim in the Garden of Eden. Then he spoke about the halachic (legal) interpretations read from the rabbi's book, offering his own profound and probing comments, in a lengthy discourse on the subjects discussed. When he finished, he told the *mekurav* to write endorsements for both books, for the storybook and then for the book of talmudic interpretations.

The Habad hasid, Rabbi Yitzhak, watched everything with great interest—the way visitors were received, how the rebbe interacted with his hasidim—and he was very impressed by the extraordinary depth and unique approach exhibited in Rabbi Israel's impromptu talmudic discourse. However, he found it puzzling that the rebbe had first spoken about the hasid's book of stories and had its endorsement written out first, before the rabbi's book of talmudic interpretations.

Two days later was *Rosh Hodesh*, the New Month, and Rabbi Yitzhak was invited to the festive meal. Rabbi Israel said words of Torah at the table, and before the Grace After Meals, he said: "The Lithuanian[2] *gaon* is surprised that I spoke about the book of stories of tzaddikim first, and only afterward about the talmudic interpretations, and that I also had the storybook's endorsement written first.

"This is an ancient question, and the holy Rashi, who was a *gaon* in both the revealed and concealed Torahs,[3] asks about the first verse of Genesis: 'The Torah could have begun with [the first commandment to the Jewish people] "This month shall be unto you"—Why did it start with "In the beginning" and all the stories that follow?—The reason is that "He hath declared to His people the power of His works"—[He wanted to declare and make known] the divine vitality—the soul—that infuses the works of creation and keeps them in existence every hour and minute. My great-grandfather, the holy Maggid of Mezritch, learned from the holy Baal Shem Tov how to see the soul in everything.'

"You see," said the rebbe to Rabbi Yitzhak, "we follow the same order that God, blessed be He, followed in the Torah: putting the Book of Genesis, with its tales of tzaddikim—the Patriarchs and others—first. As it says in the *Midrash*: With whom did He consult before creating the world? With the preexisting souls of the tzaddikim.[4] Only afterward comes the Book of Exodus, with 'This month shall be unto you.' [That is, God created the world for the sake of the tzaddikim, who are its "soul," so of course He placed their stories first.]

"Both authors are fine hasidim, and both books reveal extraordinary creative power. The innovative Torah interpretations demonstrate great learning and the clear lines of reasoning that the one author created and innovated in the holy Torah, and the stories of tzaddikim show the great creative power of God, blessed be He, in the world.[5] Therefore, I gave my endorsement first to the book of stories, before the one for the book of Torah novellae."[6]

The Power of Stories

Rabbi Nathan of Nemirov, Rabbi Nahman of Bratzlav's foremost disciple, also commented on Rashi's question and explained that the Torah begins with stories because they inspire a person to do and fulfill the teaching that follows. He wrote:

> The Torah has two parts: the commandments and explanations of them, which teach us how to act; and the stories, particularly in Genesis and Exodus. These two categories are also found throughout the *Tanach* [Bible] and the Oral Torah [Talmud, *Midrash*, etc.]. Why then does the holy Torah begin with stories? As the rabbis have said: "The Torah could have begun with 'This month shall be unto you.' The reason is that: 'He hath declared to His people the power of His stories' [*maasav*; Rabbi Nathan understands this word, which can mean either "His works" (deeds) or "His stories," in the latter sense, and interprets the verse contrary to its literal meaning]."

Since the purpose of the Torah is to lead to correct action, the commandments are of prime importance. Yet even on the simple level, aside from the hidden wisdom and secrets the Torah stories contain, they have a tremendous power to awaken a person's heart to fulfill the Torah. In the same way, the stories of the tzaddikim have the power to set a person's heart on fire to serve God, to learn the teachings of the rebbes and fulfill them truthfully and sincerely, according to His will, blessed be He.[7]

The Sweetness of Stories

Lastly, we can note the charming comment of Rabbi Levi Yitzhak of Berditchev. Rashi asked: *Mah taam patah bivreishit?* "What is the reason the Torah begins with the Creation" and other stories, and not the laws? Making a play on words with the Hebrew *taam*, which means "reason" or "taste," the Berditchever paraphrased Rashi's Hebrew question with the Yiddish: *Vos fur a zeese taam pasah bivreishis?* "With what a sweet taste did the Torah begin—with the stories of Creation," instead of the strict laws![8]

THE STORYTELLING OF THE PATRIARCHS' SERVANTS:
ELIEZER, THE SERVANT OF ABRAHAM

The second scriptural support most frequently used by the hasidic rebbes to explain and justify their high opinion of stories and storytelling is another teaching of the *Midrash*. In the Book of Genesis, Abraham sends his servant Eliezer back to the city of Haran in Mesopotamia to find a wife for Isaac. Once there, Eliezer meets Rebecca at the well, and then her brother Laban at their home. Eliezer then recounts to Laban all his doings to that point (24:33-49), essentially repeating what the Torah had already reported rather fully earlier (24:1-27). The rabbis took note of the unusual length of Eliezer's speech as he narrated his story. They were amazed that whereas commandments of practical significance are sometimes merely hinted at in the Torah, Eliezer's "storytelling" is of tremendous length. In the *Midrash*, Rav Aha comments: "The conversation of the Patriarchs' servants is superior to the Torah teaching of their descendants."[9] Thus, Eliezer's storytelling shows that Jews of later times are so far below the spiritual level of Abraham, Isaac, and Jacob that they are even inferior to the Patriarchs' gentile servants. Although the rabbis were descendants of the Patriarchs, none of their teachings were worthy of being included in the Torah, yet even the casual conversation and drawn-out storytelling of the Patriarchs' servants had been included.

The Hasidic Interpretation

The hasidic rebbes interpreted Rav Aha's midrashic comment to justify their emphasis on storytelling, even in preference to Torah teaching.[10]

The Rizhiner

Rabbi Israel of Rizhin, for example, used this *midrash* to explain why he attempted to influence his hasidim primarily by private conversations and storytelling rather than Torah teaching. According to Hasidism and the Kabbalah, the tzaddikim accomplish a cosmic mystical repair of the world by "raising up the divine sparks" that have fallen into the power of evil and unclean forces. Usually this is effected through Torah, prayer, and other *mitzvot*. But Rabbi Israel said that some sparks had fallen too deeply to be extracted and released by those means. What then should be done? Certainly they could not be left unredeemed? He said:

Abraham taught us a new and different way to free the sparks: by means of storytelling and conversation. That is the method that Abraham's servant and disciple Eliezer used when he went to get Rebecca, for when he saw that he could not extricate her from her impure environment by Torah or prayer, he said, "If I am unable to do this by means of Torah, prayer, or other *mitzvot*, I must do it by storytelling and conversation." [He reads *lo ochal*—"I won't eat" (Genesis 24:33)–as *eineni yochol*—"I am unable." According to the Rizhiner, who interpreted hasidic beliefs about mystical storytelling into the Torah text, Eliezer's storytelling had a mystical effect in causing the wicked Laban to release Rebecca.] That is the meaning of Rav Aha's comment: "The conversation of the Patriarchs' servants is superior to —more effective than—the Torah teaching of their descendants."[11]

I will later discuss hasidic ideas about the mystical effects of storytelling but, on the simple level, this teaching shows that Rabbi Israel intended to rescue his hasidim from the place to which they had descended and from their worldly and unholy environment in the same way that Eliezer rescued Rebecca—by storytelling.

STORIES BECOME TORAH

Rashi observed that the Book of Genesis is largely stories. Among them, of course, is the story of Abraham's servant, Eliezer. Rabbi Shlomo of Radomsk combined the two midrashic teachings—about the Torah beginning with stories and about Eliezer's storytelling—and said:

We see that the whole Book of Genesis is stories of the Patriarchs— the tzaddikim—which shows that telling stories of the tzaddikim is Torah. Therefore, the rabbis said: "The conversation of the Patriarchs' servants is superior to the Torah teaching of their descendants." Why? Because the conversation of the Patriarchs' servants *became* the Torah of the Patriarchs' descendants.[12]

It is indeed an important insight to realize that stories about the lives of holy people become Scripture. Thus, the stories about the first tzaddikim, such as the Patriarchs and Matriarchs, *became* our Torah. Should we not learn from this, Rabbi Shlomo asks, the importance of telling stories about the tzaddikim of later generations also?

The Stories We Tell Will Also Become Scripture

Rabbi Meir Shalom of Kalishin took Rabbi Shlomo's thought a step further and said that when the final Redemption comes, all the stories told now about the tzaddikim of later times will *also* become part of the Torah. The stories of the generations who lived before Mount Sinai became part of our Torah. The same will happen for the generations after the Giving of the Torah on Sinai. God said through the prophet: "For a Torah shall go forth from Me" (Isaiah 51:4), and the *Midrash* teaches that this means that there will be a new Torah at the final Redemption.[13] When this verse and teaching are fulfilled, then the stories told in later generations and until today about the tzaddikim will also become Torah.[14]

12

Storytelling among the Misnagdim *and Non-hasidim*

STORYTELLING AND PERSONALITY

The opponents of Hasidism, the *misnagdim*, generally viewed hasidic storytelling as excessive and even frivolous. Although they also told stories occasionally, they did not encourage or promote it as did the hasidim. As mentioned in Chapter 10, this indifferent and sometimes dismissive attitude derived from their religious perspective, which concentrated on Torah study, and specifically the Torah's legal teachings, rather than on its stories. They were generally less interested in the ideal personalities of tzaddikim as portrayed in stories and more interested in teachings about the commandments and their fulfillment.

Furthermore, leaders among the *misnagdim* were not generally charismatic and, unlike hasidic rebbes, did not form sects. A great *misnagid* rabbi's followers primarily respected his Torah learning and genius, rather than his person as such (although he, of course, had to meticulously fulfill the Torah's teachings). Thus, they were less oriented than hasidim to telling admiring stories of their leader's greatness. Another related reason why *misnagdim* were less enthusiastic about telling stories is that they were usually more sober personality types, who simply were not attracted to religious singing and dancing, or to storytelling, as were the hasidim.

A DIFFERENCE IN EMPHASIS

However, the difference between hasidim and *misnagdim* was not absolute. The *misnagdim* also had their tzaddikim,[1] their Torah teachers and leaders, whose stories they cherished and told. The same is true for non-hasidim in the traditional community today. Although there may not be quite as many stories about non-hasidic tzaddikim, there are still countless stories about them, many preserved orally, some collected in books. And that is only to be expected, for whenever people revere and admire exceptional individuals, they will always tell stories testifying to their greatness. The difference between hasidim and non-hasidim lies in the emphasis the former put on the practice of storytelling and the extent to which they elevated a more or less natural social activity to sacred status as a *mitzvah*. Hasidism even produced a mini-theology of storytelling, with numerous teachings about its use as a spiritual practice. While many people in the non-hasidic traditional community also tell religious stories, the whole enterprise operates at a lower level of intensity and intention. Hasidism alone brought storytelling as a spiritual practice to the fore, discussing it, analyzing it, and encouraging it. Instead of a mere conventional activity, usually pursued somewhat "unconsciously" during spare time, it became conscious and intentional, a spiritual activity engaged in for the benefit of the teller as well as the listeners. This perspective, in all its ramifications, simply does not exist outside of Hasidism, nor is there any comparable body of teaching about storytelling from non-hasidic sources.

Another factor distinguished the hasidic renewal of storytelling. The main, if not exclusive, use of storytelling by non-hasidim had always been by rabbis and *maggidim* (preachers). But there is a significant difference between the age-old use of storytelling as a teaching tool by religious teachers and its widespread adoption by masses of ordinary hasidim, who made it an integral and vital part of their religious activity. There is little that is new or interesting about preachers telling stories, but there is something new when a whole community begins telling and knows why they are doing it. That is the reason I have almost exclusively concentrated on hasidic storytelling and the teachings of the rebbes. Other Jews have always told and still tell stories, but having done so somewhat unreflectively, they produced few, if any, teachings about the subject, and there is much less to say about their involvement.

THE *MAGGIDIM*[2]

The tradition of storytelling *maggidim* (preachers) in Judaism goes back to ancient times.[3] In more recent centuries in Eastern Europe, the rabbi's primary function was to rule on questions of Jewish religious law, and his infrequent sermons were usually scholarly in nature. It was the itinerant *maggidim*, traveling from town to town and from synagogue to synagogue, who specialized in preaching and in telling parables and stories. Although they were not professional religious storytellers as such,[4] they frequently and effectively used stories in their sermons. In the earlier years of the hasidic movement, there were many hasidic preachers as well as non-hasidic ones. Later, the rebbes—some of whom had been preachers—absorbed many of the inspirational and storytelling functions of the *maggid*. One of the most famous non-hasidic practitioners of storytelling, particularly of telling parables, was the Dubner Maggid, Rabbi Jacob Kranz (eighteenth century), who was closely associated with the great Torah genius and the supreme opponent of Hasidism in his generation, Rabbi Elijah, the Vilna Gaon.

The Dubner Maggid was renowned for his enormous repertoire of parables and his ability to extemporaneously produce a parable for any topic under discussion. A story relates that when the Vilna Gaon once asked his friend how he so quickly found a parable suitable to any particular subject, the Maggid replied, as usual, with a parable:

"A student at a military academy, who was returning home after graduation, stopped at a village inn to rest his horses. When he went to the barn, he noticed on its side a number of targets, with a bullet hole in the exact center of each. Astonished by this extraordinary display of marksmanship, he asked to meet the person responsible. A barefoot boy came over and introduced himself. 'Where did you learn to shoot like that?' asked the military student, 'What is your secret?' 'To tell you the truth,' replied the boy, 'I first shoot the gun and only later draw the circle around the hole.'

"It's the same with me," continued the Maggid, "When I hear or create a good parable, I commit it to memory. All I have to do later is apply it to a suitable subject that arises."[5]

Presumably, this parable too had been stored in the Dubner Maggid's memory, waiting for an appropriate application. Parables are generally more flexible than true stories in this regard and can often be applied to many different subjects.

Today, only a few traditional *maggidim* remain, such as the famed Maggid of Jerusalem, Rabbi Sholom Schwadron, who is an exceptional teller of stories and parables.

STORYTELLING ABOUT AND
BY THE HAFETZ HAYIM

As said previously, the non-hasidim in the traditional community also have their heroes, whose stories they tell. Today, the lines between hasidim and non-hasidim are not as sharply drawn as in former days. Hasidim occasionally tell stories about non-hasidic greats, and non-hasidim, perhaps more frequently—because of the plethora of excellent, readily available tales—tell stories about famous hasidic rebbes. One of the most famous and exceptional non-hasidic tzaddikim of the last few generations was the great Hafetz Hayim, Rabbi Israel Kagan. The following tale, which contains stories within stories, must be read carefully, and its storytelling elements should be noted. It was told by Rabbi Sholom Schwadron, the Maggid of Jerusalem, and the exciting rhythms of his speech can occasionally be heard through the written word.

"This story," said the Maggid of Jerusalem as he began his tale, "was told to me by a famous Torah scholar, who in his youth studied at first in Radin, in the *yeshivah* of the Hafetz Hayim, and then in Kamenitz, with Rabbi Baruch Ber. The home of Rabbi Baruch Ber was a story in itself, for it was completely open, as if ownerless. The boys who were students came and left at will and did everything else in the house that they needed—cooking their food and so on. Rabbi Baruch Ber sat in his room studying, oblivious to the hubbub around him. The *rebbetzin* (the rabbi's wife), for her part, totally gave up her house; she had not a corner to herself. The students did whatever they had to do there.

"The exception was when an illustrious guest visited her husband and wanted to speak with him privately. Then, the *rebbetzin* asked the students to depart, after which she shut the door, and Rabbi Baruch Ber could be alone and converse with his guest.

"Once, at the time of the evening prayers, Rabbi Baruch Ber returned to the *yeshivah* with a very important guest, Rabbi Shalom from Eishishuk, who had been one of the leading students and intimates of the Hafetz Hayim in Radin. The [unnamed] rabbi and Torah scholar who told me this story said that he knew immediately that after prayers Rabbi Baruch Ber would invite Rabbi Shalom to his house, where they would talk about the Hafetz Hayim. He burned with curiosity to hear their conversation. He already knew the custom that the *rebbetzin* would ask the boys to leave and then the *rosh yeshivah* (head of the *yeshivah*) would converse privately with his guest. So before they had finished the evening prayers at the *yeshivah*, he entered the rabbi's house when students were still there and, taking advantage of the usual commotion, slipped into the rabbi's room and hid under his bed without anyone noticing.

"While he was lying there, the prayers at the *yeshivah* ended, and Rabbi Baruch Ber and Rabbi Shalom returned to the house. As usual, the *rebbetzin* asked the boys to leave and they did. Then, the two rabbis sat down, the *rebbetzin* served them tea, and Rabbi Baruch Ber asked Rabbi Shalom to relate something about the Hafetz Hayim. Rabbi Shalom consented and began to tell a story:

"'The Rebbe [the Hafetz Hayim] taught a special class for his best students every morning, until noon. But on Friday, he ended at eleven and told stories until noon. Once he told us how when he was fifteen years old he went to study in the *yeshivah* of Rabbi Nahumkeh Horodner, of blessed memory. And who was Rabbi Nahumkeh? Who was he?! . . . He was one of the thirty-six hidden tzaddikim [in whose merit the world exists]! He hid his greatness and served as the community's *shammos* (synagogue caretaker). Yes, the *shammos!* Later he was the pillar of kindness for the whole community and every act of kindness was performed through him. He administered a major charity fund and supported many modest, pious people about whose poverty no one knew. In fact, it seems that he also supported the thirty-six hidden tzaddikim,[6] for he knew their identity. In any case, in his later years, when he became famous as a holy tzaddik, he had a *yeshivah*, and students from all over flocked to study with him. The Hafetz Hayim also came to this *yeshivah*, as a young man, to study with Rabbi Nahumkeh Horodner.

"'On that Friday, when the Hafetz Hayim was telling this story, he said that over the course of time the students became aware that every night, after midnight, Rabbi Nahum disappeared, no one knew where. "Of course, we wanted to know what Rabbi Nahumkeh was doing at that hour. Our curiosity was so intense that we began to spy on him and discovered that he was going to the synagogue, which at that time of night was completely empty, with not a soul there. What did I do?" said the Hafetz Hayim. "I went to the synagogue for the evening prayers, and when they were finished and everyone was leaving, I went into the Women's Section, which was screened off from the main room, and hid under a bench while the whole synagogue emptied out. After the caretaker walked around to check that everyone had left, he locked the door of the synagogue and departed.

"'"Exactly at midnight I heard someone opening the door. A shiver ran through my whole body and I began to tremble. It was the Rebbe, Rabbi Nahum. He went up on the *bimah* (synagogue platform) and took out of a chest that was used as a storage place for discarded sacred items—old books, torn-out pages with divine names on them, and worn tallises—a book, probably of Kabbalah, that he began to study. Suddenly I saw that he was surrounded by fire! I was terrified and began to shake. I wanted to cry out 'Gevalt! There's a fire!' I quickly realized, however, that this was not ordinary fire, so I kept silent and did not utter a sound. But I continued to tremble and shake and felt that my soul was about to fly out of my body. He stood there studying for about an hour, and I felt every moment that I was about to die. Afterward, when he finished, closed the book and returned it to the chest, the fire suddenly disappeared and he left! At that moment, I began to feel better and recover. I lay there trembling until the morning, but before people arrived for the morning prayers, I got up and left the synagogue."

"The rabbi who was telling me this heard it all as he was lying under the bed. Rabbi Baruch Ber responded to Rabbi Shalom Eishishuker's story by saying, 'That there was fire around Rabbi Nahum is simply what would be expected, but it is amazing that the Hafetz Hayim was able to see it when he was only fifteen!'

"The rabbi told me another amazing story from Rabbi Shalom of Eishishuk that he heard as he lay under the bed. Rabbi Shalom said that just as the Hafetz Hayim had seen something wondrous from his master, Rabbi Nahumke, so [at an earlier time] had he seen something wondrous from the Hafetz Hayim. 'Once,' he said, 'we saw the Hafetz Hayim put on his hat and coat, take his walking stick, and go out. I sensed that something unusual was happening and wanted to know what it could be. I followed him to the fields outside Radin, to a small garden by a stream. The Hafetz Hayim stood in the garden, marked out a circle on the ground with his walking stick (like Honi ha-Maagal),[7] entered it and said, "Master of the World, I've entered this circle and will not exit until You fulfill my request!" It goes without saying that I trembled to hear such words! But with my own eyes I saw that after just a few minutes, he left the circle, certainly because Heaven had fulfilled his prayer!'

"Rabbi Shalom of Eishishuk concluded, 'When the Hafetz Hayim told his story about Rabbi Nahumke, I dared to say to him, in the presence of all the students, that just as he had caught Rabbi Nahumke in the miracle with the fire, so had I caught him with the circle he drew and what he had said then. . . . The Hafetz Hayim listened to what I said—as did the other students—but kept his silence and uttered not a word, of admission or denial.'

"This whole story was told to me," concluded the Maggid of Jerusalem, "by the rabbi who heard everything as he lay beneath Rabbi Baruch Ber's bed. And it seems that Rabbi Shalom Eishishuker continued telling stories about the Hafetz Hayim, but meanwhile the *rebbetzin* discovered that he was hiding under the bed, took a broom and chased him out of the house!"[8]

Considering that Rabbi Shalom of Eishishuk told a story of the Hafetz Hayim hiding under a bench to discover what his rabbi was doing in secret, and how, in a similar way, he, Rabbi Shalom, had followed the Hafetz Hayim to spy out his secret activities, one might assume that as Rabbi Shalom spoke he knew that the student (and later rabbi, who told this tale) was under Rabbi Baruch Ber's bed, even before the *rebbetzin* chased him out.

This story makes clear that non-hasidim also value and tell stories praising their great Torah teachers and leaders. Not only did one rabbi share precious stories about his master, the Hafetz Hayim, with another, who asked him to tell them, but a student was so eager to hear the stories that he employed stealth to eavesdrop on the rabbis' conversation.[9] Among other things, he heard that the great Hafetz Hayim had a special storytelling session late Friday morning on *erev Shabbat*. When the student later became a rabbi, he told the whole story to the Maggid of Jerusalem, Rabbi Sholom Schwadron, who in turn told it in his sermons to large audiences. So Hasidism did not "invent" storytelling in Judaism; it only raised it to a new and unprecedented level of intensity and purpose.

II

HASIDIC TEACHING ABOUT THE METHODS AND PRACTICES OF STORYTELLING

How to Learn, Tell, and Listen

13

Deriving Lessons from Stories

THE "THEREFORE"

According to hasidic tradition, all teachings and stories have a "therefore"—
a lesson for each person's divine service; indeed, there are usually multiple
"therefores" for whatever level he or she is on. The previous Lubavitcher
Rebbe, Rabbi Joseph Isaac Schneersohn, emphasized in his talks and letters that the most important aspect of everything studied or any story told
is the *bechein*, the "therefore," the practical guidance it offers with respect
to divine service.[1] This view is not limited to hasidim, however. A favorite
saying of the Maggid of Jerusalem is: "The most precious part of a story is
its lesson!"[2]

LESSONS AND THE POWER TO FULFILL THEM

The present Lubavitcher Rebbe, Rabbi Menachem Mendel Schneersohn,*
in a comment connecting the inspirational and instructive aspects of hasidic
stories, said that not only does a holy story contain lessons, it also provides the motivational power, encouragement, and blessing necessary to
fulfill the lessons, depending on the willingness of the listener.[3]

LESSONS FROM STORIES, STORIES FOR LESSONS

I earlier quoted the first Lubavitcher Rebbe, Rabbi Shneur Zalman of Liadi,
who said that when the disciples of the Maggid of Mezritch heard teaching

---

*During the preparation of this book, the Lubavitcher Rebbe passed away to his eternal world.

from him, they considered it to be like the Oral Torah, and when they heard a story, they considered it like the Written Torah.

Rabbi Joseph Isaac Schneersohn of Lubavitch explained an aspect of this, saying that according to Habad Hasidism the distinction between the Written and Oral Torahs is that the former is Wisdom (Hochmah; the spark of insight) and the latter is Understanding (Binah; the development and expansion of an idea). This means that the philosophical teachings of Hasidism are Binah and the stories hasidim tell are Hochmah. The kabbalistic Sefer Yetzirah teaches: "Understand (gain Binah) through Wisdom (Hochmah) and become Wise (gain Hochmah) through Understanding (Binah)." Applying this to explain Rabbi Shneur Zalman's saying, Rabbi Joseph Isaac said it means that one should approach the wisdom of hasidic stories with understanding, seeking to draw out the comprehensible teachings and lessons that can be learned from them; and one should approach the understanding contained in hasidic philosophy with wisdom, seeking the stories and spiritual lifestyle that harmonize with the particular teaching at hand.[4]

Thus, when pondering a religious story, a person should try to understand its practical teaching and guidance for his own spiritual life, and when he confronts a religious teaching, he should try to recall a story that illustrates the lifestyle it recommends.

PRACTICE MAKES PERFECT

A frequent hasidic setting for sharing stories is the often joyous gathering called the farbrengen, where comradeship is celebrated with teaching and stories and with liquor, song, and dance. Some farbrengens are led by the rebbe himself; other, smaller and more informal gatherings by one or more veteran hasidim. Rabbi Joseph Isaac Schneersohn said that the rabbis teach that the true way to acquire the Torah is by being in the company of those who embody its teachings. Usually this refers to being in the presence of one's teacher, but it equally applies, he said, to

> a hasidic gathering—a hasidic farbrengen—when it is of the kind conducted by the elderly hasidim of every generation, where they tell stories of tzaddikim and hasidim, bringing out the religious lessons of the tales and explaining and expounding what must be learned from them. They become aroused with a spiritual fervor appropriate to the content of the stories and, to a significant degree, bring their arousal into action, in avoiding evil and pursuing good. That is why

our holy rebbes, the princes of Habad and the famous rebbes of the hasidic movement as a whole (the memories of holy tzaddikim for a blessing for the life of the World-to-Come, their souls being in a peaceful Paradise, may their merit protect us) loved hasidic gatherings and hasidic stories.[5]

MORE THAN THE JOY OF TELLING

As Rabbi Joseph Isaac taught, one must not only draw out the lessons of the stories but fulfill the lessons in practice. Although a person may love to read, hear, tell, and retell inspiring tales about tzaddikim who were not only greatly learned in the Torah but lived it, he must ask himself a pertinent question: Is he interested in the stories because he wants to live their teachings, or merely because he seeks the sheer joy of reverently telling the stories as an end in itself? How can he gauge his own motives? One sign that a person's desire for spiritual improvement is sincere and his determination to achieve it firm is his persistence in staying with a story, mulling it over and digesting it fully, not letting go of it, until its lesson is fully absorbed and its teaching translated into practice.[6]

STAYING POWER

Rabbi Zev of Zhitomir, a disciple of the Maggid of Mezritch, said that when he traveled with a group of his fellow hasidim to the Maggid, as soon as they reached the town limits of Mezritch, they attained everything they desired. But if there was anything they did not attain on entering the town, they received it when they reached his house. If when they arrived at his house there was still something lacking, they attained it when the door of their master's house was opened or, at the most, when they saw their master's face. Then they attained everything they desired.

Once, one of the disciples traveling in their group to the Maggid said, "Why should we stay with the rebbe, since we achieve everything we want simply by looking at his face?" So they told their wagon-driver not to unharness the horses from the wagon when they arrived, because they were simply going to their master's house to see his holy face, and would travel home immediately.

When they came to the Maggid's house, he told them a story of twenty-four words, and they had to stay until he finished telling it. When they were leaving immediately afterward to return home, they told their wagon-driver to travel slowly, and they would walk alongside the wagon on foot. So they walked that whole day and night, until dawn the next morning, and all their conversation and thoughts were on that story, to fathom the depths of every word they heard from their master, the Maggid.

In the morning, the wagon-driver began to yell at them and rebuke them, saying, "Is it a little thing that you didn't pray *Minhah* and *Maariv* yesterday?[7] Do you also want to omit *Shaharit* and saying the *Sh'ma* on time today?" He shouted this twice, but they didn't even hear him. Only when he yelled a third time did they awaken and, seeing the sun rising in the sky, realize that a day and night had passed while they were immersed in probing the depths of their master's words.[8]

Among other things, this story teaches the effect of the mere sight of a rebbe on a hasid who is prepared to receive his spiritual influence. It also teaches how he should "take home" what he has heard from his rebbe. The peculiar reference to the Maggid's story being twenty-four words is explained by the fact that the disciples actually pondered every single word of the story and knew the exact number.

Of course, most of the tales a person hears will not be from the mouth of a rebbe, but this story still contains a valuable lesson about sticking with a story until one drains from it every last ounce of spiritual nourishment.

EVERY DETAIL INTENTIONAL

The present Lubavitcher Rebbe, Rabbi Menachem Mendel Schneersohn, states that when a tzaddik tells a story, he is so exactingly intentional in everything he says that the story can be minutely analyzed and lessons learned from every detail.[9]

> When an ordinary person tells a story, one cannot be certain about his intentions and the degree of care he took in expressing himself. However, when the teller is someone of stature, and particularly a rebbe . . . one can be certain that his telling was utterly intentional, and each person—male or female—who the story reaches, should be instructed by it.

> Stories told by our [Lubavitch] rebbes . . . are exact in all their details, both in relation to understanding the story—for every detail aids

in understanding the story itself—and also in relation to understanding the story's meaning and lesson, for every detail contains instruction about the service of God.[10]

TWO LESSONS OF A STORY

The Lubavitcher Rebbe (who is the seventh rebbe in the Habad line) always emphasizes the lessons of stories he tells. Here is an example in a tale he told about his predecessors, the third and fifth Lubavitcher Rebbes. He once said:

As a boy, the Rebbe Rashab went in every year on his birthday, to his grandfather, the Tzemah Tzedek, to receive his blessing. Once, when he entered, at the age of four or five, he burst into tears. When his grandfather asked him why he was crying, the child answered that he had learned in the Humash (the Five Books of Moses) that the Holy One, blessed be He, had appeared to our father Abraham (it was the week of the Torah portion Vayera), and he was crying because God had not appeared to him!

The Tzemah Tzedek said to him, "When a Jew ninety-nine years old decides to circumcise himself, he deserves that the Holy One, blessed be He, appear to him."

The Tzemah Tzedek's answer calmed the child and he ceased crying.

[The Lubavitcher Rebbe continued:] The fact that the Rebbe Rashab told this story [about his childhood] to his son [the previous rebbe, Rabbi Joseph Isaac Schneersohn], and he [the previous rebbe] told it [publicly] with the intention to publicize it in the world, proves that it relates to us too. This story teaches us two things: One, we can learn from the Rebbe's crying, that every Jew, even one not on the level of being educable (that is, not only is he unable to understand on his own, he is not even qualified to receive from another), is permitted to demand that the Holy One, blessed be He, appear to him, just as He appeared to our father Abraham, and to make his demand so forcefully that it is expressed with tears (which indicate that the matter is above understanding and, since the mind cannot contain it, it produces tears, which are the "overflow of the brain"). . . . Two, we can learn from the Tzemah Tzedek's answer that the prerequisite for God's revelation is . . . that a person realizes that he must circum-

cise himself, for his spiritual situation is deficient and he must radically change and improve. This general self-nullification is the prerequisite that prepares him to be spiritually elevated to the highest
levels, even to the level of "God appeared to him" [Genesis 18:1], just
as he appeared to Abraham after he circumcised himself.[11]

ACTING ON INSPIRATION

A religious person must not only assimilate a story intellectually but prac-
tically, by acting on the inspiration it provides, to fulfill its lesson or lessons. The Baal Shem Tov appreciated the quality, particularly developed
in simple, devout workingpeople, of being an *oved*, a servant or "worker"
for God, not only studying Torah but, simply and directly, laboring to fulfill what one learns. While a scholarly person might expertly analyze a Torah
teaching or a story to delve into all its nuances and depths, a simple person, although much less adept intellectually, and only understanding the
matter incompletely, might be more powerfully oriented to surely translate his knowledge into appropriate action. A hasidic tale displays this laud-
able quality in a simple man, who heard a story from the Baal Shem Tov,
when the Besht was still a hidden tzaddik, and acted on the story's lesson.
      Reb Eliezer Lippa was a simple but devout Jew who lived in the town
of Tarnow in Galitzia. He was not able to study Torah, nor did he know
the meaning of the Hebrew words of the daily prayers or of the Psalms
that he recited regularly, but he was a good and righteous man. He always
prayed with the congregation and said "*Amen*" and "*Amen, Y'hei Shmei
Rabba* . . ." in response to the prayer-leader; he listened attentively to the
reading of the Torah scroll, following along word by word in the *Humash*;
he never conversed about worldly matters in the synagogue and treated
Torah sages and scholars with great deference.
      Eliezer Lippa earned his living with his hands, and he possessed a
number of useful skills: He was a builder of simple ovens, a woodchop-
per, a gardener, and also a harvester. At the time this story takes place,
however, he was working as a water-carrier, drawing water from the river
that was about a mile from the town. From this hard work he derived a
decent living according to his modest standard, for four of his customers
were prosperous merchants who paid him generously for his efforts.
      Once, when the holy Baal Shem Tov was still a hidden tzaddik, he
passed through that town and no one knew who he was, because he dressed
in rough clothes like a villager and mixed with the other villagers, to whom

he told stories from the *Aggadah* (legends of the Talmud). He also told them about the great pleasure that the Holy One, blessed be He, derives from the sincere prayers and Psalms said with simple faith by ordinary Jews. One day Eliezer Lippa was taking a barrel of water through the marketplace in his horse-drawn cart when he saw his friend and fellow watercarrier, Reb Zalman Dov, and other acquaintances of his standing and listening with evident concentration to the words of a poor wayfarer (namely, the Baal Shem Tov); so he also drew near and attended to what was being spoken about.

He heard the wayfarer telling a story about Temple times: A rich man was bringing a large and healthy fattened ox to the Temple to offer as a sacrifice. The ox was a massive, powerful animal, and the men were unable to budge it when it refused to be led. A poor man happened to pass by on his way home from the market, carrying a bunch of vegetables for his family's meal. Seeing the difficulty and sympathizing with the plight of the man who was trying to bring a sacrifice to the Temple, he held the bunch of vegetables in front of the animal to let it nibble at them, and led it along peacefully, until they brought it to the place of sacrifice.

That night the owner of the fattened ox was shown a vision in his dream, and he heard a voice saying: The sacrifice of the poor man, who gave up his family's meal of vegetables to help you, preceded your offering.

God desires the heart, said the wayfarer to his audience. The rich man brought as his burnt-offering a large fattened ox, and he was so happy he had merited to sacrifice such an animal that he also sacrificed a sheep as a peace-offering and made a celebration feast for his family and all his friends and acquaintances. He also gave the priests their shares of the sacrifices. All this because of his intense joy at the great *mitzvah* he had performed.

The poor man, who was broken and crushed by his poverty, was bringing home some vegetables for his family's meal. What were his few vegetables—that he gave up to help his fellow Jew—compared to the massive ox and the sheep that the rich man sacrificed? But He who sits in heaven, blessed is He and blessed is His name, had more pleasure from the offering of the poor man's few vegetables than from the rich man's fattened ox. For the rich man offered much, but his family sat down that night to a hearty meal; the poor man sacrificed his family's food, everything he had, to help his friend, and that night his family went hungry.

The Besht explained to his audience of simple Jews that anything a Jewish man or woman does because God commanded it is judged according to the intention of the person's heart. Therefore, even the least thing in the world—that costs just one penny—that a Jew does for the sake of God, and does it willingly and joyfully, with purity of heart, is very precious and dear to the Creator of the world, blessed is He and blessed is His name. He proudly describes it, so to speak, to the ministering angels, and says: "Look at the good deed that this one of my sons or daughters has done!"—and He blesses him or her.

When the Besht concluded and left, Eliezer Lippa returned to his work, and although as usual he cracked the whip over his horse to get it to pull, and in the sweat of his brow he also pushed his cart loaded with the barrel full of water, his mind remained on the story the wayfarer had told—about the poor man's bunch of vegetables—and his explanation that even the smallest act performed for the glory of God, blessed be He, if done joyfully and with a pure heart, is dear and precious to the Creator of the world, blessed is He and blessed is His name. This story and its meaning bore into his brain and gave him no peace. Eliezer Lippa sorely envied that poor man with the vegetables and in his heart he pleaded with the Holy One, blessed be He, to allow him to do some *mitzvah*, to serve God joyfully and wholeheartedly.

When Eliezer Lippa returned home he told his wife what he had heard from the wayfarer, and he explained to her, in his own words, that although the Temple no longer exists, every Jewish man or woman who performs a *mitzvah* joyfully is as if offering a sacrifice.

A week passed, then two and three, yet the wayfarer's story about the sacrifices of the rich man and the poor man stayed with Reb Eliezer Lippa and gave him no peace.

One day, when Reb Eliezer Lippa was delivering water to Reb Naftali, the head of the community, who was one of his four wealthy customers, a novel idea fell into his mind, an idea that warmed his heart and immediately gave him immense pleasure.

Eliezer Lippa's four wealthy customers paid him for his water deliveries a fair amount more than the usual price, and almost half his livelihood was from them. On the other hand, Reb Zalman Dov the water-carrier supplied the town's four synagogues, and they paid only half price for their water deliveries. Reb Eliezer Lippa thought: "Why don't I switch with Reb Zalman Dov—my four wealthy customers for his four synagogues?" For Eliezer Lippa valued the opportunity to serve God by providing water for the handwashing of the worshipers more than he valued the profits from his best customers. After conferring with his wife about his plan, which would significantly diminish their income, and after receiving her warm approval, Eliezer Lippa approached Zalman Dov.

Reb Zalman Dov happily agreed to the transfer that Reb Eliezer Lippa suggested to him. No one in town noticed the switch or gave any thought to the matter, but Reb Eliezer Lippa and his wife were overjoyed. In fact, his wife was so inspired that some days she also went to the river with her husband to draw a number of buckets of water, just for the synagogues, and all the while she did so, her mind and heart were directed to heaven, intending for this water to be used for the holy purpose of Jews washing their hands before prayer, because she too wanted a share in this great *mitzvah*.[12]

This story shows a scene of the Baal Shem Tov's street-corner storytelling from the viewpoint of the listener. We see again how the Besht selected stories—here an aggadic tale from Temple times, comparing the offerings of a rich and a poor man[13]—that were appropriate for his audience of simple Jews, and also how he explained a story, when necessary, to draw out its lesson. But especially interesting is to note how a simple workingman, like Eliezer Lippa, could be inspired by such a tale and how he mulled it over until he found a way to translate its inspiration and message into action. This story may also illustrate the present Lubavitcher Rebbe's teaching, mentioned previously, that a holy story imparts the motivational power necessary to fulfill its lesson. Other storytelling elements are Eliezer Lippa's silent pleading with God to allow him to imitate a story's hero and his immediate retelling of a moving story to his wife. In fact, a good way to acquire a story as a spiritual possession is to immediately retell it one or more times.

Another valuable lesson from this memorable tale is that a person should emulate Eliezer Lippa and his wife in being a "laborer" for God, by making energetic efforts to translate the inspiration and lessons of stories into the actual practice of his divine service.

TELL AND TALK

In the story of Eliezer Lippa the water-carrier, the Baal Shem Tov explains to his audience the meaning of the aggadic tale he tells them. Although it may be unsuitable for a secular storyteller to explain a story's meaning, a hasidic storyteller is encouraged to discuss the meaning of a tale and draw out its lesson. This can even be done in the middle of the story, when some element there requires immediate explanation or discussion. Indeed, sometimes a point in a story is elucidated and explained by means of another, usually brief, story. And after a tale is told, listeners may also be invited to participate and share their own insights and exhortations.

As a storyteller, I often point out, briefly, at the end of a story, its lesson or lessons, when that is necessary or appropriate. Sometimes stories contain elements or motifs that listeners unfamiliar with Hasidism may not notice or grasp.[14] However, I always try to remember that an overly didactic approach can easily spoil a story's magic. In addition, what a story means to a listener may differ from what it means to the teller, and a premature explanation may stifle a listener's insight and throw a smothering blanket over a spark just about to ignite.

The other approach, which I also use and recommend, is to discuss the meaning of a story and its lesson with the audience by inviting their comments and opinions. Not only does this have the virtue of involving them directly, but I am often surprised by their perceptive and often unexpected insights that increase my own understanding of the story and that can be made use of in my next telling.

Puzzling and Straightforward Stories

Over the years I have found that hasidic stories can be divided into two categories: straightforward and puzzling. A "puzzling" story is one that makes a strong impression on me, that attracts, interests, and intrigues me, even if I do not understand it. When a story has such an impact on me, I take it as a sure sign that it contains important teaching, and it is my job to discover what it is. Straightforward stories can be profitably discussed with a group, because no two people will derive the same lesson from a story. But there is a special reward in discussing puzzling stories, because together you will often be able to elicit meanings that would have eluded you individually. Indeed, when you tell a story that fascinates you but that you do not understand, and ask for help, listeners are aroused and stimulated; they become eager to participate and share their views. This puzzling kind of story is often particularly appropriate for an audience composed of people who are highly educated and literate, who know how to analyze a story, but are not well educated Jewishly. Instead of being forced into passivity by their limited Jewish knowledge, a puzzling story challenges them and allows them to become actively engaged and exercise their intelligence. As a result, they enjoy it more and get much more out of it. When I started telling stories to groups, I used this method for another reason as well: It takes some of the pressure off the teller. If you are just beginning to tell stories and lack the confidence to simply plunge in, it is an easy way to slide into the water.

A FAVORITE STORY WITH SOME LESSONS

To conclude this chapter, here is a favorite story of mine and some of the lessons that I typically mention when telling it.

The Holy Clock

When Rabbi Jacob Isaac, the holy Seer of Lublin, died, and the seven days of mourning had passed, his heirs cast lots and divided up his clothes and various other objects that he had used during his life. The Seer's son, the tzaddik, Rabbi Joseph of Turchin, inherited his father's white silk Sabbath garments, his *gartel* (a silk belt worn by men during prayer), and an old clock that was in his holy father's room, and by whose chimes he regulated the hours of his divine service.

Rabbi Joseph folded the clothes and made a package of them, to put the clock in, so it would not be broken. Then he put the package in his knapsack, swung it over his shoulder, and started out for home with his attendant. Being poor, he went on foot. While they were on the road, a drizzle started to fall, followed quickly by increasing rain, until it was pouring. After a quarter of an hour, the downpour was so great that he could not continue traveling and had to seek shelter. By the time he reached a village, he was drenched and his clothes soaking wet. He went into the house of the Jewish innkeeper to stay there for a few hours and rest. When the rain let up, he would continue on his way. He waited an hour, then two, but the rain kept coming down. It poured the whole night, with sporadic thunder and lightning.

He got up in the morning, prayed *Shaharit*, and ate breakfast, but the rain had not stopped. The skies opened and were pouring down torrential rains. No one was entering or leaving the village, and he was forced to stay there. He remained in the inn, eating, and then sleeping there that night, both he and his attendant.

The next day, when the rain finally stopped and the skies cleared, he prepared to leave, and the innkeeper brought him the bill for his expenses. Rabbi Joseph took out his wallet, looked in it, but found only enough money to pay for one day. "I want to pay everything I owe you," he said to the innkeeper, "but I don't have enough money with me. But I do have some articles that are worth something: some holy personal effects that I inherited from my father, may he rest in peace. They're right here. Take a look at them, and maybe you can find something that appeals to you, to take for what I owe you." As he spoke, he took the package out of his knapsack, untied it, and showed the innkeeper the silk clothes, the *gartel*, and the old clock.

The innkeeper looked the things over, turned them this way and that, to see what they were and to get an idea of what they were worth, but he did not know what to say. So he called his wife over, told her the story—that the guest did not have enough money and wanted to pay with these items—and said, "Let's take them into the other room where we can talk privately and decide if they're of any value to us and if we should take them." The woman carefully gathered the things together, tied them up again, and took them into the other room, her husband following after her. They spread the clothes out on the table, and the woman began to feel them, to see what they were made of and assess their value. They did not want to be cheated. She rubbed the silk clothes between her fingers and said, "These are actually expensive clothes, real silk, but they're worth nothing to us. Not many people would be interested in buying them from us, and you have no use for them: They're holy garments, they're not for a village Jew like you. We'll just take the clock, if it works. Although it's old, it's still running, and we can use it to know the exact time to milk the cow—morning, afternoon, and evening. We'll be able to milk her every day at the same time; it'll be good for her and good for us."

Her husband agreed. He returned the clothes and the *gartel* to the guest, but they kept the clock, which he hung on the wall in his bedroom. Rabbi Joseph then left and continued on his way home. The clock chimed out the exact time, every hour, and no one paid any attention to it.

Years later, a great rebbe, Rabbi Dov Ber of Radoshitz, who had been a disciple of the Seer of Lublin, passed through that town on a journey somewhere. When he arrived the sun was setting and he had to stay there overnight. He went in to the innkeeper and asked for a separate room, so he could continue his Torah study and divine service as usual, without being disturbed. The innkeeper told him that he did not have any private rooms; there was just one large common room for all guests. But since the innkeeper knew that he was a famous rebbe, he offered him his own room and said he would sleep in the guest room. Seeing that there was no other choice, the tzaddik accepted his offer and went into the inner room.

When the innkeeper was preparing for sleep, he heard the footsteps of the rabbi pacing about in the adjacent room, singing joyfully and then dancing. He waited for a while and fixed his bed, thinking, "In a little while he'll stop dancing and singing, and go to sleep." But that is not what happened. When the innkeeper was in bed, tired from his hard day of work and drifting in and out of sleep, his guest was still joyfully singing and dancing; and he could not fall asleep. He was turning in his bed the whole night. He became very angry but did not go in to him or complain, because after all, this was a great rebbe! What could he say to him? Shortly before dawn the innkeeper finally fell asleep, and when he awoke it was already broad daylight. He hurried and got up from his bed. But when he went out of his room, and saw the rabbi going out from the other room, he remembered what had transpired during the night. He wanted to ask the rabbi why he had been singing and dancing until dawn but did not know how to bring up the subject in the right way. While he was standing there, scratching himself and thinking, the tzaddik came over to him and asked, "Tell me, where did you get that clock in your bedroom?"

The innkeeper was taken aback by the question. Why was the holy Rabbi of Radoshitz interested in his clock? But since he asked, he told him that many years ago someone stayed at his inn for two days, eating and sleeping, and when he did not have enough money to pay his bill, he gave him the clock instead.

"You don't know what a treasure that clock is," said the rebbe. "That is the clock of the holy Seer of Lublin. As soon as I went into the room and heard its chimes, I recognized it." The innkeeper was even more surprised now and asked, "How did you recognize it? Is there some kind of identification on it? And what's different about its chimes? It sounds to me just like any other clock."

"When an ordinary clock chimes," said the rebbe, "it tells those who hear it that the years of their lives are passing on; one more hour is lost and gone, never to return. Now even though this information is important, because it spurs people to repent and perform good deeds, it is still permeated with gloom and sadness, because it reminds them of the day of their death.

"But the clock of the holy Seer of Lublin, of blessed memory, is different. The holy Seer used this clock for many years to regulate his daily schedule of divine service. So its hourly chimes ring out good news, of joy and happiness: 'I'm one hour closer to the goal, one hour closer!' When I heard that chime, how could I sleep? I was so happy that I had to sing and dance the whole night."[15]

What are the lessons of this story? There are of course many, and everyone will see different meanings in it. One lesson can be expressed through a question, and that is how I sometimes end this story when I tell it: "How do we live *our* lives? So that each hour that passes is one more hour gone and we are closer to death—or that we are one hour closer to our goal?" (I usually leave it to be understood that I mean our spiritual goal.) Sometimes I might speak about the difference between the sad way of serving God from fear, concentrating on our faults and sins, and the joyful way of serving Him from love, aware of how we are constantly coming closer to Him. If our Judaism makes us happy, we will make more spiritual progress than if we constantly discourage ourselves. Another perspective on this lesson is to see the two types of clocks as representing two different types of teachers. One type, like the Lubliner, who is represented by his clock (which reminded the Radoshitzer, to his delight, of his great rebbe), encourages people to look forward, to be positive—seeking what is good, striving to go higher and higher. The other type of teacher is negative, directing people's attention backward to their sins and failures. Sometimes when I tell this story I also end with a saying of the Baal Shem Tov, that it is not the fear of death or punishment that leads people to religion but the yearning to approach the source of goodness and holiness. Of course, this beautiful story has more meanings and lessons than one can count. What thoughts occurred to you when reading it? What "therefores" do you see?

14

How to Tell, How to Listen

KAVVANAH

The Lubavitcher Rebbe, Rabbi Menachem Mendel Schneersohn, says that a person must have holy intentions (*kavvanah*) when telling a story: "A Jew must fulfill 'know Him in all your ways' [Proverbs 3:6], and in everything he does must draw down Godliness, goodness and holiness. Obviously, then, when he tells a story, he must also intend to draw down goodness and holiness."[1] Reb Arele Roth said that tellers and listeners both must have *kavvanah*: "Stories have tremendous power to arouse a person to the service of God . . . especially when the teller speaks in singleness of heart and all the listeners bend their ears to hear—then the stories cause great things to happen, and they have a powerful and beneficial purifying effect on the soul."[2]

COUNTLESS TIMES

Reb Arele said that even if a person has heard a story several times before, he should still listen as though he had never heard it, because his intention should not be to hear something novel, as if it were gossip or news, but to attain the spiritual benefit of the listening. So it is irrelevant if he heard it previously.[3]

It was said of a contemporary hasidic storyteller, the late Rabbi Hayim Tzvi Eisenbach of Israel:

Every tale he told about a tzaddik was for him actually like Torah study. He could tell the same story many times. Once, when he began a story, one of his listeners said that he had already heard it a number of times before. Rabbi Hayim Tzvi said to the man, "Did you pray today?" "Of course," he answered. "If you already prayed yesterday," said Rabbi Hayim Tzvi, "why did you also pray today?"[4]

A Sadagorer hasid, Isaac Even, writes that a hasid may discern something new in the same story each time it is retold. "Although a hasid may have heard certain stories many times, he is always ready to hear them again and again, since they have a mysterious attractive power, so that each time they are retold they seem different."[5]

Elsewhere, he writes:

Hasidim do not care if they have already heard certain stories a hundred and one times. They still open their ears anew to thirstily take in every word, as if hearing it for the first time; for stories about tzaddikim, whether old or new, infuse heavenly inspiration—of joy and illumination—into all hearts, so they listen and enjoy the radiance of the Divine Presence.[6]

TO SEPARATE LIGHT FROM DARKNESS

Holy stories must be told with faith and with a firm conviction that they contain the meaning of life. Rabbi Nahman of Bratzlav said that there are two ways a person becomes fit to tell stories of the tzaddikim: if he can see the difference between the stories of the tzaddikim and the sometimes similar stories of the wicked, or, lacking that holy discernment, if he has an unshakeable faith that there is such a difference, and that it is as great as the difference between light and darkness.

Rabbi Nahman of Bratzlav taught: "To separate between the light and the darkness" (Genesis 1:4). The *Midrash* explains: "The light refers to the *maasim* of the tzaddikim, the darkness refers to the *maasim* of the wicked."[7] The Hebrew word *maasim* has two meanings: deeds and stories. The *Midrash* teaches that the difference between the deeds of the tzaddikim and the stories about them and the deeds and stories of the wicked is as great as the difference between light and darkness. The deeds of the tzaddikim and the stories about them are full of light.[8]

BETWEEN HOLY AND PROFANE

A prime requirement for religious storytelling is the realization and conviction that holy stories are not "simply stories" like any others. A person who does not sense their profound difference from profane stories—regardless of the latter's excellence or charm—is not fit to tell them.

There can also be a question as to whom they should be told. If an audience is insensitive to the sanctity of the tales, a religious storyteller can feel inhibited in telling them. In the tale of The Storyteller and the Bishop, the storyteller sent out by the Baal Shem Tov wondered if his inability to recall any stories was because it was inappropriate for him to tell tales of the Besht in a country where his master was virtually unknown. How could they appreciate what they were hearing? He finally discovered that the actual cause, one similar in kind, was the incomplete repentance of his host. Thus, the ability of a storyteller to remember and bring forth a story depends on the spiritual receptivity of his listeners. I mentioned earlier my concern as a storyteller about telling sacred stories in a secular setting where they might not be appreciated.[9]

As a *maggid*, a religious storyteller, I try, as best as I can, to share the spiritual treasure of Judaism with others—especially those to whom it is unfamiliar. Sometimes I tell stories in secular contexts, where the audience comes from many different backgrounds, Jewish and other. On some occasions, I have also done storytelling in gatherings where people were telling mostly secular folktales. Although I also enjoy such stories, I have sometimes found it difficult to tell my own in that environment, because if the audience does not sense the difference between holy stories and the others—since everything is being told together—I have trouble opening my mouth. There are other traditions, besides Judaism, in which stories are considered holy, and one does not tell them at any place or at any time. On the other hand, one of the main teachings of Hasidism is to expand the borders of holiness.

THE HIDDEN LIGHT

Rabbi Nahman said that a person has to know *how* to tell a story because every story has something that is concealed.[10] What is concealed is the Hidden Light. (The Book of Genesis says that God created light on the first day, the sun on the fourth. What light existed before the sun? The tradition says this was spiritual light, and God hid it for the future use of the tzaddikim. Where was it hidden? In the Torah—or in holy stories.) I myself have seen the difference between one storyteller and another; I have seen how a holy storyteller—someone on a high spiritual level—can take a story that I am familiar with, that appears to my eyes plain and dull, and can, so to speak, open it up to reveal its hidden light until it glows with holy charm.

IN THE LAND OF ISRAEL

Rabbi Nahman also taught that visiting the Land of Israel makes one able to tell stories of the tzaddikim. He said:

> The Land of Israel is the essence of all holiness, and by being there one is able to divest oneself of a belief in "Nature." Instead, one comes to know and believe that everything happens just by divine providence—and that is the essence of holiness. Then one is also able to be like God, blessed be He, to separate and distinguish between light and darkness; then one is able to tell stories of tzaddikim....[11]

What is Rabbi Nahman saying here? Rabbi Nahman actually visited Israel and said that his previous spiritual level could not be compared to what he achieved by going there. The Land of Israel represents a level of consciousness where a person sees that everything, even all "natural" events, is brought about by divine providence. Someone who thinks that Nature alone rules all events through a mechanical cause-and-effect determinism fails to perceive what glimmers behind the veil. A tzaddik sees clearly what others must accept by faith: that the light of Godliness infuses all reality and directs the world. It is this holy vision or faith that is necessary to be able to truly tell stories of tzaddikim, because the ways of the tzaddikim and what happens to them can be grasped only by someone sensitive to the higher plane of godly reality.

Rabbi Hanoch Henech of Alexander said: "Hasidim are always telling stories of all kinds of astonishing miracles. Why? To accustom themselves to have simple and pure faith, to train their eyes to see things that are beyond the bounds of Nature."[12]

EVERYONE ON HIS OWN LEVEL

Everyone understands a story on his own level; only a tzaddik can fully understand stories of tzaddikim and know how to tell them to make their message perfectly clear to others. Sometimes I have seen people interpret the stories about Abraham, Isaac, Jacob, Moses, Miriam, and the other heroes and heroines of the Torah as if they were speaking about people just like themselves, not tzaddikim of awesome holiness. The smallness of thinking that everyone is like himself, and no one higher, may comfort a person, but it will surely prevent him from understanding the godly truth of the Torah stories. There have been tzaddikim of radiant holiness and goodness even in recent times. How then can one imagine that a person like Abraham was ordinary?[13] Usually, however, this same skeptical, leveling inclination denies that there are tzaddikim at all.

A hasidic tale explains the situation: A *misnagid* went to visit Rabbi Nahum of Tchernobil, to see with his own eyes why so many people were praising him as a holy man. When he was with him at a meal, he looked at Rabbi Nahum, who was eating varnishkes (noodles), and saw—to his astonishment—that he was catching two noodles that were sticking out of his mouth with his hands, and butter from the noodles was dripping down his beard! But since this *misnagid* was a very religious man, he went over to a corner and prayed, "God, if things are as they seem, I ask nothing from You. But so many people say that this man is holy. Perhaps it is because of my sins that I don't see it. I beg You to show me the truth." He went back to the table and when he looked this time he saw something completely different, and the rebbe's light was shining from one corner of the world to the other.[14]

Certainly, even the holiest people are still human and have human faults, but without admitting that there were and are people who attain higher states of godly consciousness—prophets and tzaddikim—a person will never understand the Torah or hasidic stories. Tales of tzaddikim contain light, but only someone who sees it or believes it is there can draw it out.

STATURE

Tales told by a tzaddik always have a special grace. Since a tzaddik himself has holy charm, all the stories he tells are sweet and charming. The rabbis said that what comes from the heart enters the heart. When a tzaddik tells a story from deep within himself, it penetrates deeply into the heart of his listeners and sets them on fire to serve God. In teaching about hasidic stories, the previous Lubavitcher rebbe, Rabbi Joseph Isaac Schneersohn, repeated the following words of his father [the Rebbe Rashab]:

What we have said so far in praise of the stories and conversation of hasidim has related to their innate value, without particular reference to the stature of the narrator. After all, what counts is the story. But the stature of the narrator has its importance too—not insofar as the story itself is concerned, but certainly as far as the *effect* of the story is concerned.

When my father [the Rebbe Maharash] told a story . . . one had to listen attentively with all ten faculties of one's soul, noting the choice of every single letter—for every word of his was meaningful to all the ten faculties of one's soul.[15]

PREPARATION

The Rebbe Rashab of Lubavitch said:

Someone telling a story has to prepare himself even more than if he were repeating the deepest teaching [of one of the rebbes], and the one hearing the story—even if he is the best of listeners, and the one telling the best of speakers—requires more preparation than if he were preparing himself to hear the deepest teaching.[16]

ALIVE

A lively imagination and a capacity for visualization are valuable aids for story telling and listening. Rabbi Nahman of Bratzlav said: "Others *tell* a story; I *see* a story."[17]

The Rebbe Rashab also said:

One has to know *how* to tell a story, so that it becomes alive. Even more important, one has to know how to *listen* to a story, so that the listening conjures up a complete picture, and one feels as if he is actually experiencing what is being described to him.[18]

Elie Wiesel writes that as a boy he accompanied his hasidic grandfather to the *Beit Midrash*, and he loved the storytelling there. "And when, at the conclusion of *Shabbat*, I listened to the old men speak about their respective rebbes, I closed my eyes to see what they were seeing."[19]

RABBI JOSEPH ISAAC SCHNEERSOHN

Like Rabbi Nahman of Bratzlav and Elie Wiesel, Rabbi Joseph Isaac Schneersohn, the Rebbe Rashab's son and successor as Lubavitcher Rebbe, often spoke about how as a boy he came to love the hasidic stories he heard from his family and teachers. He had a vivid imagination that his rebbe father consciously cultivated and he himself worked to improve. He developed a strong desire to repeat stories, not only to others but to himself, mentally, and to ponder their lessons. So he would sit and with closed eyes meditate on a tale he had heard. He said:

> By my diligence in listening to stories and my love of repeating them to myself or others at every opportunity, I developed the ability to vividly imagine every story, as if [I was living through what was happening, and] the events were taking place before my very eyes.[20]
>
> My powerful imagination turned every story into a living picture, a vision, as if I was actually watching the faces of the heroes of the stories.[21]

The previous chapter included Rabbi Joseph Isaac Schneersohn's teaching about the importance of the *bechein*, the "therefore," and how one should strive to learn the lessons of the stories about tzaddikim and hasidim. We see that even as a boy he fulfilled his own teaching, meditating on the stories to make them come alive and to draw out their lessons. He also passed the "test" we suggested for spiritual seriousness by his perseverance in holding on to each story to extract from it as much spiritual nourishment as possible.

THE KELMER MAGGID

The Kelmer Maggid,[22] Rabbi Moshe Isaac, one of the greatest non-hasidic *maggidim* of the nineteenth century, could depict a scene so vividly that people listened entranced and felt they were actually witnessing the event he was describing. When he came to a town, he sought out from informants the aspects of Jewish life that needed reinforcement and improvement, and as he stood on the *bimah* (elevated platform) in the synagogue delivering his talk, he minced no words and even singled out for rebuke individuals who were notorious wrongdoers. Nevertheless, people flocked to hear him whenever he came.

Once, in the month of *Elul*, a month of introspection in preparation for the holy days of Rosh HaShanah and Yom Kippur, he was in the town of Bialystock, where each trade had its own synagogue. There were separate synagogues for the carpenters, leatherworkers, and tailors. One night, in the Tailor's Synagogue, with great flamboyance, he depicted how the town of Bialystock appeared before God on the Day of Judgment. For over an hour he detailed the city's virtues and faults, describing the debates among members of the Heavenly Court concerning the fate of the townsfolk. Then the Maggid announced, "The moment of truth has arrived for the tailors of Bialystock, the people of the Tailor's Synagogue. Listen," he thundered, "the voices of the Heavenly Court call, 'Tailors of Bialystock, stand at attention!'" And incredibly all the tailors in the audience actually got up and stood at attention. The scene he described was so real to them that they felt they were actually witnessing it, and so they stood up, as if they were in the dock about to hear their judgment from the Heavenly Court![23]

OUR LESSON

Everyone knows that a person can develop his speaking ability and his listening ability and can learn to increase his powers of expression or of concentration and comprehension. This same kind of training can be used for telling or listening to stories. Whether preparing to tell or hear a story, a person should be aware that, just as with praying, he should have *kavvanah* during storytelling. He should consciously focus his attention, call up his faith in the holiness of the story, and try to visualize the people and events, imagining himself as actually present in the action. When meditating on a story in solitude, he should visualize its scenes one after the other, going slowly and not leaving any scene until it has taken on a luminous form in his mind.[24] But all his efforts—in telling, listening, and meditating—should be motivated by joy and delight and a desire to make himself more receptive, to open his heart to the divine light of the story, and what God wants to tell through him or to him.

15

Hearing the Hints in Stories

STORYTELLING WITH THE HOLY SPIRIT

When a rebbe teaches or tells a story, his words can arouse a person's heart to the service of God and to repentance. But aside from the evident religious and moral lessons in what he says, his hasidim have faith that his words often also have hidden meanings—sometimes even prophecy and the holy spirit—and that if studied carefully they can be seen to probe the past and predict the future.

PAST SINS

RABBI KALONYMUS KALMAN EPSTEIN OF CRACOW

Not to Shame

Rabbi Kalonymus Kalman Epstein of Cracow writes, in his famous book, *Ma'or v'Shemesh* (Luminary and Sun), that sometimes a tzaddik tells a story to inspire or to teach a good practice. At other times he wants to reproach people for their sins, but lest he embarrass them by speaking directly, he tells a story. The story spares his listeners any shame or humiliation because it only hints at certain sins, and also because it applies to everyone, so no one is singled out before others. Nevertheless, each person who hears the story recalls his own sin and takes from the story his own lesson. Rabbi Kalonymus Kalman said that he himself had seen tzaddikim telling stories, where if even a hundred people were listening, each one thought that the tzaddik told the story because of him and just for his sake, and each one took his own lesson from it. Yet no one was embarrassed or shamed, because the story was not directed to anyone in particular, and no one knew for whom it was intended. Yet each one thought it was told for him.[1]

A State of Mind

To explain the mindset that leads to this remarkable and beneficial effect, Rabbi Kalonymus Kalman says that when a person goes to a great tzaddik he becomes anxious and troubled: How can he appear before him, with his low behavior? He is certain that the tzaddik will look right through him and, by his holy spirit, know all his sins and bad deeds. So he is repentant and feels very humble. When he enters the tzaddik's presence, he is so embarrassed and ashamed that he actually becomes confused and is even afraid that the tzaddik will say something about his low deeds in front of everybody. The tzaddik, however, says nothing about this, but when he tells a story, everyone listening is in a state of mind where he sees in the tale a reference to his own deeds and believes he told it to hint to him about his sins. This is so even though the tzaddik may have told a story simply to inspire them or teach them a good practice.

Rabbi Elimelech of Lizensk

Rabbi Kalonymus Kalman reports how he once saw his own master and rebbe, Rabbi Elimelech of Lizensk, standing in front of his home, in the middle of a circle of avid listeners, telling a story, and each one there thought that the rebbe had told the story for his sake and had hinted at sins he had committed.

For the Rebbe's Own Benefit

Sometimes, he says, people benefit from a story even though a tzaddik tells it for his own spiritual needs. A tzaddik continually examines his actions to see if his character traits are thoroughly pure, for the sake of God alone. When he scrutinizes himself so carefully, there sometimes falls into his mind a slender doubt about some character trait; for example, it might seem to him that he is somehow lacking in faith or trust in God. He then immediately seeks to repair this deficiency and ponders it deeply. At such a time his conversation and the stories he tells reflect his anxious concern about this matter, so he tells a tale about faith or trust in God, and everyone who hears him recalls how *he* has been lacking in faith or trust in God. Because the tzaddik's words were said for the sake of heaven, to repair the fault that arose in his mind, they enter the listeners' hearts, and each one is inspired to repent and fix what he damaged by his sin. Later, the tzaddik may have a doubt about his love or fear of God and tell another story about love or fear, and whoever hears it recalls his own deficiency and will seek to fix it. So depending on the subject of the tzaddik's story, the person listening recalls to himself what he needs to repair. Today he may hear a story and be reminded how he sinned yesterday, or he may be reminded of a sin he committed in his youth long ago, because the stories the tzaddik tells are from the doubts that arise in the tzaddik's mind.[2]

RABBI ISRAEL OF RIZHIN

This is told about Rabbi Israel of Rizhin:

Once when the Rebbe was in Jassy [Romania], he visited the homes of seventeen of the town's prominent citizens and told each of them a story. Later every one of them came to visit the rebbe in his home and confessed his sins, having realized that his evil deeds were hinted at in the story he was told.[3]

Is it not remarkable that Rabbi Israel chose this surprising way to communicate with each and all of these people? We will have more to say later about how he taught mainly by storytelling.

THE LESSON

What is the lesson from these stories and teachings? Perhaps it is to be sensitive to divine hints when hearing a religious tale. Even if a person is listening to a friend or an acquaintance—not a rebbe—why is he hearing this story at this time? Nothing happens except by divine providence. If this story was "sent" to him, what is being hinted at, even if the teller is unaware? If a person is listening to a tale with others present, or someone is telling it casually, he can still consider it as if it is being told *just for him*, to encourage and inspire him to greater efforts in some area where he is deficient or to hint at some sin he had forgotten or a character trait that needs improvement.

Rabbi Kalonymus Kalman of Cracow said that when a tzaddik wants to improve some trait or repair some deficiency, he may tell stories about that subject. Anyone can adopt that same approach by calling to mind and telling (in appropriate circumstances) stories that relate to his present spiritual concerns.

FUTURE MIRACLES

IN RETROSPECT

Rabbi Nahman of Bratzlav said:

Hungarian hasidim tell miracle stories about their rebbes because they are pious and believe in tzaddikim. Miracles come about through faith in the words of the tzaddikim. In truth a tzaddik is full of miracles, and when a person has faith in him and sincerely and carefully attends to everything he says, to each and every word, believing that everything he says is absolutely true and uttered with full intent, then when he goes home (after his visit to the tzaddik's court) and pays careful attention to everything that happens to him, he will understand in retrospect all the tzaddik's words and what he was hinting at, and what his intentions were when he was speaking to him. And he will see in retrospect how the tzaddik's words hinted at each and every thing that happened to him. As a result of this miracles come about and are revealed.[4]

LIFE-STORY

The Baal Shem Tov sometimes told a story or parable or made an oracular comment to a new disciple to show him the correct religious path. He told the irritable Rabbi Jacob Joseph of Polnoye a story about driving a wagon and its horses, with the lesson to "slacken the reins," to "loosen up," as we say today in the vernacular. When he made the ascetic Maggid of Mezritch a disciple, he said to him: "My horses don't eat matzah (unleavened Passover bread)!" meaning that he must strengthen his body with sufficient food and cease fasting.[5] These two great disciples were present when the Besht told a story to another new disciple—a boy who later became a great rebbe, Rabbi Menahem Mendel of Vitebsk. But the story he told Menahem Mendel was of a different kind: We can call it a "life-story."

As a boy, Menahem Mendel studied in the house of the Maggid of Mezritch, and when he was ten years old he already amazed everyone with his phenomenal knowledge of *Gemara*. His rabbi, the Maggid, was very fond of him. One Sabbath, after the morning meal, the Maggid saw that the boy was jauntily walking around the house in a self-congratulatory mood and his yarmulke had slipped to one side. The rabbi stood in the doorway of his room, holding the knob of the open door in his hand, and said, "Mendel, how many pages of *Gemara* did you learn today?" "Six!" the boy answered proudly. As if speaking to himself, the rabbi muttered, "If the yarmulke is already tilted to one side from learning six pages, how many pages will it take before it falls off completely?" He then turned around and closed the door behind him.

Understanding the seriousness of the matter, the boy began to cry. Then he ran to the rabbi's door and banged on it, shouting, "Open the door, master! Tell me what to do, because I know that I was proud of my learning!" The rabbi opened the door and said, "Fear not! We'll travel to my master, the Baal Shem Tov, and he'll show us both the correct path."

They set out on Tuesday and arrived in Medzibuz on Friday. The Maggid went to the Besht immediately, but the boy delayed, while he shampooed and bathed, for even after he grew up he paid meticulous attention to his appearance and dress, more so than anyone else. Later, the Baal Shem Tov was in the synagogue ready to welcome the Sabbath, for his custom was to do so early in the day, and he was standing by the prayer-leader's stand. But instead of beginning, he waited two hours, until the boy came; then he prayed *Kabbalat Shabbat* (the Sabbath Welcoming Service). However, he did not greet the boy or speak to him on the Sabbath. [Although the holy Baal Shem Tov waited two hours (!), thereby showing his high regard for the level of the boy's *neshamah* (soul), he did not speak to him because of the boy's seeming lack of respect in not coming to greet him immediately and in delaying his arrival at the synagogue. Probably the Besht also had other reasons.]

When he was smoking his pipe after the Sabbath, he called the boy Mendel to him and—in the presence of the Maggid of Mezritch and Rabbi Jacob Joseph of Polnoye—told him a story about oxen and a plow. The story contained hints of everything in Menahem Mendel's life, from the moment he left the womb, until the day of his death in the Holy Land. The Maggid said that he understood the whole story, and Rabbi Jacob Joseph said he understood half. The boy Mendel said that he understood the story just up to that moment when he was standing there.

Later, the Besht told the Maggid not to worry about the boy's seeming arrogance and vanity, that, on the inside, he was lowly in his own eyes. Indeed, all his life the holy rabbi signed his letters, "The truly lowly Rabbi Mendel." When Rabbi Mendel reached adulthood, he said that he already understood the whole story.

When he had become a great rebbe in Vitebsk and was ill and unable to speak, all the people broke down and wept, thinking that his death was near, and the Holy Ark would be taken from them. But Rabbi Mendel awoke from the sound of their weeping and said, "Fear not. From the story that the Baal Shem Tov, of blessed memory, told me, I know that I'll be in the Holy Land." And so it was: He recovered, with the help of God, and traveled to the Holy Land.[6]

Problems and Resolutions in Storytelling

16

Miracle Stories:
What to Believe

Today, when many people have difficulty believing in miracles, we must ponder their frequent presence in hasidic stories. How should we, as storytellers and listeners, relate to these miracles? Should we refrain from telling tales that contain miracles we do not believe happened? Can we gain anything by listening to such tales?

A TRADITIONAL PLACE

Traditional Judaism has always had a place for miracles and stories about them. Indeed, such stories are valued for showing the miraculous exceptions that prove the rule—of God's control of Nature. Some stories also show how God performs miracles through the tzaddikim, according to the rabbinic saying: "When a tzaddik decrees, the Holy One, blessed be He, fulfills." Others reveal how He rewards the righteous and punishes the wicked.[1] But miracle mongering has usually been discouraged.

AN ARGUMENT FOR THE SAKE OF HEAVEN

Nevertheless, a proliferation of miracle stories about various rebbes led to controversy within the hasidic movement. Some rebbes emphasized, while others disparaged, miracles and miracle stories. Those who approved of such tales felt that they fostered belief; those who disapproved considered them among those things good in small doses, bad in large. They felt that many were false and that they turned people's attention from spirituality to spectacle, as if the Jewish People at Mount Sinai had become fascinated by the sound and light show of thunder and lightning and failed to pay attention to the Ten Commandments. This same argument continues today, but of course attitudes have changed radically since the time when most of these hasidic stories came into being. Today a strong belief in miracles is much less common.

SKEPTICISM VERSUS PIETY

Skepticism is not something invented recently, but modernity and modern science have reinvigorated it—and justifiably so. However, there is healthy and sickly skepticism. The Torah says that only a simpleton believes everything (Proverbs 14:15). But today the pendulum has swung way too far in the direction of the sickly variety of skepticism. Piety, which is the very life of faith and belief, is grievously lacking. Rabbi Nahman of Bratzlav said that it is better to be a fool and believe everything, and then one will also believe in the truth, than to be skeptical of everything and reject the truth also. But one need not be a fool to be pious and believe.

HASIDIC VIEWS

The Besht's Opinion

In Chapter 10 I told the story of how the Baal Shem Tov appeared to his disciples after his death, when they were collecting his teachings, and urged them to tell stories of his piety. In another version of that tale, he protests against their concentrating on miracle stories.

One time when the Besht's circle of disciples had gathered after his death, and were telling stories about him, the Besht's son, Rabbi Tzvi, fell asleep. In his dream he saw his holy father, who said to him, "Why are they telling miracle tales about me? Let them instead tell of my service to God, blessed be He. Then they as well as I will benefit!"[2]

They would benefit by being able to imitate his actions (they could not imitate his miracles); he would benefit—as would any other deceased tzaddik about whom stories are told—by his soul being elevated in heaven, due to the continuing good effect his life and actions were having on Earth.[3] Another story, with a similar message, tells: "Once, when Rabbi Menahem Mendel of Rimanov returned from a visit to the grave of the Baal Shem Tov, he said that the Besht was angry at those who were telling stories of his miracles, rather than of his piety and fear of God."[4]

Levels Above Levels

It is important to realize that there are stories on all different spiritual levels, depending upon the level of the teller or the collector of the stories. When I once asked a hasidic storyteller if he had seen a certain book of hasidic tales, he said simply: "They're not soul-stories." Stories that touch the soul are the ones most fit to tell. But, unfortunately, some hasidic stories are on the level of the crudest peasant folktales; and some books of hasidic stories have an exclusive interest in miracles, materialistic rewards for piety— of children, wealth, and long life—and a small-minded pleasure in divine punishment of the wicked. Not that such stories are always unworthy, but if that is all a book contains, it is deficient and distorted. There are, then, stories on all levels, up to the very highest and purest. A person reading hasidic tales, particularly in Hebrew or Yiddish (the few English books are more selective), should not imagine that they are "all the same."

Shivhei ha-Besht

A prime example of the lower end of this scale is the first book of hasidic stories, Shivhei ha-Besht, translated into English as In Praise of the Baal Shem Tov. Although it certainly contains some fine stories, much of it is concerned with various low matters. It is also teeming with miracles. While many rebbes accepted it (presumably because of its good part), others were less approving.[5] When Shivhei ha-Besht was first published, Rabbi Yehudah Tzvi of Strettin exclaimed, "Are these the praises of the Baal Shem Tov? All these miracles? I can do these miracles. The true praises of the Baal Shem Tov are his love and fear of God!"[6]

A hasidic storyteller once said to me that the rebbes felt that Shivhei ha-Besht was "a joke." I can add that not only is the original book unworthy of the holy Baal Shem Tov, but the English translation makes matters even worse. It was not translated as a religious book but as folklore by anthropologists, who include an appendix classifying the stories according to folkloric categories, such as "Tabu" and "Magic"! Thus, a reader is hindered in approaching the text with a religious frame of mind. Perhaps this is only poetic repayment for the original book's sins.

SUGGESTIONS

By Rebbes

What should our attitude be to miracle stories? Or, to ask the question more specifically, what should our attitude be to the truthfulness of the stories? Here are some suggestions from the rebbes.

Lest one think them naive, consider this comment of Rabbi Shlomo of Radomsk: "Whoever believes all the stories about the Baal Shem Tov in *Shivhei ha-Besht* is a fool; but whoever denies them is an *apikoros* (wicked and a nonbeliever)."[7]

Rabbi Mordechai of Neshkiz said:

> I do not give much credence to miracle stories told about the tzaddikim—because many of them are fabricated and others are riddled with errors—except for the tales told about the Baal Shem Tov, may his memory be for the life of the World-to-Come. For even if a story about him never actually occurred, and there was no such miracle, it was in the power of the Baal Shem Tov, the memory of a tzaddik for a blessing for the life of the World-to-Come, to perform everything.[8]

The Rebbe of Lublin said, "If someone came and told me that he saw the Baal Shem Tov make a ladder and go up into heaven while alive, bodily and with his clothes on, I would believe him. Because it is fitting to believe everything told about the Baal Shem Tov."[9]

There is an important thought here that can serve as a guide not only for Baal Shem Tov stories but for all hasidic miracle stories: It is that all things are possible for God; He may not have done that particular miracle, but He could have. On the other hand, just because He could do them, does not mean He did. This perspective may help to resolve the problem some people have with miracle stories.

By Others

Franz Rosenzweig, the German-Jewish philosopher, who was born into an assimilated family and found his way back to Judaism after almost being lost, wrote:

All the days of the year Balaam's talking ass [Numbers 22] may be
a mere fairy tale, but not on the Sabbath wherein this portion is read
in the synagogue, when it speaks to me out of the open Torah. But if
not a fairy tale, what then? I cannot say right now; if I should think
about it today, when it is past, and try to say what it is, I should probably only utter the platitude that it is not a fairy tale. But on that day,
in that very hour, it is—well, certainly not a fairy tale, but that which
is communicated to me provided I am able to fulfill the command of
the hour, namely, to open my ears.[10]

Rosenzweig found it difficult to communicate the core of his intuition.
A modern writer, Yael Mesinai, in a preface to a book of hasidic stories,
beautifully conveys the truth he struggled to express. She writes:

Everybody knows such stories are for children. But the Tzanzer
Rebbe once said: "If you believe them, you're a fool. If you don't believe them, you're wicked."[11] Most people heedlessly drift between
these extremes of innocence and evil, but the stories welcome and
encompass all listeners, whether or not they believe. The story is
a ritual, a healing event weaving together wisdom and action, the finite
and infinite, the world of beyond and the worlds in between. The
story, like a dream, is a vessel that codifies and transmits precious information, the innermost secrets of the heart. The story is the story of
the world—the place of hiddenness where God seeks refuge even as
He longs for us to know, to listen to Him, to obey His innermost will.
    The story is preceded by the deed. Rabbi Nahman [of Bratzlav] says
that a deed done with your whole being never stops happening; it
goes on, even after we, the actors, have finished. A story too has that
eternal momentum. It can be tapped, unveiled, shown as alive. And
if a story is about tzaddikim, the righteous men of the past, who better can relate and bring these tales to life than another tzaddik? For
when the tzaddik speaks, he has the power to transform the story
into a living event. The story is real in the moment of telling. It is not
an intellectual event, but one that strives for joy, the "holy shiver"
that speaks to our soul. "Does the soul dream facts?" Rabbi Nahman
asks us. The story represents another way of knowing. It addresses
itself not to our hunger for information, but to the need to confirm
what we already know. Thus, we can read a story again, or hear the
same tale from a new tzaddik in each generation, the style slightly
transformed by the times, but there is always the same impetus to

renewal, some new insight or stirring inspired by listening. For each time we hear, some restlessness in our heart is abated. Our quest is answered.[12]

Elie Wiesel, a master storyteller and popularizer of hasidic tales, says about his devout, hasidic grandfather:

> My first hasidic tales I heard from him. He made me enter the universe of the Baal Shem Tov and his disciples, where facts became subservient to imagination and beauty. What difference did it make that events and chronological dates no longer matched? I surely didn't care. What mattered to me was not that two and two are four, but that God is one. Better still: that man and God are one.
>
> I can still hear my grandfather's voice: "There will, of course, always be someone to tell you that a certain tale cannot, could not, be objectively true. That is of no importance; an objective hasid is not a hasid."[13]

FICTION MAY BE TRUER THAN FACT

Stories are a world unto themselves. They float midway between heaven and earth. When a person reads Kafka, for example, he need not ask if the story occurred. Certainly Kafka's mysterious tales emerged from incidents in his own life. But which contain the deeper truths? Would we have been better off if he had instead written biographical stories—what "really" happened? Obviously not; the transformed "fictional" stories are truer than what happened in real life.[14]

Perhaps I can illustrate this by analyzing a hasidic tale. When the Baal Shem Tov was still a "hidden tzaddik"—his identity concealed under the guise of a simple villager—he was once the guest of a wealthy and charitable Jewish farmer who had a special house where wandering poor people could stay for a week or so. Late one night, when the farmer had undressed and was about to go to sleep, he was surprised by a brilliant light entering his window and went over to see where it was coming from. Seeing that it was from the poor people's house, he became afraid that a fire had broken out there, so he quickly dressed and ran over to check. When he looked in the window of the Baal Shem Tov's room, the source of the light, he saw the Besht sitting on the floor, reciting *Tikkun Hatzot* (the Midnight Lamentation): His outstretched hands were raised to heaven and his face was glowing with a brilliant, supernatural light, as tears ran down his cheeks. Startled, the farmer fainted and fell. The Besht heard the sound, went out, and revived him, but he made him promise not to reveal that he was a hidden tzaddik.[15]

In those earlier times some pious people woke up at midnight to recite *Tikkun Hatzot*, study the Torah, and recite Psalms. This might be expected of a rabbi or other learned and pious person but not of a simple villager. To stay awake one needed a candle. So if a visitor arrived in a town late at night—and there were no streetlights then—he could tell who was up and who might offer him hospitality simply by seeing where a candle was still lit. Since hidden tzaddikim kept vigil during the night to engage in acts of piety, it was not unheard of for a "simple laborer" to be discovered to be a hidden tzaddik because he was found with his candle lit, studying Torah and so on. That might be the origin of this story about the Besht. The farmer noticed a light and went over to see why one of the poor people had a candle burning so late (candles were not cheap either, by the way, and for a poor person to burn one late would itself be unusual). He looked in the window and found a hidden tzaddik, the Baal Shem Tov, reciting *Tikkun Hatzot* by candlelight.

Perhaps over time, as this story passed from one person to another, it was transformed into something more dramatic: The farmer thought there was a fire and fainted when he saw a supernatural light. The fire, light, and fainting graphically represent truths that cannot otherwise be easily expressed. The brilliant light stands for the tzaddik's holiness, the fear of fire first heightens the drama and then represents the fear and dread that descends on someone who comes in contact with awesome holiness beyond his ability to contain the experience. Many hasidic tales have someone fainting, because that is the most obvious, visible demonstration of a person's being profoundly affected. That fact of emotional turmoil is communicated much more effectively by having someone faint than by referring to invisible feelings or by saying, "He was deeply moved." We can also note that in the midst of an intense divine mood, the Besht's face might indeed have been "shining" in a way not ordinarily seen.

Which story would be "more true?" What might be a more realistic story, about a farmer seeing candlelight from a room of the poor people's house, rushing to investigate, and finding a man whom he had thought a simple villager piously reciting *Tikkun Hatzot* being profoundly moved; or the possibly fictionalized tale that now exists, with its dramatic effects and miraculous light? If the purpose of the story is to impress us with the Baal Shem Tov's humble piety and awesome holiness, perhaps the miracle tale is superior.[16]

BELIEVING IN THE STORY

The lesson from this example is that even someone who might not believe that events happened exactly as described in a story can still tell and hear the story with perfect faith, if he can believe in the story itself. As for me, I *can* believe that there actually was a supernatural light radiating from the Besht's face *or* that that was added to a more naturalistic story. Either way, the basic meaning is the same. In essence, it is not important to me as to which was actually the case. Why let idle skepticism intrude and disrupt my relation to the story? When I hear or tell a story, I am not concerned with facts and am not attending primarily with my mind and intellect, but with my heart and soul. What is necessary is to *believe in the story itself*, that it contains the meaning of life, and that it is a leaf from the Tree of Life.

THE TEST OF THE BAAL SHEM TOV

Let me conclude this chapter with a story about the Baal Shem Tov that mentions miracle tales circulating about him during his lifetime and that illustrates his own teaching about the relative places of miracles and piety.

A rabbi in a city not far from Medzibuz, where the Baal Shem Tov lived, had heard many stories about his miracles but considered them to be just the fantastic imaginings of the ignorant simple people. He believed that the Baal Shem Tov was like the many other *baal shems*, faith healers, who plied their trade of folk remedies, incantations, and interpreting dreams— and whose doings were not to be taken seriously. But finally it became impossible to ignore him any longer; some people were saying that he was the leader of the generation, and many great men of Israel and people of exceptional piety were streaming to him to hear his teaching. He realized he could not continue simply to dismiss him; he had to test him and see for himself. So he decided to visit the Baal Shem Tov and evaluate him from first-hand knowledge, not hearsay.

When he came to the Baal Shem Tov in Medzibuz he carefully and minutely observed everything the Besht did; not the slightest movement escaped his scrutiny. In a short while he saw that the stories about the Besht's miracles were true, not imagined. However, although he saw him perform miraculous healings, he did not detect in him any outstanding Torah knowledge or piety. He was not impressed by miracles alone. What were miracles worth without fear of God? So he was not satisfied and considered all his labors of investigation as being for nought.

To get to the bottom of the mystery he carefully listened to every word the Baal Shem Tov uttered, hoping to discover why many people thought him so wonderful. The Besht, however, knew how to hide himself from those who came to test him. Days and weeks passed, but the rabbi did not succeed in finding in him even one of the virtues that the sages enumerated as characterizing the great leaders of Israel. He saw that the Besht spent most of his time in the company of the simple people, conversing with them in the marketplaces and on the streets; he was occupied with incantations and with medicinal herbs that he searched for in the fields and woods and which he distributed to the sick people who came to him from near and far. When the rabbi saw all this day after day, he finally decided to leave the next morning, after prayers, and return home.

However, early the following morning, an innkeeper from a nearby village arrived in Medzibuz and begged the Baal Shem Tov to come to his home, because his son, who had fallen ill a number of days ago and was bed-ridden, was not getting well. The Besht agreed to go and ordered his servant to prepare the coach so he could leave immediately for the village. The rabbi decided to take this opportunity to closely observe the Baal Shem Tov one last time. He asked to go along and the Besht consented. They climbed into the coach and set out. On the way each of them learned his regular morning Torah lesson from memory, so as not to allow the journey to interfere with his Torah-study.

When they arrived in the village, the Baal Shem Tov climbed down from the coach and entered the innkeeper's house; the rabbi followed him in. The man's large house was used as an inn, and the Besht began to walk back and forth in the central room; he did not sit down but kept on pacing ceaselessly, engrossed in his thoughts. The householder had the table set with food and invited them to sit down and eat the morning meal, although the Baal Shem Tov had still not gone in to see the sick boy he had come to heal. The rabbi stood there waiting to see what the Baal Shem would do. When he saw that he went to wash his hands to eat, he did the same, and they both sat down at the table.

But as soon as they had eaten the first bite of bread, the innkeeper's wife rushed in, crying out that her son was dying. The Besht remained seated, seemingly unconcerned; the rabbi also stayed seated but looked on in amazement. How can he sit there and not rush in to the sick boy who he came to heal?

While the rabbi was observing this in wonderment, the wife came in a second time, wailing that her sick son had already given up the ghost and was no longer among the living. When the rabbi heard this he imme-

diately jumped out of the window next to where he was sitting, for he was
a *cohen* (a hereditary Jewish priest) and forbidden to be in the same house
with a corpse. That same moment the Baal Shem Tov rose from the table,
entered the boy's room, and closed the door behind him. He stayed inside
for a few minutes, then opened the door and told them to give the boy a
little soup to strengthen him.

When the Baal Shem Tov sat down again at the table, the rabbi—who
was viewing this scene through the window—realized that the boy must be
alive, and reentered the house. When he went into the bedroom to see what
had happened, and saw that the Besht had actually revived the dead, a great
fear and dread came over him.

Nevertheless, although he witnessed this awesome miracle, he had still
not seen any sign of special piety from the Baal Shem Tov. And what were
miracles worth without fear of God! He spent the rest of that day with the
Besht in the village, and he remained thoroughly perplexed, because he
saw no reason at all why the Besht merited these extraordinary powers.

Then the Lord of Compassion took pity on him; he saw the Baal Shem
Tov in all the greatness of his fear of God and all the depth of his holiness,
and he realized who he was. This is how it happened.

Before evening they left the village to return to Medzibuz, but when
they reached the forest night fell. It was Thursday night, and the Baal Shem
Tov wanted to arrive home before midnight, for he had made a "fence," a
rule, for himself—in order to keep the Sabbath with the utmost holiness—
never to travel on Friday. That is the way of holy people, to always make
fences to keep themselves far from anything wrong. But when the coach
reached the forest, it was so dark they could no longer see the road. The
horses continued on, but the driver had no idea where they were going or
where they were. The journey from the village to the city took just one hour;
they had been traveling already for more than two hours and the outskirts
of the city were nowhere in sight. The Baal Shem Tov himself tried to drive
the coach and to speak to the horses in their language—but without success. The gates of wisdom had suddenly shut before him, and he was unable to open his mouth.

The Besht was deeply grieved and distraught at being delayed on the
road and saw in this the work of the Satan who wanted to make him stumble
by violating his fence not to travel on *erev Shabbat* (Friday before the Sabbath). He climbed down from the coach and disappeared into the woods,
away from the road, and people. When the rabbi saw this, he too climbed
down and quietly went among the trees after the Baal Shem Tov, who was
so grief-stricken he had no idea someone was following him. When he came

to a small clearing, the Besht threw himself prostrate on the ground and began crying and pleading loudly, "Master of the World! You know that everything I do is only for Your sake, to increase the glory of Your Name in the world. I've made a fence for myself not to travel on *erev Shabbat*, and if I violate it, it is actually like desecrating the Sabbath. I beg You, God of Compassion, have pity on me and save me from this terrible distress. Show me the road that leads to the city, so I'll arrive before Friday and not transgress the fence I made for myself." He lay on the ground this way for a long time, pouring his heart out before the Creator, blessed be His name, while tears streamed down his face. And all these anguished supplications were only so he would not be put in a situation where he would be tempted to transgress, God-forbid, the stringency he had willingly accepted on himself, to be supremely careful and zealous to keep the Sabbath and sanctify it. [If they were still lost at midnight, the Besht had the option of stopping in the forest and staying there Friday and the Sabbath—without food, water, etc. Although the Besht would certainly *not* violate his rule, he did not even want to be tempted, and there certainly would be a temptation, since staying in the woods might be dangerous to life, in which case breaking the rule would be permitted.]

At that moment, the rabbi saw the Baal Shem Tov's greatness and holiness, his true fear of God, a fear utterly pure and unalloyed, that came from love of God and the Torah. As he stood there, observing this awesome scene, he wholeheartedly accepted the Baal Shem Tov as his spiritual master.

Later, however, the rabbi began to suffer when he thought of all the vain suspicions he had harbored against someone so pure and holy as the Baal Shem Tov. He finally decided to go to him and confess his former suspicions and beg the Besht's forgiveness and pardon. But before he could open his mouth, the Besht forestalled him and said, "I already know what you want to say. And I'll answer you with the words spoken to Moses, 'I have forgiven you, according to your desire.'" [Numbers 14:20][17]

When the Besht appeared in his disciples' dreams he urged them to tell stories of his piety and fear of heaven rather than his miracles. This story, in a complex and delightful way, illustrates that teaching. The rabbi was skeptical when he heard miracle tales about the Baal Shem Tov, but even when he discovered they were true, he was not convinced of his greatness until he saw his piety and fear of heaven. This kind of pious skepticism would have pleased even the Besht.

The Kotzker Rebbe, who was a vociferous critic of miracle mongering and laughed at the kinds of miracles reported of some other rebbes, once said that a *real* miracle was for a rebbe to bring people to actually repent and return to God. The Baal Shem Tov may or may not have revived the physically dead, but he certainly performed the Kotzker's kind of miracle and revived countless people who were spiritually dead.

Some people—and I am among them—can believe that the Besht could have performed the miracle of reviving the dead boy, or that he was worthy of performing it—whether or not it actually occurred; others may not believe in miracles at all. But the most important thing is simply to *believe in the story*.

17

Different Story Versions: Issues of Truth and Falsehood

A PROBLEM

One remarkable aspect of an oral tradition of storytelling is the way stories are transformed in the telling. Stories change when passed from one person to another and even when an individual tells the same story on different occasions. As a result, there are commonly multiple versions of an oral tale, a phenomenon that sometimes troubled hasidim.

One hasidic author, noting the different versions of hasidic and other religious tales throughout the history of the tradition, asked if in each case only one version of a story is true and the others are false.[1] He was not the only compiler of a book of hasidic tales who felt compelled to try to answer this disturbing question in his preface.

ONE PERSPECTIVE

The typical hasidic reaction to this phenomenon of multiple versions was and is to try to stem the tide of variation and restrict changes in the stories. Many rebbes and hasidim stress repeating tales exactly as they were heard. Some accept and retell only a tale that has a line of transmission through reputable pious people who can be relied on not to have altered it. This is especially true for miracle tales, where there is a well-known tendency to fabricate and exaggerate. The Tzanzer Rebbe remarked humorously: "If a hasid says he saw something, he may have heard it; if he says he heard it, it certainly never happened."[2] Storytellers who are rigorous about attribution try to give a tale's "lineage" back to the person to whom the event occurred, or to someone who witnessed it, or who heard it directly from the original person. However, there are limits to possible success in this endless task of preventing the proliferation of story versions and of invalidating untrustworthy stories. Moreover, there are other approaches and attitudes to these problems of variability and veracity that afflict any oral tradition.

ANOTHER PERSPECTIVE

Rabbi Israel of Rizhin

According to His Spiritual Level

A disciple of Rabbi Israel of Rizhin, who wrote a book about him that includes a selection of the stories he told, says:

> Among the stories are some that the holy and pure Rizhiner told in different ways, and with different words, but both these and those are the words of the living God. It is simply that he told the story, about himself or about some other tzaddik who preceded him, according to his spiritual level at that time and place. As a result, there were various changes in his holy words. I have heard that the tzaddik, the hidden light, Rabbi Baruch of Medzibuz, the merit of a tzaddik for a blessing, also sometimes told the same story in different words. . . .[3]

One must assume that the differences in the versions told by the Rizhiner caused confusion among some hasidim.

According to the Needs of the Hour

One of the Rizhiner's sons attributed his father's variant tellings not to the varying spiritual level of the teller (his father) but to the varying situation and circumstances:

> They once told Rabbi David Moshe of Tchortkov, a son of the Rizhiner and also a great rebbe, one of his father's stories, and re-

marked that he told it often, and each time differently. Rabbi David
Moshe said that when tzaddikim tell stories, they adapt them to fit
the need of the hour. And, indeed, he also told the same story differently on different occasions.[4]

False Endings

The Rizhiner, an accomplished storyteller who reflected on the nature and purpose of storytelling, seems to have been well aware of how
hasidim sometimes unconsciously altered stories in the telling.

The Rebbe [the Rizhiner] once spoke about the matter of not engaging in idle conversation [or worldly concerns] before morning
prayers. He told a story about a certain hasid who made a good living by going to the market once a year to buy his merchandise—warm
winter clothes. One year he traveled to the market as usual and returned with a large quantity of merchandise. But that winter was
extremely mild and no one bought his stock. His financial situation
was so desperate he was not even able to properly feed his family.
   One morning before prayers, the poritz (gentile landowner) of the
district came to buy all of his merchandise. But the hasid told him, "I
don't do business before prayers." The Rebbe concluded, saying,
"Everyone asks, 'What is the end of the story?' But I say, that is the
end of the story—that a simple hasid can have such faith."[5]

   We saw in the previous chapter about miracle tales how people tend
to tell stories according to their own spiritual level. They also change them
in that direction. The Rizhiner knew that many hasidim expected a miraculous and materialistic ending to the story he told. Typically, such a story
would end, for example—and to make the point most blatantly—that the
poritz went off to buy elsewhere, but when the faithful hasid left the synagogue after prayers he stumbled over something and looking down found
a gold brick half buried in the dirt of the street.
   When some of the simpler hasidim repeated a tale like the one the
Rizhiner told, it "acquired" this kind of ending, for people on a lower spiritual level are not satisfied until a story demonstrates a material reward for
faith. From the Rizhiner's comment, we can assume he understood how
hasidic tales often acquired such miraculous endings. Truly spiritual people
not only do not require a story to have a material reward for piety, but find
it a distraction that degrades their religious ideal. As a storyteller, the

Rizhiner changed stories according to his spiritual mood and to fit the situation, but it seems he was also aware how other people, perhaps unconsciously, changed stories according to their own lower spiritual level.

Form and Matter

The hasidic author who asked whether the existence of different versions meant that one is true and the others are false answered his own question philosophically, stating that everything, including stories, is composed of form and matter, and that as a story assumes its form in the act of telling, the facts—its "matter"—may have to change. What is essential, he argued, is the potentiality, not the actuality—that the story *could* have happened this way, not that it did.[6] This view is certainly more radical than most.

Read It One Time

I have heard Rabbi Shlomo Carlebach, who is a master hasidic storyteller, tell the same story differently on different occasions in a way that sometimes amazed me. I have also compared stories he has told to the book version that is the probable source (although one cannot be sure; perhaps he had oral sources) and noted the differences. He has said: "I never read a story more than once. After I read it, I walk away and begin to tell it. I say it as I know and understand, without ever going back to the book." It is clear that such a method focuses not on the accuracy of details but on faithfulness to the basic meaning.

He explained his approach by saying:

I don't change a story, but I like to make it more heavenly, with more *hein* (charm), give it more pepper and salt—but not by changing it. You see, the people who collected and wrote down hasidic stories were not always the big hasidim. I heard from the Bobover Rebbe: Who were most of the people who came out with books of hasidic stories? A *Yid* has to marry off his daughter, so he needs money. He can't write a book of Torah. So he gathers all the stories he can find, and puts them in a book. So sometimes you read a story and you realize that part of it is not true; it *couldn't* be like this! You know, the story's true, yet. . . . When I tell a story as I do [changing, but not changing it], I trust my nose that that's the way it happened."[7]

Memory and Meaning

Oral stories commonly undergo changes due to the natural workings or deficiencies of memory. But not every change is bad; since the mind remembers what is meaningful, stories often change in ways that make them more meaningful and better.

The Purpose

Religious stories always have an underlying *purpose*, which is to inspire people with faith and communicate wisdom and values. That purpose determines the "form" the hasidic author was speaking about. For example, when a teacher tells a story to illustrate some point, he naturally emphasizes the part relevant to his theme in a way that changes the shape, the "form," of the story.

Sometimes tales must be adapted because an element in a story might not be understood or might offend a particular audience. Perhaps a hasidic story has an element that a particular group of listeners will not understand. Should the teller leave it in and explain it? Or should he alter or omit it? What I do depends on the individual case and circumstances, the "need of the hour." Sometimes it is fitting to simply eliminate the incomprehensible element, other times to briefly explain it, occasionally even to make a digression to explain it—providing that does not distract the audience and cause the story to lose the effect it was created to produce. Certainly something must be done. Why tell a story if the listeners will not understand it?

Occasionally a story has an element that will disturb or offend a particular audience. Perhaps it motivates the action of a character in a way that was fine when it was originally told or written but that is unacceptable to many people today. Why should I include that element if it will prevent the listeners from absorbing the lesson of the story? Why tell the story at all?

Perhaps some character in a story makes a comment that denigrates women. If this is just one peripheral element in a complete story, why include it if it offends the audience and prevents them from accepting the actual lesson? The original story was told to communicate a religious message, not to preserve extraneous facts for a historical record. Instead of losing the "form" to preserve the "matter," one should save it by changing the facts and adapting the story to the "need of the hour."

However, some qualifications are necessary here. First, a storyteller with religious integrity will not pander to an audience, cutting and trimming tales to fit their taste. Second, a storyteller does not have a free hand to change things at will. There is a difference between altering details and main elements of a tale. If the line between truth and fiction is blurred by a casual attitude to facts and to story elements, the listeners' faith in the essential veracity of the stories will be destroyed.[8] Balance is needed here. There is no absolute rule and no substitute for wisdom. Only a knowledgeable person, faithful to the tradition, can know what to change and how. Of course there may be differences of opinion as to who is qualified to do this, who succeeds and who does not. In our generation, where the carefree and careless attitude of "do your own thing" approaches the chaotic situation in the time of the Judges, when "everyone did what was right in his own eyes," there is certainly a need for some stringency, although not the kind that outlaws all flexibility. But if a storyteller is zealous for the tradition, always trying to preserve, not change, he or she can make changes, when needed, without fear.

Hasidic Rebbes:
The Theory and Practice
of Their Storytelling

18

How Rebbes Use Stories

Most hasidic tales are about tzaddikim, and rebbes most commonly tell stories about other tzaddikim. But they also tell stories about hasidim and simple people, as well as parables and religious folktales. Rebbes tell stories of many different types, in many different settings, for many different purposes. The following tales will give the reader at least a taste of the rich variety.

ALLEGORIES FOR NEWCOMERS

People constantly come to rebbes for help in solving their problems, both material and spiritual. Many ordinary people seek their advice, blessings, or prayers concerning material problems of livelihood, children, sickness; more spiritual people seek knowledge of how to get close to God, how to develop love and fear of God, how to pray. It was from the latter class that the rebbes of earlier times traditionally sought not just hasidim but disciples. Whether they were dealing with disciples or simple hasidim, they sometimes communicated by means of stories and parables. The following story shows a tzaddik using storytelling when a young rabbi, a "disciple candidate," came to test him to see what religious teaching and guidance he had to offer.

Rabbi Moshe Leib of Sassov paced back and forth, puzzled and upset. He had not been excited about coming to Mezritch to visit the Maggid, and now, after having met him, he wondered why any learned man would want to speak to him.

He had been told that the Maggid was a distinguished talmudist, a scholar of repute. If so, why hadn't the Maggid spoken a single word of Torah to him? All he did was tell him childish stories. He began by talking about a farmer who had stuffed a lion skin with straw and placed it in his field to scare animals away. At first the plan worked and the animals had kept their distance. After a while, however, they realized that the lion was not alive and began to use it for sport, ripping it apart, piece by piece.

Why did he waste my time with that tale? Moshe Leib thought. Suddenly, it occurred to him that the Maggid's words might have been an allegory. Our sages refer to the lion as the "king of beasts" and to the rabbis as "kings" because of their halachic authority. Perhaps the Maggid was intimating that, although Moshe Leib was a rabbi, he was merely a straw lion, lacking life and true power.

He started to review the Maggid's second story. A poor man discovered a treasure. He sought out the advice of friends, invested the money wisely, and became very wealthy. As his wealth grew, he felt it proper to upgrade his wardrobe. He hired a tailor to sew him a custom-made suit, as other wealthy men did.

Everything went well until the tailor called him to make a final fitting. He had never ordered such a suit before and did not understand what the tailor wanted from him. He would have taken the suit, put it on, and walked home. Instead, the tailor told him to stand straight, put his feet together, turn around. . . . He kept tugging at all the corners of the garment and sticking pins in here and there. The man could not understand what he was doing. The suit had looked fine to begin with. Finally, he concluded that all the tailor's activity was intended to make fun of him, taking advantage of the fact that he had never bought such a suit before. Enraged, he pulled the garment away from the tailor, threw him the fee he had promised, and stalked out of the shop.

Perhaps this also was an allegory, Moshe Leib thought. Garments are metaphors for our means of expression: thought, speech, and action. Was the Maggid telling him that he was being offered a chance to develop a new approach to self-expression and that he was too boorish to appreciate the opportunity? It did not take Moshe Leib much further reflection to decide to become the Maggid's disciple.[1]

Rabbi Moshe Leib at first reacted boorishly to the Maggid's tales and fables and was rushing to leave Mezritch. Only on reflection did he realize that the Maggid was telling him these stories to take his measure in order to fit him for a "new suit."

Rabbi Nahman of Bratzlav said: "By telling tales of tzaddikim . . . a person merits fine clothes."[2]

Rabbi Nahman intended this literally and metaphorically: By storytelling a person would actually merit nice clothes. But his statement was based on the deeper spiritual meaning: that stories about tzaddikim provide a person with finer "soul-garments" of thought, speech, and action.[3]

In Chapter 15, we saw that the Baal Shem Tov, in first conversations with disciple candidates, sometimes showed them the correct religious path by speaking in allegories. He told Rabbi Jacob Joseph a tale about "slackening the reins" when driving horses and made an oracular comment to the Maggid of Mezritch that "My horses don't eat matzah!" We see in the story about Rabbi Moshe Leib that when the Maggid of Mezritch succeeded the Besht as leader of the hasidic movement he also sometimes employed this method of allegorical storytelling for newcomers.

TEACHING HIMSELF

The following story shows a rebbe storytelling when a hasid sought his help in a personal crisis.

A man once came to Rabbi Samuel Tzvi of Alexander to tell him about his trouble. He was being taken to court and the chances of his being found innocent were absolutely nil. He begged the rebbe to help him elicit divine mercy so he would be saved. The man was crying profusely as he told the rebbe his desperate plight, but the rebbe said that he had no advice and didn't know how he could help him.

When he heard that his situation was hopeless, the man began to weep again and called out, "To whom can I go, what will I do?" The rebbe then told him a story:

"A hasid once came to the Vorker Rebbe and poured his heart out to him about a serious problem. The rebbe then gave him leave to go. But when he had started on his way home, together with other hasidim who had spent the Sabbath in Vorki, they saw the rebbe's carriage from afar coming after them. (The holy Vorker's custom was to go out on excursions in his carriage. The Old Alexanderer Rebbe said about him that this was because his intense fear of God made him so restless that he couldn't stay home.) Needless to say, when the hasidim saw the rebbe coming up behind them, they stopped and waited for him.

"When he reached them, they conversed and drank a *l'hayim*. Then the hasid spoke again to the rebbe, brokenhearted and with tears in his eyes, telling him that he would not be able to stay in his house because of the suffering and anxiety this problem was causing him, and he had no idea what to do about it. His only hope was for the rebbe's prayer to save him.

"'Believe me,' said the rebbe, 'I don't know any way to help you,' and as he said this, tears streamed from his eyes. Of course, these tears elicited divine mercy and brought his salvation."

After telling this story, Rebbe Samuel said to the man who had come to him about his court case, "Believe me, I don't know any way to help you." And as he said this, tears streamed from his eyes and ran down his cheeks. With those tears he ripped up the heavenly decree against the man and saved him from his trouble.[4]

Rebbes often use stories to teach practical lessons about behavior. A rebbe can even teach himself that way, as here, where Rebbe Samuel "reminded himself" what to do, by means of this story about the Vorker Rebbe.[5]

THREE STORIES TOLD BY THE RIZHINER

The stunning variety in the types of stories and the settings and situations in which they are used is revealed in three tales that show the storytelling of Rabbi Israel of Rizhin, who more than any other rebbe taught and communicated by means of storytelling.

The First Story: Clapping

The Rizhiner told a tale to instruct a hasid who prayed in his synagogue and used to clap his hands—as hasidim sometimes do—but without fervor or energy.

Once, after the morning prayers, the Rizhiner called this man over to him and said, "I'll explain to you what is really called clapping.

"Before the Shpoler Zeideh[6] was revealed to the world and became a famous rebbe, he taught Torah to children. Since he was tenderhearted and compassionate, people brought him children that other teachers could not help. One of these children, a boy who was almost unteachable, and used to run wild the whole day, became, when he grew up somewhat, a thief.

Once, this young man was caught after stealing something from the church in the town. The gentiles put him on trial and ruled that he could save himself from being burned to death only if he agreed to convert (God save us!).

"Because this thief had been a pupil of the holy Shpoler Zeideh, it's understood that some spark of holiness had clung to him. He courageously faced his tormentors and said he would rather be burned alive than change his religion! Those cruel and wicked people immediately stood up, poured boiling oil on his head, which flowed all over him and down to his feet, and then they lit his fingers. At that moment," said the Rizhiner, "that Jew began clapping his burning hands together and shouting, 'I don't care! I'm staying a Jew!' *That*"—said the Rizhiner, ending his story—"is what is called clapping your hands."[7]

In an encounter on the road, Rabbi Samuel told a hasid a story to remind *himself* what to do about the man's request for help. In the synagogue, the Rizhiner told a hasid this story "about clapping" to teach him how to pray with self-sacrifice and fervor. Note that although the Rizhiner used it that way, the story itself is not about praying or clapping but about the unflinching faith, even to martyrdom, not of a tzaddik or hasid but of a simple Jewish thief.

The Second Story: The Ignorant Villager

The Rizhiner Tzaddik once came into his *Beit Midrash* and said to his hasidim: "Let me tell you an amazing story.

"A villager once came into the nearby town to pray with the congregation on Rosh HaShanah. He was a simple country Jew who did not even know how to recite the Hebrew of the prayers. On Rosh HaShanah he stood in the synagogue looking around, without even opening his mouth. When the congregation reached the *Shemoneh Esreh* [the central prayer of the service], many of the worshipers began to weep. The villager was very surprised at their sudden crying: 'There wasn't any argument or dispute in the synagogue, or any disaster—why are they crying?' He couldn't understand it. But finally an idea occurred to him: 'They must be hungry! They've been standing here the whole morning without having eaten anything, so they're crying.' Since he also was hungry, he began to cry too.

"After the *Shemoneh Esreh*, the worshipers ceased weeping. Again the villager was surprised. 'Why have they stopped crying? They haven't eaten yet!' Then another thought occurred to him. He remembered that he had seen food being prepared in the kitchen for the festive meal after the services, and they had put a tough piece of meat into the pot. 'It would certainly take a long time to make such a tough piece of meat soft and tender. It must be that the people praying remembered that the dish was being cooked and were consoled, knowing that if they continued waiting, the food would be much better and tastier. So they stopped crying and are waiting patiently.' The villager then also stopped weeping.

"But when they reached the *shofar*-blowing [another high point in the service], the congregation once again broke out in tears. 'Now why are they crying?' he asked himself again. After thinking it over, he decided, 'It's true that the dish will taste better if it cooks longer, but they're so hungry they can't wait anymore. That's why they're crying.' So as before, he too began to cry with the rest of the congregation."

As soon as the tzaddik finished the story, he left the *Beit Midrash*. The hasidim said, "This is a parable about the Exile."[8]

Rebbes often have a private room for their study and devotions, next to the main hall of their *Beit Midrash*. Here the Rizhiner came in to his hasidim, who were studying in the *Beit Midrash*, specifically to tell them a story and then immediately left.

He either created this story or, perhaps more likely, used an already existing humorous folktale. Regardless, there is a tension here, because the rebbe was not simply telling it as a joke. Why then did he tell this story? That was the question the hasidim had to answer. Note the rebbe's teaching method in telling the tale without explanation and leaving. He wanted them to discuss it. The story is worthy of a long discussion, isn't it? The single sentence comment of theirs at the end is perhaps the main conclusion they came to about its meaning.

According to hasidic teaching, exile can be cosmic, national, or personal: Cosmically, the Divine Presence on earth is in exile; nationally, the Jewish people are in exile from their land; and personally, each individual suffers his own spiritual exile. What strikes me about the story is the way it illustrates how all religious actions, such as praying, can be performed and experienced on many different levels, from the lowest to the highest, and how tragic it is when a person ignorantly drags exalted matters down to his level. That is the "personal exile." If the story is allegorical, with the rustic villager portraying the Jewish people performing their divine service without the proper intention, it explains the spiritual cause of the national exile and even of the cosmic Exile, because the Congregation of Israel represents the Divine Presence on earth. What do you think about this story?

The Third Story

As background to the following story the reader should know that Rabbi Israel of Rizhin was from a family of incomparably holy *yihus* (lineage): His great-grandfather was the Maggid of Mezritch, the Baal Shem Tov's successor as head of the hasidic movement; his grandfather, Abraham the Angel; his father, Rabbi Shalom Shachna of Prohobitch—all tzaddikim, all holy. The Rizhiner was raised in an atmosphere of the most profound piety and was from early on considered a holy child. Even in his youth, many older rebbes praised his awesome sanctity. When he became a great rebbe, the Rizhiner followed a spiritual path of kingly glory, conducting himself like a king of Israel, with a court that had the trappings of royalty. Not unexpectedly, this style attracted a fair share of criticism. But holy and pure tzaddikim, whose word and integrity cannot be doubted, testified that the Rizhiner's desire for wealth and opulence was utterly pure and for the sake of God alone; it was part of his spiritual path and there was nothing low or impure about it. The Rizhiner occasionally revealed his attitude about this matter and reacted to criticism against him.

The Two Badhans

One Sabbath night, Rabbi Israel of Rizhin took the wine cup in his hand and began to recite the *Kiddush*: "And there was evening and there was morning, the sixth day. . . ."[9] But then he put the cup back on the table, sat down, and began to tell a story:

"The son and daughter of two very wealthy men were getting married, and since this would be an expensive wedding, with a large number of guests, many *badhans* [traditional Jewish jesters] wanted to entertain there. Two of the most famous among them—Reuven and Shimon—were determined to win the job. Both of them went to the future in-laws, saying they were top *badhans*. Since neither would admit that the other was better, the two wealthy men, who did not know which of them to choose, offered a compromise: Let each one of them entertain at the beginning of the affair and try to amuse the guests, and the one whom they liked the most would remain for the whole wedding. The two *badhans* agreed, and when they drew lots to see who would perform first, it was determined that it would be Reuven. Reuven immediately jumped up on a table and began:

"'Friends,' he called out in a loud voice, 'let me tell you an amazing story that happened to me. When I came of age, I married, as a person should. After some time, my wife gave birth to a son. I said to her, "My dear, as the rabbis say, there are three partners in a child: the Holy One, blessed be He, his father, and his mother.[10] Therefore, this son of ours is also the son of the Holy One, blessed be He. So you must be very careful about his upbringing—to watch over him and raise him in holiness and purity, so he'll be holy, as befits someone who's a son of the Holy One, blessed be He." My wife took my words with the utmost seriousness, and forsaking everything else, devoted all her time and energy to guarding and caring for the child, with holiness and purity.

"'Every day she took him in his crib to the *Beit Midrash*, so his ears would hear the sound of holy words of Torah study and prayer. She protected him from everything unclean and tainted and kept him from even looking at things and places that were not pure. She continued this until the child became completely holy, and he was worthy having said about him what was said about Rabbi Joshua ben Hanania [a rabbi of talmudic times]: "Happy the one who gave birth to him."[11]

"'The next year my wife had another son, and the following year still another. She protected these two children also, in holiness and purity, but not like our first son, for all her thoughts were on him.

"'When our oldest boy reached the age of three and the time arrived to begin training him to perform the *mitzvot*—as it is said: "When a child begins to speak, his father should begin to teach him Torah etc."[12]—I said to my wife, "The Holy One, blessed be He, has given us three sons. Since there are three partners in a person, why don't we divide our three boys equally between the three partners. It's only right that our first one fall to the lot of the Holy One, blessed be He; and in order to fulfill the verse, 'Train a youth in the proper way, and when he is old he will not depart from it,' I'll drop everything else and concentrate all my efforts on directing this child in Torah and holiness, until he'll truly be fit to be called a son of the Holy One, blessed be He."

"'That's what I did: I forsook all worldly activities, took this child, wrapped in a tallis, to a feast I made for the poor and at which I distributed great amounts of money to charity, and then I hired a special *melamed* [Torah teacher] for him.[13] I paid the *melamed* generously and asked him to devote all his time and effort to tutoring this son of mine. And, with God's help, the boy grew in Torah, going from strength to strength, until he reached his bar mitzvah.

"'I made him a big feast for his bar mitzvah and gave away tremendous sums for charity. The boy, whose success in Torah and holiness I constantly prayed for, delivered a wonderful bar mitzvah Torah discourse, showing profundity and erudition in both the revealed Torah and the Kabbalah. He astonished everyone present. They were so impressed by his piety and scholarship that they said there was not another boy like him in the whole world.

"'When my son reached the age of marriage, many prominent people proposed matches to me. There wasn't a wealthy man who didn't yearn to make this precious boy his son-in-law. But I didn't know what to do or whom to accept. I couldn't help thinking that the truth was, there was no one worthy of having him! After all, who is worthy of taking for his daughter the son of the Holy One, blessed be He?! Meanwhile, the boy grew up and I became worried that he'd never marry, God-forbid. Isn't it true that the Holy One, blessed be He, "did not create the world to be desolate but to be inhabited," that He, blessed be He, intended for people to marry and have children? So I became depressed.

"'One day I went out for a walk in the country, and there, in a pure place, I poured my heart out before the Creator of the world and said, "O Lord God, You know everything I've done for this boy, until I merited that he's now a *gaon* [Torah genius], holy and pure, so there is none like him in all the world, and so that he should be called by Your name—the son of the Holy One, blessed be He. God, You know that there's no one in the world fit to make a match with You, to be Your in-law! Everyone knows that in-laws should be of equal status, and isn't it written, 'There is none beside Him,' and 'There is none but You and no one is like You'? Nevertheless, our sages, of blessed memory, have said (*Yevamot* 63b): 'Go down a step [in social standing] in taking a wife.'

"'"Therefore, I'll agree to an in-law who'll be on the level of our teacher, Moses, on him be peace. In other words, that he should be the greatest tzaddik of the generation, on the level of our teacher, Moses—as the sages say: 'Well said, Moses!' in referring to a great scholar, where Rashi interprets: the greatest of the generation.

"'"But although my son is incomparable," I said to God, blessed be He, "what tzaddik will want to make a match with the father, with Reuven the *badhan*?! So I beg You, Master of the World, grant me great wealth, so that the greatest tzaddik of the generation will agree to be my in-law."[14] And God, blessed be He, heard my plea and, in His abundant compassion and mercy, He summoned His Heavenly Court and they decreed that I was in the right. I immediately heard a heavenly voice proclaim, "Reuven! Stand up and hold out the edge of your coat." I did so, and there fell into my garment an incredible treasure of gold coins and jewels. Overjoyed, I lifted my legs and ran home.

"'While I was on the way, this person here came in my direction—this Shimon, who always apes everything I do and chases after me wherever I go. When he saw the fabulous treasure I was carrying, he—who always begrudges me the least good—took one look at the gold and silver, the precious stones, and greedily asked, "Aren't you a *badhan* like me? Where'd you get this incredible wealth?" I am a generous person and happy when good comes to others, so I didn't hide a thing from him. I told him how the treasure came into my possession and the place in the field where it fell down to me.

"'Shimon didn't wait a minute. As always, he imitated me now too. He ran there and began to cry out that his children are also the children of the Holy One, blessed be He, like my children. He also pleaded and argued before the Holy One, blessed be He, and asked for riches in order to make the best match for his eldest son.

"'The Holy One, blessed be He, who loves justice and truth, heard his pleas, and summoned His court. The Heavenly Court investigated his case and decreed that this Shimon is a liar, whose only interest is copying Reuven's truthful deeds. Since the Upper World is a world of truth and they can't bear falsehood, they decreed that Reuven slap Shimon's face once, on the cheek, before all the assembly and congregation, and push him from the place where he's standing—as is fitting for cheats and liars—so other wrongdoers will not do as he did.'"

"After saying these words, Reuven carried out the decree: He jumped off the table, ran over to Shimon, slapped him soundly, and pushed him out of the house."

The Rizhiner Tzaddik stopped his tale here, rose from his seat, took the cup in his hand, and said *Kiddush* over the wine with tremendous fervor.[15]

The Tale's Interpretation

What a story! This amazing story, spoken before God and congregation, is, among other things, Rabbi Israel's reaction to criticism of his rich lifestyle. Particularly, the Rizhiner seems to have been concerned with those who confused him with fake "rebbes," who amassed wealth and surrounded themselves with regal trappings but who were corrupt within. Doesn't this tale speak for itself and for the integrity of the one who told it? Could a hypocrite and fraud tell such a story?

How remarkable that the Rizhiner chose to express his thoughts about this matter with a story of such complex beauty, a story that (like the previous one about The Ignorant Villager) he either created or adapted from a humorous folktale. Most of it is a story within a story, told in a tone of righteous indignation by Reuven the *badhan*, and how happily humor is mixed in with piety and holiness! (The story about the ignorant villager on Rosh HaShanah also uses humor to convey a holy lesson.) Note the typical method of the *badhan*, who not only amused but showed off his Torah knowledge and expertise by sprinkling his talk with numerous quotes from the Torah and the rabbis.

The *Kiddush* on Sabbath evening is a time of special holiness, and many rebbes recited it in a state of exalted mystic consciousness. That the Rizhiner interrupted the *Kiddush* to tell a story is certainly remarkable; it also reminds us of the incident when he told stories before the morning prayers and forgot to pray.[16] Perhaps he told this story during the *Kiddush* because reciting the *Kiddush* over the wine is traditionally considered as giving testimony that God created the heavens and the earth. It is a time for testifying in holy matters. (Testimony before the Heavenly Court enters the story twice, with the court convened to consider first Reuven's and then Shimon's prayers for wealth.) Certainly the Rizhiner told this story before God as well as those at his Sabbath table.

He not only was justifying himself before God, as being different from the hypocrites and presenting himself as innocent and humble, but in the motif of slapping and pushing out the fake, he also intended to cast out the Other Side (Satan, the Accuser and Adversary), so as to recite the *Kiddush* in holiness and purity.

My own impression is that the Rizhiner identified with both the holy child and his *badhan* father in the story. With the humility of an awesome tzaddik, he proclaimed both his innocence and his lowliness before God. He saw himself as a child of God but also as a *badhan*, a lowly entertainer and storyteller for his hasidim. Was he perhaps also influenced by the *Zohar* (the main book of the Kabbalah), which calls King David "the jester of the King" because he effected supernal joy?[17]

I do not at all think that my comments even begin to touch the depths of this story or its complex variety of motifs. As Hillel said: "Go and complete it!" Certainly this story is worthy of intense discussion and study.

VARIETY, COMPLEXITY, AND DEPTH

These three stories told by the Rizhiner—about fiery clapping, about the confused and ignorant villager on Rosh HaShanah, and about the two *badhans*—show the striking variety of stories told by rebbes, of the settings in which they told them, and of the purposes for which they told them. Plainly, the Rizhiner not only was a gifted and prolific storyteller but was bold in how he used stories. In the tale of The Two *Badhans* one can begin to sense the complexity and depth involved in the stories and storytelling of the rebbes. Perhaps the Rizhiner was influenced by the other rebbe most famous for storytelling, his older contemporary, Rabbi Nahman of Bratzlav— who is the subject of the next chapter.

19

An Exceptional Case: Rabbi Nahman of Bratzlav

FANTASY TALES

Rabbi Nahman of Bratzlav loved stories and was an extraordinary story-teller. As I noted earlier, he said that many tzaddikim originally became aroused to serve God after being inspired by hearing stories of the tzaddikim. This was true of Rabbi Nahman himself. But although he also told stories about tzaddikim, Rabbi Nahman became famous for his religious fantasy tales that were based on kabbalistic teaching and whose characters were kings and princesses, warriors and wanderers, sages and simpletons.

WHEN HE BEGAN TO TELL

Such fantasy tales were something new in Hasidism. They seemed more like the secular tales popular among the nonreligious and the gentiles than the pious Jewish folktales people were familiar with. But the stage had been set earlier by Rabbi Nahman's great-grandfather, the Baal Shem Tov, who had occasionally used secular tales allegorically to express kabbalistic concepts. In Chapter 5 I discussed the Baal Shem Tov's use of the risqué tale of The Wife's Test, a story also found in Boccaccio's *Decameron*. The influence of the Baal Shem Tov's storytelling on Rabbi Nahman appears in a teaching Rabbi Nahman gave preceding his first telling of fantasy tales:

The stories [folktales and fairy tales] that people tell contain many deep secrets and exalted concepts. However, they are flawed, and have numerous deficiencies. They are also confused, because people do not tell them in the correct order: Something that belongs at the beginning of a story is told at the end and the reverse is also the case, and there are many other confusions of this nature. Nonetheless, it is unquestionably true that the stories people tell contain awesome secrets and hidden wisdom.

The Baal Shem Tov, the remembrance of a tzaddik and holy man for a blessing, was able to bring about a kabbalistic mystical unification [a *yihud*, which unifies two spiritual forces that have been separated] by telling a story. When he saw that the supernal channels were defective, and it was not possible to rectify them through prayer, he would rectify and unite them by telling stories.[1]

Rabbi Nathan, who wrote the introduction to the book of Rabbi Nahman's stories, comments:

When the Rebbe (of blessed memory) began telling stories, he said, "I am now beginning to tell stories." . . . as if to say, "I must tell stories because my Torah lessons and conversations are not having any effect in bringing you back to God." All his life he made great efforts to bring us close to God, but when he saw he was not succeeding with us, he began telling stories.[2]

There are a number of important issues to discuss in relation to Rabbi Nahman's comments about his motivation in telling stories—first of all, his remark about the confused wisdom of secular tales.

Folktales and Fairy Tales

Rabbi Nahman was aware of the charm of secular folktales and fairy tales and wanted to lift them into the religious realm by using them for the holy purpose of attracting people to God. But he saw that although they contained profound wisdom, it was not godly wisdom. According to the Kabbalah, attributes like wisdom, love, beauty, and glory are cosmic principles that can be manifested or expressed on higher or lower levels. Not only beauty but all the others as well are in the eye of the beholder. Thus, if something worldly is beautiful and attracts, it is natural to ask what the "true," spiritual form of this beauty is. The same logic holds for worldly wisdom. If these secular tales contain wisdom, what is the true form of that wisdom, and what are the "corresponding" sacred tales? The rabbis say: If people tell you that the nations have wisdom, believe them; but if they tell you that they have Torah, do not believe them. How then can secular wisdom be elevated and "transformed" *into* Torah? By rearranging and reordering it, according to a God-centered perspective. That is the kabbalistic process that Rabbi Nahman described as correcting the confused order of secular stories. The Baal Shem Tov had occasionally transformed secular, gentile melodies into holy songs. Later hasidic rebbes also appropriated gentile songs and melodies saying that they had originally been sung in the ancient Temple in Jerusalem or by David when he was a shepherd boy on the hills of Judea but they had been in exile for hundreds of years and the time had come to "redeem" them. Rabbi Nahman said that the purpose of Jewish melodies was to include and elevate the melodies of all the nations of the world. The Baal Shem Tov, Rabbi Nahman, and a few other hasidic rebbes similarly appropriated elements and motifs from gentile folk and fairy tales. Thus, a captured princess in a tale they told might represent the mystery of the exile of the *Shechinah*; a blind beggar, a humble tzaddik who does not even "look" at material things; a robber, the forces of evil that try to subvert piety.[3]

Secrets

If Rabbi Nahman said that even secular folktales contain "awesome wisdom and hidden secrets," how much more so his own stories, which were based on the Kabbalah! He said that every word of his stories was intentional—like the Torah itself—and they should not be changed or altered in the slightest way. Moreover, "they contain extraordinary, hidden, deep meanings. They are fit to be preached in public and one may stand in the synagogue and tell any one of them."[4] The obvious moral and religious lessons found in Rabbi Nahman's tales can be appreciated at face value. As for the deeper level, of kabbalistic "secrets," he claimed it was not even necessary that they be understood. "It is best not even to hint at the mysteries contained in the stories," he said, "for when something is completely hidden, it can accomplish the most." Rabbi Nathan, Rabbi Nahman's foremost disciple and interpreter, remarks, after reporting this comment, "Still, the Rebbe revealed some of the mysteries in his tales, so that people would realize that they contained hidden things."[5]

Rabbi Nahman's view that a story's mysteries need not be rationally understood applies to secular art and literature also: The effect of a work of art does not depend on its being "understood." When a person reads a novel or hears a folktale, if it works it has an immediate effect in changing his *kishkes*, his insides. In fact, that a novel, for example, has to be explained, indicates it is *not* effective as art. Therefore, Rabbi Nahman felt that his stories worked best if their kabbalistic underpinnings were left concealed. After all, if he had wanted to teach Kabbalah directly he could have done so. Why stimulate a person's intellect when the tales were engaging his imagination and operating on deeper levels of consciousness? Indeed, it was when he saw that Torah teaching and conversations were *not* succeeding that he chose to elevate his hasidim by storytelling.

That does not mean, however, that the tales should not be studied, probed, and analyzed. In fact, there is a rich body of Bratzlav literature that does just that. The point is that there is a time for this and a time for that. It is the same with secular art. For example, if someone cannot experience a novel or movie without simultaneously cogitating about it, he is losing out by substituting an intellectual experience for an aesthetic one. The same is true for the spiritual-aesthetic experience of one of Rabbi Nahman's fantasy stories. It is fine to reflect on it but only after a decent interval that allows time to absorb its imaginative meaning. Why spoil the experience by premature intellectualizing?

STORYTELLING AS INDIRECT COMMUNICATION

Stories contain secrets, hidden wisdom, according to Rabbi Nahman, and their particular virtue, what makes them potent and effective, is that they are a form of indirect communication.

Waking from Sleep

When Rabbi Nahman felt that his Torah teaching and conversation were not producing the kind of progress he wanted for his disciples, he began telling them stories. Rabbi Nahman believed that many people, even very religious people, lacked a true spiritual awareness, and he expressed this metaphorically by saying that they were "asleep," sleep representing a state of lowered consciousness. The only way to "awaken" them was through stories. But just as a person who has been in darkness for a long time cannot suddenly be exposed to glaring sunlight, so one who is spiritually asleep cannot receive the light of Torah directly; it must be veiled at first—in stories.[6] Rabbi Nahman once quipped that he was contradicting popular wisdom, for "most people say that stories help you fall asleep; I wake people up with stories."[7]

The Beggar with the Crooked Neck

Rabbi Nahman clothed the Torah's light in stories. In the previously quoted comment, he also said that when ordinary prayer would be ineffective, the Baal Shem Tov prayed by clothing the prayer in a story. Undoubtedly, Rabbi Nahman did the same. Thus, storytelling can clothe either Torah or prayer and be a means of indirect communication. Rabbi Nahman's tale of The Seven Beggars tells of the wedding of an orphan boy and girl, at which each of seven beggars gives them a wedding gift. All of the beggars have handicaps—they are lame, blind, or hunchbacked—yet their "defects" are only apparent and actually mask excellences. One of the beggars has a crooked neck, yet his "defect" allows him to throw his voice in an extraordinary way. He tells the newly wed boy and girl of a mated pair of birds, separated in two lands, who piteously wail for each other and must be brought together. The beggar says: "I can throw my voice so that while no sound is heard here, it is heard at a distance. I can therefore throw the voice of the female bird and make it reach the place of the male bird and also throw the voice of the male bird and make it reach the place of the female bird. By doing this I can bring them together, and everything will be rectified."

According to Jewish mystical teaching, there is nothing other than God. All existence is really one. But now there seem to be two: God and the world. In truth, however, the world is also God, and the messianic goal is that God as immanent, the female *Shechinah*, will be united with God as transcendent, the Holy One, blessed be He. Bringing together the boy and girl in marriage or the mated pair of birds symbolizes the unification (*yihud*) of the "male" Holy One, blessed be He, and the "female" *Shechinah*. Since the Community of Israel represents the Divine Presence on earth, uniting Israel with God unites heaven and earth. How is this unity to be effected? By the divine service of Israel, particularly the tzaddikim.

The seven beggars represent different aspects of tzaddikim, and their apparent defects are "deficiencies" in the activities of the tzaddikim necessitated by the constraints of the exile. Their wedding gifts are their varied forms of divine service that redeem the world and bring about the unity, the wedding, of heaven and earth, the Holy One, blessed be He, and the *Shechinah* (His Divine Presence). The beggar with the crooked neck represents, among other things, the tzaddik as storyteller and gives us insight into Rabbi Nahman's view of storytelling by tzaddikim. The "defective" *crooked* neck, which symbolizes *indirect* communication, allows him to "throw his voice," that is, he has the ability to disguise Torah and prayer in stories. By this he can "unify the two birds"—God and His *Shechinah*. When the normal methods of Torah and prayer are ineffective in uniting Israel and God, because the suffering of the exile makes Jews spiritually dull and unreceptive, the unification can be accomplished by means of storytelling.

One English version of Rabbi Nahman's stories has a commentary from Bratzlav sources. The comment on "throw my voice" says:

> The tzaddik can bring God and the *Shechinah* together by throw-ing his voice. One way of doing this is by clothing his [Torah] les-sons in stories. . . . Telling stories is therefore throwing one's voice at the Israelites.
>
> The tzaddik can also clothe his prayers in stories. Because of spiri-tual barriers, he cannot make such prayers directly, and to all prac-tical purposes they seem like stories. But in the place where they are needed, they are heard. In this respect, he is throwing his voice toward God.[8]

When people are unable to hear Torah directly, the tzaddik must clothe it in stories. Speaking Torah, God's word, by means of a story, to Jews who are separated from Him, is "throwing the voice." Conversely, when God cannot, so to speak, hear a prayer directly, the tzaddik must also clothe it in a story. Usually a tzaddik prays for a person in need, but sometimes it is impossible to pray directly (for example, because the individual is un-worthy of having the request fulfilled) and he must clothe his prayer in a story, that is, tell a story as a prayer, disguising it from contrary spiritual forces. Thus, the tzaddik "throws his voice" this way or that, to the people or to God, by telling stories that disguise Torah or prayer. His having to speak indirectly is represented in Rabbi Nahman's story by the beggar's crooked neck.

These methods were Rabbi Nahman's own and were based on those of the Baal Shem Tov. Rabbi Moshe Hayim Ephraim of Sudilkov, Rabbi Nahman's uncle and the Baal Shem Tov's grandson, wrote that the Besht had a special ability to serve God by storytelling and to use seemingly worldly stories to "clothe" his wisdom.[9] He also quoted him as saying that some people could be elevated only by stories.[10] In a previously quoted comment, Rabbi Nahman mentions the Baal Shem Tov as a precedent for using tales to accomplish mystic purposes, saying that sometimes when the Besht wanted to make a *yihud* to help someone, he saw that the supernal channels were disrupted and could be repaired only by clothing prayers in stories. (I will later discuss more fully how the rebbes used storytelling in place of prayer.)

OPPOSITION AND JUSTIFICATION

If the usual types of storytelling by hasidim were sometimes considered frivolous by the anti-hasidic religious establishment, how much more so Rabbi Nahman's fantasy tales! Even some of the other hasidic rebbes opposed this new kind of storytelling.[11] These were not the familiar stories of tzaddikim or standard religious folktales, in which the heroes were rabbis and other pious men and women; they were hardly distinguishable from secular fairy tales. Consequently, some rebbes considered it dangerous to draw religious people into this alien realm.

Sleep and Deep Slumber

Rabbi Nahman discussed in depth what led him to begin telling such tales, and he made efforts to justify his innovation.[12] He said that there are two types of stories, those "amidst years" (or of "seventy years" [the usual life span] or "seventy faces" [the traditional number of Torah perspectives]) and those of "ancient times." The usual type of story—that "amidst years"— is able to rouse people from their spiritual sleep, but when someone has fallen into a deep slumber, it is no longer sufficient or effective. Then, a deeper type of story, which can reach into the most central core of consciousness, must be used. This is the type of his fantasy tales, which are stories of "ancient times," in other words, myths. He said that his generation could no longer be roused by normal means; their slumber was too deep. Even people who outwardly seemed very pious were asleep and without an awakened God-consciousness.

Dreams and Stories

How do you communicate with people who are asleep? Through dreams. Rabbi Nahman said that his dream-like fantasy tales could stir up the more profound levels of consciousness and rouse people to true spirituality. They would replace an impure imagination with a pure one, leading finally to a renewed faith.[13] Rabbi Nahman also frequently related his dreams and "visions of the night" to his disciples.[14] The sleep and dreams of a person on a high spiritual level are not like those of ordinary people. Certainly, Rabbi Nahman's dreams were mostly visions in which he was "conscious" or "superconscious" during sleep. These dream-vision "stories" that he told his disciples obviously affected his other storytelling. They may explain his previously mentioned comment: "Other people *tell* stories, I *see* them."

Types and Archetypes

According to the traditional concept, the Torah has seventy "faces" (perspectives). The usual stories, which Rabbi Nahman categorized as those of the seventy faces—clothing the seventy faces of the Torah—represent the normal, accepted variety of Torah views and stories, in their diverse kinds. He considered his innovative fantasy tales as being *outside* of that range. He claimed that they represented a deeper level that supplies meaning to all the seventy kinds, that is, he was telling stories using the mythic *archetypes* behind all the more familiar, varied *types* of stories.[15] But when Rabbi Nahman admitted that they were not among the traditional seventy kinds, he also indirectly gave recognition to why they were not readily accepted.[16]

CHILDREN FROM STORYTELLING

Rabbi Nahman said that his new form of storytelling could wake people from their spiritual slumber. He also claimed that these deeper stories could make barren women produce children. He meant this statement literally—that the stories could mystically release the pent-up energies of barren women so they could have children[17]—but also metaphorically and spiritually—that the stories could "produce a newborn child" by elevating a person to true spirituality. He said that "Just as I was born through storytelling . . . so will my children be born from storytelling."[18] As a boy, Rabbi Nahman was set on the quest for God-consciousness by hearing stories, and he believed that the same stimulus, although of a stronger sort, would work for his spiritual "children," his disciples.

A PRAYER ABOUT STORYTELLING

Rabbi Nahman encouraged his disciples to compose prayers based on his Torah lessons and to pray to attain what he taught them. Here is a prayer of that type, composed by Rabbi Nathan of Nemirov, based on Rabbi Nahman's teachings about storytelling. Although it focuses primarily on miracle tales, the concepts alluded to have a broader application.

Great are God's deeds and the stories about them; desirable in every way. How great are Your deeds, O God; Your thoughts are indescribably deep. O Master of the World, You are the God who performs miracles; by means of the true tzaddikim, You do wonders in every generation. Our ancestors have told us all the wondrous miracles and awesome signs You performed through Your true tzaddikim in each generation, from the earliest times until today. In this generation too there are certainly true miracle-workers. Therefore, in Your abundant mercy, help, strengthen, and inspire me that I merit to tell stories of the deeds of true tzaddikim—what happened to them, their children, and all those associated with them; and all the great and awesome miracles and wonders, both revealed and hidden, they did in the world, and all the holy ways and revelations of divinity that they drew down into the world.

May I merit to hear all this well, with my ears and heart, and may I speak and tell about these things constantly. May my mouth be full of the praises of the tzaddikim, all the day occupied with their glories, for their praises and glories are Yours. May I be occupied daily with telling stories of the deeds of true tzaddikim, in a manner that their awesome holiness will be drawn onto me. And through this I'll merit to purify my mind of all confusion and disorder, and free it from all kinds of foreign and external thoughts and all sorts of bad musings, and from every manner of confusion in the world that derives from constricted consciousness. May I leave small consciousness and attain expanded consciousness. And through this, save and rescue me from all the troubles, afflictions, and judgments in the world, for they all come from confusion and small consciousness. In Your abundant mercy, save and rescue me from them all by helping me to be occupied constantly in telling stories of the deeds of the true tzaddikim, who are on the level of and represent expanded consciousness.

Help me . . . always to believe with perfect faith in Your providence. Completely remove from me any false belief in "natural" events; let me finally realize that there is no "Nature" at all, just Your providence alone. For Nature too is directed by Your providence. You alter Nature time and again by means of the true tzaddikim who perform miracles and wonders in every generation, as we have heard from our ancestors. Have mercy on us and on all Israel, for the sake of Your name. Help us to be like You—to make a division and know the difference between light and darkness, until we can clearly distinguish between stories of true tzaddikim and stories of the wicked. May we know about whom to tell stories, and how to tell them. May I merit to tell stories about true tzaddikim, who are so great that speaking about them and telling stories about them has the power to purify my mind. You have enabled me to understand that for each story of the tzaddikim there is a similar story about wicked and false people, and deceptive stories about those who do what appear to be miracles— by tricks, magic, or other means—and no one can discern or differentiate between them, except someone who knows how to tell the difference between light and darkness, as You have shown us, in Your abundant mercy. But because of our pitiful condition of being so far from You, we, certainly, are unable to distinguish between light and darkness. Therefore, have mercy on us, help and save us, so that [if we do not have true discrimination] we will at least attain to perfect faith that the difference between the stories about the tzaddikim and the stories about the wicked is like the difference between light and darkness, for then we too will be able to tell stories of the tzaddikim. Let our faith be so strong that it will be as if we were actually seeing with our eyes what we truly believe. May we believe in You, O Lord our God, that You watch over and care for everything with Your divine providence, at all times, that You perform miracles at all times through Your true tzaddikim who are in every generation. May we merit to believe that there is a great difference between miracles and wonders done by true tzaddikim, and what appear to be miracles done by the wicked or by those who combine and mix good and evil and are not yet worthy to perform miracles but nevertheless wrap themselves in a tallis not their own. For the difference between their deeds and the miraculous deeds of the true tzaddikim is as great as that between light and darkness. May I merit to always tell stories of true tzaddikim that have the power to purify my mind. May the words of my mouth and the meditations of my heart be pleasing to Thee, my Rock and Redeemer. Amen. *Selah.*[19]

This prayer expresses the earnest wish to tell and hear stories of the tzaddikim constantly, for such stories draw down holiness and purify the mind; they foster the expanded consciousness represented by the tzaddikim. As in the teaching of the Mezritcher Maggid, that praising the tzaddikim is like praising God, "their praises and glories are Yours."[20] As discussed previously, the hasidic tradition values the miracle stories emphasized in this prayer, because they reinforce faith in God's rule over Nature. But even for people who have difficulty accepting supernatural miracles, such stories can convey a luminous suggestion of something behind the veil, of God's control of Nature, even without miraculous "exceptions." They inculcate a belief in the inner, spiritual reality of the world. That perception is the purity of mind, the expanded consciousness, sought after. We previously discussed a saying of Rabbi Nahman in which he metaphorically labeled that elevated God-consciousness the "Land of Israel." But although Rabbi Nahman obviously appreciated miracle tales, he also felt that people might be misled by "miracles" performed by those who were not true tzaddikim. So he warned against the danger of a lack of discrimination. However, do not let the emphasis on miracle tales distract you from the many other concepts about storytelling that you will find in this prayer if you read it carefully.

Let us close this chapter with one of Rabbi Nahman's famous fantasy tales to offer at least a taste of their exotic flavor.

THE HUMBLE KING

Once there was a king who had a wise advisor. The king said to the wise man, "There is a king who signs his letters and documents, 'the mighty warrior and humble man of truth.'

"I know that he is a mighty warrior, because his land is surrounded by the sea, and he has a navy of warships with cannons that do not let anyone approach the land. On the side away from the sea, a swamp surrounds his land, with a single narrow path, on which only one man at a time can walk. This path is also defended with cannons, and if anyone attacks, they fire the cannons. It is impossible even to come close to his land.

"However, when he signs himself 'humble man of truth,' I do not know if it is so. I therefore want you to bring me a portrait of that king."

The king had portraits of every other king, with the single exception of this one. No king had that king's portrait, since he kept himself hidden from all people. He sat on a throne behind the curtains of an enclosed canopy, isolated from his subjects.

The wise man traveled to that land. Then he decided he must first know the essential nature of that land. How can one understand the nature of a land? By knowing its humor. In order to understand something, one must know the jokes related to it. There are many types of jokes. Sometimes a person wants to hurt another with his words. When his victim takes offense, he says, "I was only joking." It is thus written, "As a madman casts firebrands, arrows, and deadly weapons . . . and then says, 'I was only joking'" (Proverbs 26:18,19). There are also cases where someone is only joking, but nevertheless, the other person is hurt by his words. There are also other types of humor.

There is a land that includes all other lands. In the land that includes all lands, there is a city that includes all cities of that land. In the city that includes all cities, in the land that includes all lands, there is a building that includes all buildings. Here, there is a man who includes everything in the entire building. . . . Here, there is the one who composes all the humor and jokes in the entire land.

The wise man took a large sum of money and went there. He saw them telling many kinds of jokes and engaged in all sorts of humor. From the jokes, he understood that the land was totally filled with falsehood, from beginning to end. He saw that they made jokes about how people were cheated and deceived in business, and that when people went to court, all the decisions were false and they took bribes. Even when someone went to the Supreme Court, there was nothing but falsehood. Jests were made about all these cases. From this humor the wise man understood that the land was totally full of falsehood and dishonesty, and that there was no truth at all there.

After observing the humor he went to test the reality. He bought and sold merchandise, allowing himself to be cheated. He took his case to court and saw that everything was falsehood and bribery. One day he could give a bribe, and the next day they pretended they did not recognize him. He took his case to a higher court, and it too was full of falsehood. Then he went to the Supreme Court, which was also full of falsehood and bribery.

Finally, he brought his case before the king. When he came to the king, who sat hidden behind the curtain of a canopy, he said, "Over whom are you king? The land is completely full of falsehood, from beginning to end. There is no truth at all in it." He then began to describe all the falsehood in the land. Hearing this, the king inclined his ear toward the curtain to listen to the wise man's words. The king was very surprised that there was a man who was aware of all the falsehood in the land. When the ministers of state heard the wise man's words, they were very angry with him. However, he continued describing the falsehood in the land.

The wise man then said, "It would be logical to say that since you are king, you are like the rest—that you also love falsehood, like everyone else in the kingdom. But one thing shows me that you are a man of truth. Since you cannot tolerate the land's falsehood, you keep yourself at a distance from your subjects." With that, the wise man began to praise the king very, very highly.

The king was very humble. His humility equaled his greatness. When a person is truly humble, the more he is praised and made much of, the smaller and more humble he becomes. Therefore, when the wise man praised him and spoke of his greatness, the king became very small and humble, until he actually became nothing.

The king then could not restrain himself. He threw aside the curtain to see the wise man. He had to see who knew and understood all this. In doing so, however, the king revealed his face and the sage saw him. The wise man was then able to paint his portrait and bring it to his king.

"The ways of Zion (Tzion) are mourning" (Lamentations 1:4). "Zion," tzion in Hebrew, alludes to monuments of all the lands that came together. It is thus written, "One shall see a man and build a monument (tzion) next to him" (Ezekiel 39:15).

This is the significance of the verse, "See Zion (tzion), the city of our gatherings" (Isaiah 33:20). In Hebrew this is Hazeh Tzion Kiryat Moadenu. The initial letters of the words of this verse spell out metzahek, which means to tell a joke. This is the place where all the monuments come together. If a person needs to know if he should perform some act or engage in some type of business, he can know it there. May it be God's will to rebuild His Temple. Amen.[21]

The recorder of Rabbi Nahman's stories, Rabbi Nathan, concludes:

> Look, see, and understand the extent of these concepts. Happy is he who waits and reaches the point where he can know and perceive even a small degree of the mysteries of these stories. Nothing like this has been heard since ancient times.
>
> All the verses and allusions that are cited after some of the stories

are only hints so that people will realize that the story is not something devoid of meaning, heaven forbid. Rabbi Nahman expressly said that he was revealing some hints and verses alluding to the mysteries in the stories so that people will realize that he was not merely engaging in idle chatter, heaven forbid.

However, the mysteries of these stories extend far beyond the grasp of our knowledge. "It is deep, deep; who will find it?"

There is an extensive literature—including Bratzlav hasidic literature, some recently produced in English—that discusses and interprets Rabbi Nahman's stories.

Rabbi Nahman not only was an extraordinarily creative composer of stories but clearly had a developed religious perspective on his storytelling. His transformation of secular folktale motifs was kabbalistically motivated, his stories expressed kabbalistic concepts, and he sought to accomplish kabbalistic mystical unifications by means of his storytelling. All this would mean little if the stories themselves were unremarkable, but they are stunning. However, we have to disagree with Rabbi Nathan, that "nothing like this has been heard since ancient times," for even in ancient times there was nothing quite like it.

III

HASIDIC TEACHING ABOUT THE BENEFITS OF STORYTELLING

20

Stories Save

TELLING STORIES FOR ONE'S OWN BENEFIT

PURIFYING THE MIND

People tell stories of the tzaddikim because the stories give them life and bring divine sweetness and beauty into their lives. But in the process of telling and listening they are purified. The rabbis tell a parable to explain the effect of the holy company of tzaddikim, of a person who walked into a perfume shop and simply by standing among the jars of aromatic perfume came out smelling sweetly. It is the same with hasidic stories. Someone constantly occupied in praising the fragrant ways of the tzaddikim ends up emanating a sweet fragrance. According to hasidic teaching, telling and listening to tales of the tzaddikim purifies a person's mind and soul.

Someone might mistakenly think that a person who tells a story does so only to benefit the listeners. But telling stories benefits the one who tells as well as the one who listens.

Rabbi Nahman of Bratzlav taught: "Telling stories of the tzaddikim and events in their lives is something very great, because it purifies the mind."[1]

ELEVATING CONSCIOUSNESS
AND SAVING FROM TROUBLES

Why is this? It happens because the tzaddikim are on a higher plane of consciousness, and when a person speaks about them his mind is immersed in that higher world and is elevated.[2]

Storytelling not only purifies but saves. At least some aspects of this can be understood rationally. According to the mystic teachings, a person's state of mind affects what happens to him. In the most obvious sense, if someone is walking around in a constricted state of consciousness he is more likely to get into a car accident, God spare us, or into an argument. Contrarily, when his mind is elevated through contact with the world of the tzaddikim, who have expanded consciousness, good things are more likely to occur.[3] Similarly, the state of a person's consciousness affects his perception of reality and the way he experiences events. Thus, if a mishap or reversal occurs while he is in a lower state of consciousness he will understand it as being contrary to his welfare, but if it occurs when he is in a higher state of consciousness he can experience it as being God's will to help him, albeit in a painful and difficult way.[4] Thus, the holy company of the tzaddikim, even through the agency of stories, will affect a person's mind in a way that will change his experience of life.

Rabbi Nahman taught:

Telling stories of the tzaddikim . . . purifies the mind . . . and one is saved from troubles. Because troubles come from mental confusion, which is the level of constricted consciousness and also the level of judgments. But the stories of tzaddikim are on the level of expanded consciousness . . . and they purify the mind from evil thoughts that are drawn to a person due to constricted consciousness. As a result, troubles and judgments, which are the level of constricted consciousness, are ameliorated and "sweetened."[5]

Magnifying the Salvation of His King

Rabbi Nahman said:

Telling stories that show the greatness and extraordinary powers of the tzaddikim sweetens the harsh judgments and brings lovingkindness into the world. This is the interpretation of the verse: "He magnifies the salvation of His king and does lovingkindness to His anointed one" (Psalm 18:51). The Talmud says, "Who are the kings? The sages" (Gittin 62a). By magnifying the salvation of His king, that is, when we speak in magnificent terms about the help and salvation that came about through the agency of the tzaddikim, "He does lovingkindess to His anointed one." The Hebrew word for "His anointed one," meshiho, can be read as mesiho, meaning "the one who speaks about him." God does lovingkindness with mesiho, the one who speaks about the tzaddikim in magnificent terms, telling stories about their greatness.[6]

MEASURE FOR MEASURE

Rabbi Nahman expressed a related thought from another perspective. He said: "When someone tells stories of the tzaddikim, his righteous deeds are mentioned in heaven."[7]

When a person remembers and praises the righteousness of the tzaddikim, he is rewarded measure for measure, and his own righteousness is remembered.[8] And when his merits are mentioned in heaven, he receives God's blessing: Judgments against him are annulled and he is shown kindness.

THE BLESSINGS OF STORYTELLING

The hasidic editor of a book of stories about tzaddikim interpreted Proverbs 10:7—"the remembrance of a tzaddik is a blessing"—to mean that any mention of a tzaddik, such as by telling a story about him, brings a double blessing.

The *Midrash*[9] teaches the value of telling stories of the tzaddikim by saying that the Holy One, blessed be He, occupies Himself in praising the tzaddikim [as in the many stories in God's Torah that praise His servants], because "the remembrance of a tzaddik is a blessing" (Proverbs 10:7). Telling stories of the tzaddikim, who sacrifice themselves, heart and soul, to serve God, produces two kinds of blessings: One, the story itself has a holy influence on the teller; two, since he helps others, who hear the story and are aroused to serve God . . . and we know from the teaching of the rabbis that whoever influences others for good is himself protected from sin—a second blessing is that the teller will merit all manner of good things, spiritual and material."[10]

THREE MISTAKES

According to popular hasidic tradition, telling stories of the Baal Shem Tov on *Motza'ei Shabbat* (the conclusion of the Sabbath) has a specific mystic potency for *parnosseh*—for one's livelihood. But Rabbi Shalom of Belz and other rebbes[11] said that although this is basically correct, it contains three mistakes: It is not only on *Motza'ei Shabbat* but at any time; it is not only for *parnosseh* but for all good things, spiritual and material[12]; and it is not only stories of the Baal Shem Tov but stories of all the tzaddikim.[13]

THE BAAL SHEM TOV AND ELIJAH

According to a hasidic story, the Baal Shem Tov drew down this potency— that stories about him have the power to save—through prayer.

Once, the Baal Shem Tov's disciples saw him weeping greatly and then he began to rejoice greatly. His foremost disciple asked him why he had cried so much, and then became so happy. The Besht answered him: "At first I sat down and pondered over how the prophet Elijah and I both learned from the same master, Ahiyah the Shilonite,[14] but whereas Elijah merited that every time people mention him, they say—as is custom-ary—'May he be remembered for good,' I only merited that they would tell stories about me. So I wept, pleading and begging God, that when a Jew tells a story about me [he also benefits "for good," so that if the story is one] that pertains to spirituality, he attain spiritual salvation; and if it pertains to materiality, he attain material salvation. After my prayer, I heard a heavenly proclamation that everyone who believes that all the divine service and all the efforts of Israel the son of Sarah [that is, the Besht] were only for the benefit of Israel, collectively and individually, and tells stories about him after the Sabbath, at the beginning of the week—will have salva-tion and success that week; if at the beginning of the month, he will have success all that month; if he speaks of him at the beginning of the year, he will have a good and blessed year. So," the Besht concluded, "when I saw that even when I will be in the upper world, the Children of Israel will be saved because of me, I became filled with happiness and joy."[15]

For a story about the Baal Shem Tov to save, the person telling it must believe that all the Besht's actions were holy and for the benefit of Israel. This tale says that the Besht knew people would tell stories about him— indeed, they did so even during his lifetime—and he prayed that they gain merit thereby, that their pious motives receive heavenly recognition, and be rewarded. Since the rebbes say that tales of all the tzaddikim have this mystic potency to save, perhaps the Besht's prayer opened this channel of divine blessing for all storytelling about tzaddikim. Thus, a story about a tzaddik can bring God's salvation into the world, for when told with faith, it is like a prayer, and like a prayer, it saves.[16]

It is an old Jewish custom to mention Elijah the prophet, often in story or song, on *Motza'ei Shabbat*. In addition, it is a custom, whenever mentioning Elijah, to say: "May he be remembered for good," that is, for the good of those who speak about him. Certainly both these customs influenced the development of the later hasidic tradition of telling tales about the Baal Shem Tov on *Motza'ei Shabbat*, as is indeed suggested by this Baal Shem Tov story.

HOW TO TELL A STORY SO IT SAVES

In order to save, a story must be told with faith and fervor.

The Rebbe of Helish, whose grandfather had been a disciple of the Baal Shem Tov, was once asked to tell a story. He said: "A person has to tell a tale in a way that the telling itself saves. My grandfather, of blessed memory, was lame. Once they asked him to tell a story of his master, the Besht. He began to tell them how the holy Baal Shem Tov would leap and dance when he prayed, and as he recounted to them what he had seen, he stood up. And the story so aroused his fervor that he began to show them by his own leaping and dancing how his master did it. That moment he was cured of his lameness and became a healthy man."[17]

REAROUSING THE MIRACLE

Hasidic tradition teaches that recalling a miracle by means of a story rearouses the potency of the original miracle and can produce another like it. Rabbi Shlomo of Lutzk said: "Through the words and remembrance of a miracle when one tells the story, that kind of miracle is aroused and drawn down again. For that reason, it is a *mitzvah* to recount the story of the Exodus from Egypt."[18] In other words, telling the story of the first redemption will help bring the final redemption.

Rabbi Tzvi Elimelech of Dinov said:

Our holy rabbis, the tzaddikim of our generations, have written that they received a tradition from those who have the holy spirit that when someone is in need of help and salvation, of healing or success, or needs to safely make a dangerous ocean voyage, he should

verbally call to remembrance miracles that occurred, in similar circumstances, to the tzaddikim throughout the generations . . . because
by telling the stories of miracles that happened in similar circumstances he will be saved in the view of all. . . .[19]

TELLING STORIES FOR
THE BENEFIT OF OTHERS

So far I have discussed hasidic beliefs about how a person can benefit and
save himself by storytelling. But hasidim believe he can also help others.

STORIES CAN SAVE EVEN IN THE NEXT WORLD

Hasidism teaches that stories told about deceased tzaddikim benefit and
elevate them in the next world. Presumably, the same is also true for ordinary people, when stories told about their exalted moments and deeds provide a positive example for others. But remarkably, a person can even be
saved in the next world by a story that provides a negative example—of
what *not* to do.

I heard Rabbi Shlomo Carlebach tell the following tale, which he preceded by saying that certain stories are "bank" stories and others "cash"
stories: Some stories you can have stored in the bank of your mind, others
you should have ready, like cash (because they have a lesson frequently
needed). This tale about his ancestor, the Bach,[20] was, he said, a cash story.

The holy Bach had a big *yeshivah*, and the top student became rich
after he went out into the world. A poor man once came to the Bach for
help, saying he was in a trade where it was difficult to find a job. He had
heard that a certain nobleman had an opening, but there was simply no
way an ordinary Jew could talk to a nobleman. He told the Bach that when
he had lost his job, he started to have troubles with his wife; because he
could not support his family, his marriage was being destroyed and his
children were starving! What he wanted was a letter of recommendation
to the Bach's top student, Reb Abraham, so that he would speak to the
nobleman on his behalf.

The Bach gave him the letter and he went and gave it to Reb Abraham,
who told him he was ready to do the favor, but after three months. He was
just about to travel to the big fair in Leipzig and could not help him now.
The poor man was distraught because his situation was desperate. Who

knows what would happen in three months! But there was nothing he could do. So he waited. After three months Reb Abraham came back from Leipzig and took care of the situation. He spoke to the nobleman and the man got the job.

Some time later Reb Abraham became very sick, and it was clear he was soon leaving this world. The Bach visited his pupil and made him shake hands on it and swear that he would come to him after the Kiddush on Friday evening and tell him how it went with him in the other world. The Kiddush is a very holy time and tzaddikim sometimes enter into exalted spiritual moods then.

After Kiddush who could tell where the holy Bach was? His pupil came to him in a vision and told him what had happened. He had appeared before the Heavenly Court and since he had led a holy life he was going to heaven; there was no problem. But on his way there, a dark angel appeared before the court and claimed that there was a problem. Reb Abraham was brought back to the court and they asked the dark angel: "What are you claiming?" He said: "I'm not claiming that he deserves to go to Hell. But if you can let somebody wait for three months, you're no merchandise for Paradise." So Reb Abraham was crying to the Bach that he was neither in Heaven nor in Hell. The Bach said to him: "I'll learn mishnayos for your sake. [It is traditional, particularly on a yahrzeit, to study Mishnah teachings in behalf of a deceased person, to benefit his soul.] But I can't be sure that learning mishnayos will be enough. I'll leave in my last will and testament that my children and grandchildren tell this story. Then, if someone will not be forced to wait for charity or a favor because of hearing it, it will go to your credit."[21]

The Bach's student made someone wait and, measure for measure, he also had to wait. Telling his story benefited him not because he performed an exemplary deed but because he provided an example of what not to do. Rabbi Carlebach is a descendant of the Bach, and by telling this story he was fulfilling the directive of his holy ancestor.

REOPENING THE CHANNEL

Previous quotes stated that a person in need of divine assistance should tell a story of an earlier miracle to rearouse a comparable miracle. Rebbes told stories with similar intentions to benefit others.

Rabbi Yehiel Joshua of Biala said that the first instance of a miracle opens a channel, so to speak. Thereafter, telling the story of the original miracle reopens the channel to draw down salvation from that same kind of miracle. So some tzaddikim did miracles by telling miracle stories.[22] "It is said that whenever the holy Rabbi of Liska wanted to effect a miracle, he first told a story of a tzaddik, and with it drew down the salvation."[23]

And the Fire Abated

Rabbi Yitzhak Isaac of Kalev once traveled to a certain village for the holy Sabbath. While they were praying *Kabbalat Shabbat*, the Sabbath Welcoming Service, they heard cries that a fire had broken out in the barn of the farmer who was the rabbi's host. The man wanted to run out to save his property [although it is forbidden to extinguish fire on the Sabbath], but the holy rabbi held his hands and said, "Stay! Let me tell you an amazing story:

"The Rebbe Reb Zusya [of Hanipol] was once reciting Psalms with great fervor shortly before *Kabbalat Shabbat*, when a cry was heard, 'There's a fire in the house!' They shouted to him, 'Zusya, there's a fire!' but he went on with his Psalms and paid no attention to them. They yelled to him again, and then again. Finally, he answered, 'If there's a fire, doesn't it say: "And the fire abated" [Numbers 11:2]!'[24] When the holy Rabbi of Kalev uttered these words: 'and the fire abated,' they saw that the fire—just as had happened with Rabbi Zusya—was completely extinguished."[25]

The Merit of Martyrs and Tzaddikim

These miracles by storytelling were believed to rely on the merit of the tzaddik about whom the story is told. Before the holy Rabbi of Ziditchov told stories to draw down salvation, he fervently intoned the *Av ha-Rahamim* prayer:

May our Merciful Father, who dwells on high, remember, in His great mercy, the pious, upright, and innocent martyrs of the holy communities of Israel. They were precious and beloved in life and not separated in death. They were swifter than eagles and braver than lions to do the will of their Creator and the desire of their Rock. May our God remember them for good![26]

It seems that the Ziditchover wanted to add the holy power of mentioning the martyrs to the merit of mentioning the tzaddikim about whom he told stories, in order to draw down salvation to those he sought to help with his storytelling. Merely mentioning the tzaddikim or those sanctified by martyrdom has a holy potency, as it says: "The remembrance of a tzaddik is a blessing" (Proverbs 10:7).[27]

THE BESHT TELLS A STORY WHEN
THERE ARE OBSTACLES TO PRAYER

In the previous chapter, I considered some aspects of Rabbi Nahman of Bratzlav's comment:

The Baal Shem Tov, the remembrance of a tzaddik and holy man for a blessing, was able to bring about a kabbalistic mystical unification (yihud) by telling a story. When he saw that the supernal channels were defective, and it was not possible to rectify them through prayer, he would rectify and unite them by telling stories.[28]

When the defective channels blocking the flow of divine beneficence could not be rectified by prayer, he accomplished that by telling a story. When might this be necessary? Perhaps the Besht wanted to help someone whose sinfulness presented an obstacle to a direct prayer, since strict justice mitigated against his receiving divine mercy. Then, the Besht might "pray" for him indirectly, with a story. As in interpersonal dealings also, an indirect approach often arouses less opposition. It is obvious, though, that this kind of mystical storytelling, based on a kabbalistic understanding of divine dynamics, so to speak, is reserved for tzaddikim and rebbes.

WHEN THE BESHT WAS ILL

Once during the Baal Shem Tov's final illness, his disciple, the preacher in Medzibuz, Rabbi David Forkes, came in to him and asked him how to pray for a sick person by telling stories. The Baal Shem Tov began to explain the matter to him, and as he talked he became enthused and excited, so that his face glowed with his fervor. Such a great fear and awe fell on Rabbi David that he wanted to flee from the Besht's holy presence. But because the Besht was speaking to him face-to-face he could not leave.

Just then the Besht's daughter, Edel, entered and interrupted him, saying, "Father, it's time to eat; it's very late already." Immediately all the blood left the Besht's face, which had been flushed to a fiery red; he turned white and lay down to rest on his bed, drained and fatigued. "Daughter, daughter, what have you done to me!" he cried. Rabbi David defended her, saying, "She's right, it is time to eat." "Don't you know who was here?" the Besht said to him. "Elijah the prophet, may he be remembered for good, was standing on one side of me, and my master, Ahiyah the Shilonite, was standing on the other side. As they spoke to me, I was repeating to you what they said. But when she came in and disturbed me, they left!"[29]

Rabbi David probably wanted to know the secrets of praying indirectly by clothing prayers in stories in order to pray for the ill Baal Shem Tov himself.

RABBI NAHMAN HEALS HIS DAUGHTER
WITH A STORY

Rabbi Nahman of Bratzlav also sometimes told stories to perform miracles. He once visited his daughter at her house and found her seriously ill. Very worried, he sat down and fell asleep. His great-grandfather, the Baal Shem Tov, came to him in his dream and said, "Why are you so troubled?" "Isn't my daughter extremely ill?" answered Rabbi Nahman. "Isn't it written in the Psalms," said the Besht, "'He magnifies the salvation of his king, and does lovingkindness to His anointed one, to David and his seed forever'"?

(This means: "He magnifies the salvation of his king"—the Talmud says: "Who are the kings? The sages." So when someone magnifies in story the salvation that came about through a tzaddik—"And does lovingkindness"—God, blessed be He, shows kindness "to His anointed one." The Hebrew word for "His anointed one," *meshiho*, can be read as *mesiho*, meaning "the one who speaks and tells stories about him [the tzaddik]." "To David and his seed forever"—to Rabbi Nahman and his descendants [like his daughter], who come from the seed of David. [The Baal Shem Tov and through him Rabbi Nahman were descended from King David.])

Rabbi Nahman then told his daughter, Edel,[30] a story about the Maharsha [Rabbi Samuel Edels] and concluded with the verse, "He magnifies the salvation of His king" and so on. And she became well. Later, she told the same story to other sick people and they were cured. Rabbi Nahman of Tultchin[31] also told that story to sick people with the same result.[32]

Above I quoted Rabbi Nahman's teaching on this Psalm verse: that someone who tells stories about tzaddikim is saved. Here, somewhat differently, the end of the verse is brought in to refer specifically to descendants of King David, such as Rabbi Nahman.[33]

I'LL SIMPLY TELL THE STORY

The tzaddik, Rabbi Israel of Rizhin, told:

Once when there was an urgent matter of saving the life of a good boy, who was an only son, the Baal Shem Tov had someone make for him a wax candle. He then journeyed into the forest, attached the candle to a tree, and performed other mystical acts, such as meditating on various unifications, and he saved the boy, with the help of God. At a later time (after the Besht's passing) there was a similar matter with my great-grandfather, the holy Maggid of Mezritch [the Besht's disciple and successor]. He also did as the Baal Shem Tov had done, but remarked, "I don't know the unifications [yihudim] and intentions [kavvanot] that the Besht meditated on, but I'll simply act, relying on the intentions he had in his meditations." And his deeds were acceptable on high and had the desired effect. Later, there was a similar matter with Rabbi Moshe Leib of Sassov, of blessed memory [the Maggid's disciple], and he said, "I don't have the ability to do what is necessary, but I'll just tell the story, and God will help." And so it was, with God's help.[34]

The thrice-repeated "with God's help" in this story indicates why story-telling by itself can be effective: Because what ultimately causes a miracle is not esoteric knowledge of Kabbalah but simple, although total, faith and trust in God's help. Storytelling that saves is like a prayer, by means of which one says: "God, I know that You've performed this miracle before in the past and I believe, with perfect faith, that You can perform it again now!"

Such storytelling also relies largely on the merit of the tzaddik about whom the story is told.[35] The Maggid humbly relied on the Baal Shem Tov's intentions and merit when performing identical actions, and Rabbi Moshe Leib relied on the Baal Shem Tov's merit when telling the story of what the Besht had done.

It seems then from this tale that the kind of storytelling Rabbi Moshe Leib was doing was not quite mystic storytelling, such as the Besht did on other occasions (and which was based on kabbalistic unifications) but it still produced miracles.

WE CAN'T GET A FROG NOW

There is a similar story about Rabbi Joshua of Belz:

When a hasid named Rabbi Benjamin Munk, who was a bookseller in Lvov, had a baby boy, Rabbi Joshua, the Belzer Rebbe, was the *sandak*, holding the baby on his lap during the circumcision. After the bris they couldn't staunch the blood and no remedy or anything they did helped. So they sent someone to call back the *mohel* (the ritual circumciser). He said that the baby was in danger and told them to get a doctor immediately.

The hasid ran to the Belzer Rebbe to ask him to pray for the infant. The rebbe, who was sitting with his sons, said, "Let me tell you a story about the Baal Shem Tov.

"One of the Baal Shem Tov's disciples, a man of exceptional holiness and piety, had two daughters who were already of marriageable age, but the father, being destitute, had no money for dowries or wedding expenses. 'You are always traveling to the Baal Shem Tov,' his wife said to him, 'Why don't you speak to him about our daughters?' He promised to do so, but when he got there he could not bear to discuss a worldly problem of this sort. When his wife saw the situation, she went with him the next time. So he had to go in to the Besht and tell him his trouble.

"The Besht said, 'The truth is that you were not right in hiding this from me until now. But let me tell you a tried and tested remedy for an infant who keeps bleeding after a circumcision: Take a certain kind of frog, called a *zabbeh* in Russian, burn it completely, and apply the ash to the wound, and the bleeding will stop immediately. Go now, and may God give you success in everything you do.'"

Someone might wonder what this had to do with the man's problem of marrying his daughters. But the hasid and his wife had complete faith in their rebbe, the Baal Shem Tov, and asked no questions.[36]

"The hasid started to travel home and passed through a village, whose lord was a very prominent and wealthy Jew. When this lord saw him, he invited him for lunch and to stay that night in his home. Before the meal the hasid had to urinate and went outside, where he saw the lord's young son urinating against a wall—and was shocked to see that he wasn't circumcised! He said to himself, 'How can I eat with someone who doesn't circumcise his sons?'

"When he went back into the house, the lord asked him to wash his hands and sit down for the meal, but he did not want to. When the man kept beseeching him, he said, 'I won't lie to you. I can't eat with you if you ignore the commandment of circumcision,' and he told him how he had seen his little son. The lord began to weep and said that he had two other boys who were not circumcised, because before they were born he had had five other baby boys who died from bleeding after circumcision, and the town rabbi had told him not to circumcise his sons anymore.

"The hasid then remembered what his rebbe, the Baal Shem Tov, had told him, and he said, 'I know a remedy for this.' He went and got a frog, burned it, pounded the ash, circumcised the oldest boy, and applied the preparation. After a few days he healed and was healthy as always. He did the same for the two other boys and they also healed properly.

"The wealthy man was so happy he couldn't contain his joy. 'How can I repay you for what you've done?' he said, 'Name any amount of money you want and I'll give it to you.' The hasid told him that he had two daughters who had come of age and since he was destitute he had no money to marry them. The wealthy man asked him how much the dowries and weddings would cost. When he told him, he took the money from his wallet and gave it to him."

When the Belzer Rebbe—who was telling this story to the hasid whose infant son was bleeding from his circumcision—concluded, he said, "It's fall now and it's impossible to obtain a frog. Therefore, may this story be a remedy, as if we had actually done what was required, and may the child heal and return to health." And so it was. When the hasid went home, the flow of blood had stopped and the child healed.[37]

To properly understand this story and the one about the Baal Shem Tov burning a candle on a tree, it must be remembered that the Baal Shem Tov was not only a theoretical but a practical kabbalist[38] and a professional *baal shem*.[39] He was a faith healer and miracle worker. As a *baal shem*, he had an extensive knowledge of herbs, folk remedies, and incantations. Attaching a candle to a tree branch at a specific location in the forest and praying using mystical unification meditations are practical Kabbalah. Frog's ashes is a remedy of a *baal shem*. Who knows whether or not this folk remedy produces real benefits? Regardless, although many of the hasidic rebbes who followed the Besht were said to have performed miracles, few if any were practical kabbalists and none was a *baal shem*. Therefore, certain of his mystical doings were probably as much a mystery to them as to us. But they could at least tell the tales, and, with God's help, that was enough.

NOT EVERYTHING IS MYSTERY

Not everything about the saving power of stories is mysterious: In a simple and obvious way they inspire people and draw them close to God; they open hearts and minds and produce an expanded consciousness that causes good things to happen; they act as prayers. But there is no salvation without faith. Can we muster faith in the stories, if not always in everything in them? If we want to, we can, with God's help.

21

Stories Save–Continued

"LOWLY" STORYTELLING

Rabbi Israel of Rizhin once explained his emphasis on storytelling and the special potency of stories told with hidden, mystical intentions. In a conversation with some close disciples, he gave a summary of Torah leadership through the generations. He said:

Our father Abraham ordained the Morning Prayer because he wanted to pave a way to holiness. So he ordained a long and holy prayer to bring people's hearts close to their Father in Heaven.[1] When the Satan saw this, he taught himself this holy prayer and managed to get a grasp on it, so he was able to penetrate into the hearts of people praying the Morning Prayer and keep them from reaching the light of holiness. It became possible for someone to pray and nonetheless for it to be from the side of the Satan, God-forbid. So our father Isaac came and said: "My father ordained a prayer so long that the Satan became jealous of it. I'll ordain a prayer so short he won't be jealous of it and will think it not worth while to trouble himself to learn it and get a hold on it. People will be able to pray quickly and draw holiness on themselves." So he ordained the Afternoon Prayer. But it didn't help! Because the Satan was jealous of this prayer too, learned it, and got a hold on it. So it is possible for a Jew to pray the Afternoon Prayer, while Satan insinuates himself into his heart to prevent the light of holiness from reaching him. Thus, a Jew can pray the

Afternoon Prayer too and it can be from the side of the Satan. Later, our father Jacob came and said: "I'll ordain a prayer that will surely not seem worthwhile for him to take hold of," because the Evening Prayer that Jacob ordained is optional not obligatory. If a person feels inspired with holiness and purity and prays it, certainly the Satan won't be able to touch it; and if he doesn't feel inspired, he won't pray. Nevertheless, since over time the Jewish people accepted this prayer also as an obligation, the Satan also learned it, so he could enter the heart and mind of someone praying it and confuse him and prevent the light of holiness from reaching him.

Then came our teacher Moses, and the Elders, and the *Tannaim* and *Amoraim*—the teachers of the *Mishnah* and *Gemara*—who made great efforts to spread the study of the Torah in Israel, so that people could draw down the light of holiness on themselves without the Satan being able to prevent it. As the rabbis said: "If that disgusting one assails you, drag him into the *Beit Midrash* and study Torah," and they said that "God created the poisonous Evil Inclination but He also created the Torah as its antidote." Nevertheless, slowly and gradually, because they did not study from pure motives, the Satan taught himself this also, so he would not be singed by the fiery Law. In fact he sits in the *Beit Midrash* and sways over the *Gemara*. He has even become a sharp scholar and can give a credible interpretation of a *Gemara* passage, chanting it with a nice *niggun* (melody)!

So then the great kabbalist, the Holy Ari, and his students arose, to innovate a new path to holiness. The Ari said: "I'll ordain something that will be concealed from the Satan, so he won't be able to take hold of it. How is that possible? The Satan notices prayer and Torah study because they're verbal. If Jews will just sit and meditate silently, performing unifications, the Satan won't even know about it." But we have to cry *Gevalt! Gevalt!* because the kabbalists became proud of their abilities and that finally ruined this method also. Since this kind of meditation requires such rare intellectual virtuosity and intense mental exertion, some of those who are capable of it became proud that they were doing unifications, and as a result everything became known to the Satan. He then exerted himself to the fullest, breaking down walls, until he found a way to get a hold on this kind of divine service also and subvert it.

Finally, the Holy One, blessed be He, sent a holy soul from heaven, the holy Baal Shem Tov, who paved a new way that the earlier generations never thought of—to engage in seemingly idle conversations and to tell charming stories, and by means of this perform holy unifications. And since the person seems to be engaged in something trivial, because that is how it appears to simple people, he can't be proud; and the Satan is not jealous of it either, for he thinks the person is already sinning by speaking about such things. Only God understands. Therefore, this manner of divine service will last and continue until the coming of the Messiah, soon in our days. Amen.[2]

The storytelling the Rizhiner is speaking about here is used primarily to convey Torah teaching but sometimes to pray and even to effect miracles. According to the Rizhiner, there were repeated attempts to innovate new ways to approach God, because the methods of previous generations had become too easily subverted and reduced in potency. This happened, he claimed, to prayer, Torah study, and kabbalistic meditation. Although each time the old method was still pursued vigorously, the newer one, being more effective, was emphasized. Finally, the way of the Baal Shem Tov, adopted by the Rizhiner also, was to use conversation and storytelling, which seem lowlier than the other methods. However, the spiritual message in storytelling is merely disguised and clothed, as we saw earlier. According to the Rizhiner, this deceptive appearance actually makes mystic storytelling superior to the other methods and gives it a special potency to save.

TWO TYPES OF STORYTELLING

In the previous chapter I discussed the story the Rizhiner told about the Baal Shem Tov using practical Kabbalah to work miracles (attaching a burning candle to a tree, etc.), while the later tzaddikim, like Rabbi Moshe Leib, used simpler and lowlier, but still effective, storytelling. We can call that story the "decline of the generations," because it focuses on the inferior knowledge of the later tzaddikim, who do not know the kabbalistic methods and can only tell the stories about earlier tzaddikim. The above teaching of the Rizhiner, however—about mystic storytelling and the progress from Abraham to the Baal Shem Tov—indicates that the appearance that the storytelling of the rebbes is "lower" is deceptive. This teaching, which we can call the "progress of the generations," indicates that the Baal Shem Tov himself was the originator of mystical storytelling, even preferring it to previous methods. We have seen other texts confirming the Besht's use of storytelling for mystical purposes.

The seeming contradiction between the two teachings of the Rizhiner—
as to whether storytelling is superior or inferior—is resolved by recogniz-
ing that there are two different types of storytelling. Stories about the
miracles performed by earlier tzaddikim are told "simply," although with
an intention to rely on the merit of those tzaddikim. Other kinds of stories,
however, such as parables, religious folktales, and fantasy tales—like those
of Rabbi Nahman—may not be simple and may be told by the storyteller
with more complex mystical intentions.

LOWLY METHODS FOR A LOWLY GENERATION

Sometimes the Rizhiner explained his use of this latter, only seemingly
"lowly," storytelling as being due to the low generation. He said:

> In earlier generations, when the people were on a higher level, the
> tzaddikim who wanted to help them could do so by means of high
> methods, namely Torah and prayer. But now in this low generation,
> it is necessary to help by means of low methods such as storytelling
> or conversation. . . . An innkeeper, who was in danger of being evicted
> from his inn by the poritz [landowner], once came to my father [Rabbi
> Shalom Shachna of Prohobitch] to ask for his help. After he poured
> his heart out about his trouble, my father proceeded to tell him some
> totally unrelated stories. When he finished, the distraught man asked,
> "But what about my problem?" "Go home in peace," my father re-
> plied, "I've already helped you."[3]

In other words, he had helped him by telling the stories with mystical intentions.

The Rizhiner's teachings show that in his time also storytelling by a
rebbe was still held in low esteem. In one place he says that the deceptive
success of the stories is because they seem to be "trivial," in the other that
storytelling is lowly and he resorts to it only because of the low generation
(although he is not explicit about why storytelling is lowly or appropriate
for a lowly generation). Perhaps, like Rabbi Nahman, he meant that stories
"clothe" and disguise more direct and exalted Torah and prayer. Rabbi
Nahman also claimed that he turned to his "fantasy" storytelling because
his teaching was not having the desired effect in elevating his hasidim. That,
however, was not storytelling to accomplish miracles.

When rebbes innovated in any way, it was not unusual for them to justify the novelty, probably to themselves as much as to others, by claiming that it was because of the difference, usually the decline, in generations. This pious explanation preserved the traditional belief (not always maintained among hasidim) in the superiority of the earlier generations while allowing for necessary changes to accommodate the "weaker," later generation. Perhaps there is something of that in the Rizhiner's comments. However, the rebbes' motives for storytelling were probably complex, and their attitudes about it were sometimes ambivalent. The Rizhiner claimed that he resorted to storytelling only because of the low generation, yet, in that context, it was the superior method. In the tale of The Two *Badhans* he represented himself in the story as a lowly *badhan*–an entertainer and storyteller for his hasidim–yet at the same time as a holy child. Rabbi Nahman, in the tale of The Seven Beggars, represented the storytelling rebbe by the beggar with the crooked neck. As with the other beggars, this is only an apparent defect; it is actually an excellence.

FOR PREGNANCY AND CHILDBIRTH

Mystic storytelling has a particular traditional connection with helping women who cannot become pregnant or are having difficulty in childbirth. Once, after teaching about storytelling, Rabbi Nahman of Bratzlav said humorously that he was contradicting popular wisdom: "People say that talking will not make someone pregnant. I said that the tzaddik's storytelling that wakes people from their spiritual sleep, brings divine intercession for barren women to become pregnant."[4]

A Story to Help in Childbirth

Another story about the Rizhiner's holy father, Rabbi Shalom Shachna of Prohobitch–as a young man, before he became a rebbe–shows him telling a tale to perform a miracle:
Some people once came to the holy rabbi, Rebbe Reb Nahum of Tchernobil, asking him to pray for a woman having difficulty in childbirth. Rabbi Nahum sent them to his son-in-law, the holy rabbi, the Rebbe Reb Shalom Shachna. It was the eve of Sukkot and Rabbi Shalom Shachna was busy decorating his *sukkah*, to make it as beautiful as possible, as was his holy way. When they came to seek his intercession for the woman having trouble in childbirth, he–being still a young man–said to them that he had nothing to do with mysteries and didn't know anything.

They returned to Rabbi Nahum and told him that his son-in-law had said he did not know anything about such matters. Regardless, he sent them back to Rabbi Shalom Shachna and told them to say that he ordered him to help the troubled woman. When they came to him the second time, with the command of his holy father-in-law, he said, "Let me tell you an awesome story.

"In the capital city, Istanbul, some carnal and depraved Muslims, steeped in lechery and lewdness, used to kidnap chaste and pure Jewish women while they were on their way to the mikveh to ritually purify themselves for their husbands. Since this had happened a number of times, the women went to the mikveh in large groups, because of their fear of the Muslims. One day a chaste and pure Jewish woman went alone, however, and a Muslim grabbed and kidnapped her, taking her to his home, which was in the upper story of a building. The Muslim had to go somewhere briefly and, locking the woman in, was not afraid that she would be able to flee in the short time he was gone.

"When he left, the woman cried her heart out, both because she was afraid she might sin and also because her husband would certainly divorce her.[5] Seeing that the house had windows facing the street below and a balcony, she decided to go out on the balcony and throw herself off. If she survived, well and good; but if not, God-forbid, it was still good, because she would not be forced to sin, God-forbid.

"She took a dibon, a heavy robe, she saw lying there, covered herself with it, and flung herself off the balcony. And—miracle of miracles!—she survived and was not even injured. She then went home wearing the dibon and when she got there hid it under the stove.

"Sensing that something had happened, her husband did not sleep with her that night, and the next day he anguished about what to do. Istanbul is a coastal city and the custom is that when someone is troubled or has a problem, he rents a small boat and goes out for a sail, to relax and dissipate his worries. That is what the husband did, and while he was out in a boat, he came across a Muslim, taking a sail to free himself from his sorrows. Although they did not know each other, they struck up a conversation and decided that each would tell the other his problems. The Jew asked the Muslim to go first, and the Muslim told him how the day before he had forced a woman to his house and locked her in when he went out for a short while, but when he returned she was gone. He was not concerned about her, but she had taken a dibon in which he had sewed secret pouches that contained a large number of valuable coins!—because he was a very wealthy man.

"The Jew turned the conversation to something else, because he no longer wanted to reveal what had been troubling him, since the Muslim himself had told him that he had not defiled, God-forbid, his wife. He then rushed back to his house, ripped open the *dibon*, and found the concealed money. The husband and wife were so happy it cannot be described, and, as is understandable, there was a tremendous reconciliation [*yihud*] between them; they felt closer than ever before and that night, when they were together, they experienced a unique joy and ecstasy from their union. And from a union [*yihud*] like this, they of course had a true *mazal tov*: She conceived and gave birth to a healthy baby." Rabbi Shalom then said to the man to whom he was telling this story, "Return home, because you also have a blessing of *mazal tov*! now, and a healthy baby has just been born to cries of '*Mazal tov*! *Mazal tov*!'"

Afterward, Rebbe Reb Shalom Shachna said: "If told in the presence of any woman having difficulty in childbirth, this story is a wondrous *segulah* [miraculously potent], that God, blessed be He, will help her give birth easily and safely."[6]

Rabbi Shalom Shachna was a young man and surprised when his holy father-in-law sent people to *him*—as if to a great rebbe—to help them. Humbly concealing his holiness, he at first acted as if he knew nothing about such matters. If he had prayed for the woman—even if he had been ordered to help—it would certainly have seemed arrogant for a young man to set himself up as a rebbe. By telling a story he could maintain his humility, because, as he said, anyone could tell such a story. This tallies with what his son, the Rizhiner, later said, that the special virtue of mystic storytelling is that not only can it contain secret mystical intentions, but the tzaddik who tells a "mere" story can escape pride. Nevertheless, Rabbi Shalom Shachna's clairvoyant final comment to the man—that his wife had already given birth—indicates special powers.

This story provides valuable insight into how some of the rebbes used stories. The tale Rabbi Shalom Shachna told is about a chaste, religious woman who was kidnapped by a Muslim rapist when she went to ritually bathe and purify herself for conjugal relations with her husband. She seemed to have no way out; her situation was desperate. However, because of her zealous determination to risk her life and sacrifice herself if necessary by throwing herself off the balcony, not only was she miraculously saved from violation, but the rapist himself ended up informing her husband of her purity (saving her from divorce) and also of a hidden treasure. Moreover, the reunion with her husband brought them closer than ever before, and their ecstatic sexual union produced a child.

The story itself is simply a religious miracle tale. But the rebbe employed it mystically as an allegory for someone captured by evil and unclean, Satanic, forces who is miraculously saved and reunited with God. The story's end focuses on the *yihud* between the couple. This word can mean both a kabbalistic *unification* (an act or meditation uniting separated spiritual forces) or a sexual *union*. Undoubtedly, in telling this story, the rebbe had a mystical intention to free the *Shechinah* (Divine Presence) from Evil and unite the (female, so to speak) *Shechinah* with the (male, so to speak) Holy One, blessed be He. Because what happens Above is reflected Below, he also intended this story to have a mystical effect in freeing the woman giving birth, who, like her "counterpart" in the story, was "captured" by evil forces.[7]

A Shaman

I once read about a shaman (a tribal healer; "medicine man") who, when called upon to help a woman having difficulty in childbirth, told and acted out, in her presence, a dramatic story about a hero's dangerous journey, in which he overcame one frightening obstacle after another—a story that finally had a successful conclusion. The anthropologists theorized that by identifying with the protagonist of the tale, the woman in labor was led through her own struggle—her difficult journey, beset by invisible obstacles—to give birth.[8] Rabbi Shalom Shachna did not tell his tale with the woman present, but at the end he *did* say that it has a mystical efficacy if told in the presence of a woman having trouble in childbirth. Let me remark that by comparing the rebbe to the shaman, I do not intend to skeptically disparage the rebbe or the hasidic story and teaching.

Rabbi Shalom Shachna's son, Rabbi Israel of Rizhin, used an analogous tale in a similar way,[9] and said afterward: "Even if told by a simple person, this story will save a woman having trouble in childbirth." That is certainly what his father intended by his similar remark. This kind of storytelling, however, is not like telling tales about tzaddikim to arouse comparable miracles. *These* stories are not about tzaddikim and may not even be religious in nature.[10] Therefore, an ordinary person telling such a story must rely on a tzaddik's assurance that it *is* potent in such a situation; he cannot know that by himself.

A Baby From a Story

The first Bobover Rebbe, Rabbi Shlomo Halberstam, once helped one of his hasidim by telling a tale. This hasid was childless after many years of marriage and every time he visited the rebbe on Sabbaths and holidays he begged the rebbe to pray that he have a child. Rabbi Shlomo always answered that he was waiting for the right time. But years passed and the man and his wife still had no children. One year he was at the rebbe's table for the final meal before the fast of Yom Kippur. Everyone ate silently in holy awe. When the fish course was served tears streamed from the rebbe's eyes as he ate. Then he stood up holding in his hand a plate with some fish on it and looking at this hasid said, "Let me tell you a story.

"Once, a group of hasidim decided to travel to their master, the holy Seer of Lublin, for a holiday, although they had almost no money for the journey. They set out on foot, hoping they would meet someone on the road who would offer them a ride in his coach. That didn't happen, however. After a few days traveling, their money ran out. They were exhausted and famished.

"One of the hasidim got the idea to pretend that one of them was a rebbe. When they entered the next village everyone would run to welcome the visiting 'rebbe' and his hasidim, provide them with food, and give them donations that would allow them to hire a wagon and horses. Although they were unhappy about using a deception, they justified it by their desperate situation—they could hardly walk, their feet were aching so, and they were almost starving. After all, to save a life many things are permitted. So they appointed one hasid who was of imposing appearance as the 'rebbe.' He was reluctant to assume the role assigned him but his friends kept pressing him and would not let him refuse. Then, after appointing another hasid as the 'rebbe's attendant,' two others went ahead and let it be known in the village that a rebbe was traveling and would soon be entering the town. The announcement caused a great stir among the townspeople. One innkeeper whose infant son was seriously ill was especially excited. The doctors had been unable to help his son. Now his hope was renewed and he said to himself, 'I'll beg this rebbe to heal my baby with his blessing.'

"As the hasidim arrived, they were met by this innkeeper, whose inn was on the outskirts of the town. He welcomed them warmly and treated them all to a hearty meal, but immediately afterward he fell down sobbing at the 'rebbe's' feet and cried out, 'Rebbe, heal my baby!' The imitation rebbe was confused and flustered. 'What does this man want from my life?' he thought. But his friends whispered to him, 'Be quiet. Just go and bless the child.' So he went into the back room where the child's crib was and shut the door behind him, while his friends waited in the inn. He blessed the baby and then returned and blessed the innkeeper that his child have a complete recovery. The grateful innkeeper gave the 'rebbe' and his hasidim a generous donation, enough for them to hire a wagon and horses to travel to the Seer and also to buy food for the remainder of their trip.

"They went to Lublin and to their master the Seer for the holiday and none of them said anything about their escapade, of which they were not very proud. A few days after the holiday they made their return journey and passed through that same village. The innkeeper once again came running out to greet them and said, 'Rebbe, how can I ever thank you for healing my child? As soon as you left, he asked for something to eat and is now completely healthy.' This time also the innkeeper provided the 'rebbe' and his 'hasidim' with a good meal. But as soon as they left the village the hasidim demanded that their friend tell them what he had done on their previous visit. 'Since when are you doing miracles?' they said. 'We know you're not a rebbe. What's going on here?' 'I didn't do anything,' he replied. 'Leave me alone.' But they kept pestering him until he told them.

"'I'm not a rebbe,' he said, 'as you well know. But I'll tell you what happened. When I went into the back room and stood by the sick baby's crib and looked down at his little face that grimaced from his pain and suffering, I realized I had fallen into a deep pit. Then, after I blessed the baby and came out and looked at the anguished father's face and his tear-stained cheeks my heart broke within me. At that moment, a Psalm verse fell into my mind: "O God, You know my folly and my sins are not hid from You. Let not those who hope in You, O Lord God of Hosts, be ashamed for my sake; let not those who seek You be disappointed because of me, O God of Israel." I turned to God and silently prayed, "This good man believes I'm a rebbe but of course I'm not. I'm just a simple person with many sins to my credit. But why should he lose out because of that? He has true faith in the tzaddikim and believes that You listen to their prayers. Why should he be disappointed because of my faults? So I beg You to heal his child because of his faith. Because he thinks I'm a rebbe." And it seems that God listened and healed the child. That's all I did and that's all that happened.'"

Rabbi Shlomo of Bobov was telling this story to his hasid at the table before Yom Kippur, and as he told the end part tears streamed from his eyes and he repeated the final words of the imitation rebbe a few times— "Because he thinks I'm a rebbe." Everyone at the table realized that he was speaking of himself and of the hasid to whom he was telling the story, which was actually a prayer that this hasid and his wife have a baby. Then the rebbe passed the plate with the fish on it for the hasid to eat, because fish is a symbol of being fruitful and multiplying. That year this hasid's wife gave birth to a baby boy.[11]

Here again, as with Rabbi Shalom Shachna in the preceding tale, the rebbe is able to help and also maintain his humility, by "praying" with a story.

A PRAYER FOR MEDICINE

The second Bobover Rebbe, Rabbi Ben Zion Halberstam, told a tale about the mystical storytelling of his great uncle, Rabbi Ezekiel Shraga Halberstam, the Rebbe of Shinova. Someone once asked the Shinover Rebbe to pray for a sick child, whom the doctors could not help; whatever medicines they prescribed only exacerbated his condition. The Rebbe answered that if heaven agreed to heal the child, help would come from the ends of the earth! He then told a long religious folktale in which a rare medicine came to a child from far away as a result of the most unlikely circumstances. The rebbe finally finished the tale and everyone went home. Some time later it was learned that an expert doctor from a distant region had arrived in town; they immediately asked him to examine the sick child, and he prescribed the correct medicine and cured him! "Then," said the Bobover Rebbe, concluding the tale about his uncle, "everyone realized that the long story told by the Shinover Rebbe had been like a prayer to arouse heavenly mercy for the correct medicine to be sent to the child he had been asked to help."[12]

I CAN'T HELP, BUT I CAN TELL YOU A STORY

Hasidim believe that a story can save someone spiritually as well as physically and materially, as in the following tale about the storytelling of Rabbi Shneur Zalman, the first Lubavitcher Rebbe.

In a town close to Liozni, on the way to Vitebsk, lived a widow with her two daughters and a son. The son went to another town to study Torah, while the daughters helped their mother run an inn in their home. The mother married her eldest daughter to a pious young Torah scholar, who continued his studies after the wedding.

There were always gentiles in the widow's inn, who came to sip some liquor, and among them was the town's priest, who enjoyed the company of the young Jewish scholar and liked to argue with him about religious subjects. This situation continued for a while, with the young man debating the priest for hours at a time, regularly defeating him; the priest, for his part, praised him to everyone, saying he was a person of exceptional abilities.

Although this young man was pious and scholarly, he was also arrogant. Every little thing filled him with pride, and after each winning debate with the priest, his opinion of himself improved. Sometimes, outstanding Torah scholars, who stopped off at the widow's inn as they were passing through the town, overheard, and were disturbed by, his heated discussions with the priest. They tried to discourage him from continuing this practice, but he ignored their advice and went on with the debates.

Meanwhile, the priest called to his side two of his fellow priests from nearby towns, and all of them met regularly in the inn every day to sit and debate. The priest and his two comrades extravagantly praised the young scholar, saying he was a great man, and ordered all the gentile villagers to treat him with respect.

One day the priest told the young man that he had spoken to the bishop about him, and about his outstanding scholarship, and that the bishop was very impressed and had asked to meet him. The priest suggested that he travel with him to the bishop and added that if he was able to best the bishop in debate, it would win him great acclaim. At first the young man declined, but after the priest and his two friends urged him on a number of occasions, he developed a strong desire to travel to the bishop in Vitebsk and engage him in religious discussion.

The bishop received the young man with much honor and asked him numerous questions on religious topics, which the young scholar answered skillfully and intelligently. A lively debate ensued and the young man emerged the winner. The bishop then called over a few of the more prominent priests and, in the young man's presence, praised him as an outstanding scholar of the Jewish Bible, who had bested him—the bishop himself—in a religious debate. One of the priests, who was a guest in the bishop's house, then said to the young man that if he would agree to meet with them for a few days to discuss religious matters, they would all be extremely grateful.

The young man agreed and stayed for a few more days at the bishop's house, where he was given a private room. They brought him kosher food from outside. During his stay there he engaged in continuous discussions and debates with the brotherhood of priests, who treated him with deference and respect. Before he left, the bishop invited him to his home and in the presence of the other priests thanked him for coming and told him that if he was amenable and would visit again, he, the bishop, would be very pleased. The young man went home and told no one where he had been or what he had done, but a new bounce was added to his step and he walked around in a jubilant mood.

A few months later, some first-rate Torah scholars, who were passing through that town on a sweltering summer day, decided to stop off at the widow's inn until it cooled off. Meanwhile, they would discuss Torah. The young man overheard their Torah discussion and began to join in, offering his thoughts on the subject under consideration. Although he was a fine scholar, he was not on the level of these men. When they heard his opinions, they laughed and said, "A young man should listen to what his elders are saying and show more respect to Torah scholars." The young man felt his pride deeply wounded by this remark and began to harbor resentment against Torah scholars, thinking that they were not properly respectful to him or his Torah learning.

In a nearby town they had built a new monastery and planned to dedicate it at the end of the summer. Then the bishop, accompanied by many priests, came from Vitebsk to visit all the towns in the region. When they arrived at the young man's town, the bishop and his entourage went to the widow's inn to meet with him, and they stayed with him for more than an hour. After this visit from the bishop at his home, the young man's prestige among the town's gentiles soared. At the same time, his arrogance became boundless.

After the festival of Sukkot, the young man left his home for several weeks. On his return he was extremely agitated and churning with barely suppressed emotion. Several days later he left again. Before the Sabbath preceding Hanukkah, his family received a letter from him that he was staying in the house of the bishop, who was treating him with the greatest honor. He had his own apartment, and the bishop had promised him that if he became one of his men, he would achieve great honor and distinction, and everyone would treat him with the utmost respect.

His wife and mother-in-law were illiterate and could not read the letter, but before Hanukkah the widow's son came home for the holiday, read it, and, deeply pained, burst out weeping. He cried out, his voice choking, "Zev (for that was the young man's name) is staying in the bishop's house and wants to convert!" When his wife and mother-in-law heard this, they began to wail, and immediately after *Havdalah*, despite the cold and the deep snow, they all set out to travel to Rabbi Shneur Zalman[13] [the first Lubavitcher Rebbe] in Liozni. They burst into his *Beit Midrash*—where everyone was still sitting at the table for the *Melaveh Malkah* feast—crying, "Rebbe, save us! Our Zev is with the bishop and wants to convert!"

Everyone in the *Beit Midrash* became upset and agitated on hearing the widow and her children (that is, her son and her older daughter, who was the wife of the young man who wanted to apostasize) tell the story with broken hearts and dreadful crying. They begged, "Rebbe, save our Zev from spiritual suicide!" "I can't help you," replied Rabbi Shneur Zalman, "but I can tell you the story of what happened with my teacher and rebbe, the Maggid of Mezritch.

"It was the winter of 1769," he continued, "when I was in Mezritch. Not far from there was a gentile town where a few Jewish families made their homes. A boy from one of those families lost his reason and decided to convert, God save us. This happened not because he rejected the Torah but because of pride! When he went to the priest, his father went with him and argued against his decision, but his son wouldn't listen. The father then traveled to the Rebbe in Mezritch. When he came in to the Rebbe, the Maggid, he broke into tears, 'Rebbe, save my son from apostasy!' After listening to the story from the distraught father, the Maggid became totally absorbed in a holy mood and began to say Torah on the verse, 'If a person sins and commits a trepass against the Lord' (Leviticus 5:21). After repeating the Torah teaching of the Maggid, Rabbi Shneur Zalman said: "When he concluded this teaching, the Maggid told a *minyan* (prayer-quorum of ten) of his disciples to recite Psalms throughout the night until dawn. I was one of those," he said, "who chanted Psalms the whole night. At dawn the young man arrived at the *Beit Midrash* of the Maggid. None of the disciples asked him anything. He stayed for a few days in Mezritch, went in to the Rebbe, and returned home."

When Rabbi Shneur Zalman finished telling this story, he said the Grace After Meals and retired to his room. The hasidim immediately chose a *minyan* of young men, who recited Psalms throughout the night. At dawn the widow and her children returned home, but shortly after they left, a young man with a knapsack on his shoulder entered the *Beit Midrash*. When he saw everyone there brokenheartedly saying Psalms, he joined them and began to recite Psalms also, while crying profusely. Everyone realized that he was Zev, but no one spoke to him about what had happened.

The whole week of Hanukkah the young man stayed in Liozni. The week after Hanukkah, he went in for a private audience with the Rebbe and returned home. After several weeks the whole family moved to a different town. Zev arranged for his unmarried sister-in-law to wed a fine young man in the Vitebsker *yeshivah* and he himself became one of the young hasidim there.[14]

Rabbi Shneur Zalman humbly said he could not help but then accomplished with a story what his rebbe, the Maggid, had done by the mystic effect of his Torah teaching. This clarifies what Rabbi Israel of Rizhin said, that what tzaddikim formerly accomplished by Torah or prayer, they did now by storytelling, and that it is easier to avoid pride in storytelling. By praying or speaking Torah, Rabbi Shneur Zalman would have been relying on his own merit; by telling the story he could rely on the merit of his great master and rebbe, the Maggid. Therefore, he said, "I can't help, but I can tell the story."

TODAY

Can people today believe that telling a story can save? If we believe that God hears prayers, can't we also believe that He hears our stories? As it says: "Then they that feared the Lord spake one with the other; and the Lord hearkened and heard." Perhaps at least some of us might even relearn the mystic art of praying through storytelling, for certainly many of the stories people tell represent prayers that they cannot utter. But even if none of us ever learn how to do this, we can at least tell the tales of those who did.

22

Messiah

CLINGING TO FAITH IN THE GENERATION BEFORE THE MESSIAH

The Rizhiner Rebbe told: "Rabbi Velvel Chenister used to sleep with his eyes open [because he was having visions]. Once when he was sleeping, one of his chief hasidim, who was sitting by his side, saw that his eyes were closed–and was startled. He was afraid that, God-forbid, the rebbe had passed away. But the rebbe opened his eyes and said, 'They showed me, during a soul-ascent to the Upper Worlds, the generation that will be before the coming of the Messiah, and I saw that even people like you will become heretics, God save us.' The hasid began to cry, and the holy rabbi said to him, 'But the way to hold on to faith will be to tell stories of the tzaddikim–of all the tzaddikim, even me.'" When the holy Rizhiner finished this story, saying, "to tell stories of the tzaddikim–even me," he repeated the words "even me" twice.[1]

Rabbi Velvel said that even hasidim as devout as his disciple would be in danger of becoming heretics, and they would benefit by telling tales even about rebbes as "lowly" as himself. The Rizhiner agreed with the teaching of the story and, by the way he ended it, applied it to himself. He also wanted stories to be told about himself.

But fulfilling this prescription–of telling tales of tzaddikim in the generation before the Messiah–will not be easy. The Rizhiner once remarked: "Before the coming of the Messiah, a person might burst before he finds someone to whom he can tell a story of a tzaddik."[2]

On another occasion, when one of the Rizhiner's top hasidim asked him to impart some teaching that would always be of benefit, he replied:

Know that before the coming of the Messiah, faith and religion will be hanging by a thread. The way to survive spiritually will be for friends to gather on the Sabbath and tell stories of tzaddikim—that will help greatly in strengthening people's faith. Our father Jacob hinted this to his sons, saying: "*Gather* around and I'll *tell* you what will happen (*yikra*) to you *in the latter days*" (Genesis 49:1). *Yikra* can also mean "to become cold" (*kar*); "In the latter days," that is, before the coming of the Messiah, there will be great coldness in regard to faith. And the remedy for this will be to "gather" and speak about faith in God and in the tzaddikim.

The Rizhiner concluded by telling this hasid, "I'm making three conditions for you: one, that you remember my words; two, that you fulfill them; and three, that you speak about this publicly."[3]

Remember that the Rizhiner had taught that although the efficacy of various religious practices had been reduced through the ages, the storytelling method of the Baal Shem Tov would retain its potency until the coming of the Messiah.[4]

STORIES BRING THE MESSIAH

Tales of the tzaddikim will not only preserve faith before the coming of the Messiah but, according to Rabbi Nahman of Bratzlav, actually hasten his coming. He said: "Telling stories of the tzaddikim draws down the light of the Messiah into this world and expels much darkness and many troubles from the world. . . ."[5]

The tzaddikim emit the Messiah's light, and telling stories about them draws his light into the world. Telling such tales demonstrates a person's belief that there *are* holy people, whose feet are on the ground but whose heads reach into heaven. Believing in tzaddikim is like believing in the Messiah and the stories about tzaddikim establish a living connection not only backward to the tzaddikim of the past but also forward to the fulfillment of the Messiah. While the traditional daily prayers contain pleas for the coming of the Messiah, tales of tzaddikim are like disguised prayers that the final fulfillment will arrive, that *Mashiah Tzidkeinu*, "our great Tzaddik, the Messiah,"[6] will come soon in our days.

THE HOLY HUNCHBACK

In Hasidism's youth, fervent belief fused with ardent storytelling to produce countless inspiring and stirring tales about the tzaddikim. Although that original burst of creativity has long since dissipated, the time of the creation of stories is not over. I would like to end this book with a story told by a master hasidic storyteller of our generation, Rabbi Shlomo Carlebach. Rabbi Carlebach tells a personal story that contains within it a tale about Rabbi Kalonymus Kalman of Peasetzna, one of the greatest rebbes of the last generation, a generation that was swept away by the Holocaust. This tale shows that the flame of Jewish fervor was not finally extinguished, that the sparks of holy stories have been passed on to ignite the hearts of the next generation, and that these sparks will burn until the coming of the Messiah. The following story, transcribed from Rabbi Carlebach's oral rendition, is in his voice.

In the Warsaw ghetto, there was a rebbe, the *heiliger* (holy) Reb Kalonymus Kalman. He wrote a book, and knowing prophetically that he would not survive, he put the manuscript under one of the stones in the ghetto where it was found after the war.[7] He had a *yeshivah* in the ghetto, not of young people but of children. He used to say, with a smile, "My hasidim eat on Yom Kippur. Do you know why? They are not bar mitzvah yet." (Before bar mitzvah, children are not obligated to fast on Yom Kippur.) There was terrible suffering in the ghetto and many people needed help, spiritual and otherwise. A great rabbi would come to him or an old man, and a little girl of four or five. He would say to the older man, "You'll make it without me. This child needs me." With older people he would spend five minutes, with children all night. He had thousands of kids. He was their father, their mother, their best friend. So many people died in the ghetto; there were so many orphans.

My whole life I was hoping and dreaming to see one of these people, who as a child was a student of the holy Reb Kalonymus Kalman. A few years ago I was walking on the Yarkon [a street along the river of that name] in Tel Aviv and I saw a hunchback, a street cleaner. Do you know that sometimes we are all little prophets? Our heart tells us something. I had a feeling this person was special. He was a real hunchback. That means his face was very handsome, but every part of his body was disfigured. I said to him, "Hey, *sholom aleichem*, my friend." He answered me in a very heavy Polish-Yiddish Hebrew, "*Aleichem sholom*." I said to him in Yiddish, "*Mein zeisse Yid*, my sweet *Yiddele*, where are you from?" He said, "I'm from Peasetzna." I said, "Peasetzna. *Gevalt!* Did you ever see Reb Kalonymus

Kalman?" "What do you mean, did I ever see him? I was a student in his *yeshivah* in the Warsaw Ghetto from the ages of five to eleven. Then I was in Auschwitz for five years. I was eleven when I got there. They thought I was seventeen; I was so strong. They beat me up so much I never healed. That's why I look this way. I have nobody in the world, really nobody." I said to him, "You know something, my whole life I have been waiting to meet one of the students of Reb Kalonymus Kalman. Would you be so kind to give me over one of his teachings?" He kept on sweeping the street. "You really think that after five years in Auschwitz, I remember the teachings?" I said, "Yes, the words of the *heilege* Rebbe penetrate you forever."

He stopped sweeping. He looked at me and said, "Do you really want to know?" He touched me so deeply and although you shouldn't swear, I said to him, "I swear to you, and I mean it with all my heart, that whatever you tell me I'll tell all over the world." You know, he was a real *hasidisher Yid* – and didn't want to say holy words when he was not clean, so he put the broom against a wall and went to wash his hands. This is what he said: "There will never be a *Shabbos* as by my holy master, my *heiliger* Rebbe. Can you imagine – hundreds, sometimes thousands, of young people dancing with the holy Rebbe in the middle. What a sight! Not until *Moshiah* is coming will such be seen again. Can you imagine the Rebbe making *Kiddush*, sitting with hundreds of children with so much holiness. He gave over the teachings between the fish and the soup courses, between the soup and the meat, between the meat and dessert. And after every teaching he would always say, '*Kinderlach, teire kinderlach,* my most precious children, *gedenskt shon,* remember, *die greste sach in die velt ist, tun emetzin a toyva.* Children, precious children, just remember: The greatest thing in the world is to do somebody a favor.'

"When I came to Auschwitz, I knew my whole family had been killed and I wanted to kill myself. Each time I was about to, I suddenly heard the Rebbe's voice saying to me, '*Gedenkst shon,* Remember, the greatest thing in the world is to do somebody a favor.' Do you know how many favors you can do in Auschwitz late at night? People dying, people crying; nobody had the strength even to listen to their stories anymore. I would be up all night. A few weeks later I wanted to kill myself again, but always at the last moment I'd hear my Rebbe's voice. Now I'm here in Tel Aviv, but believe me, I'm all alone. There are moments when I decide to commit suicide. I go into the sea until the water reaches my nose. Then suddenly I hear my Rebbe's voice again and I just can't permit myself to do it and I run back to the streets. Do you know how many favors you can do on the street?"

My friends [said Rabbi Carlebach, finishing his story], this was before Rosh HaShanah. After Succos I came back to Israel and the first morning I went to the Yarkon and I asked the people on the street corner where the hunchback was. They said he had died on the second day of Succos. Listen to me, my beautiful friends, when the *Moshiah* comes, when all the holy people will come back to the world and the holy hunchback, the holy street cleaner, will come back, he will clean the streets of the world. Do you know how he will clean the world? He will go from one corner of the world to the other and he will say, "*Yiddelach, gedenkst shon,* Precious Jews, remember, the greatest thing in the world is to do somebody a favor."[8]

* * *

In the deepest darkness of the Holocaust, this hasid held on to his faith, remembering the scenes of his holy rebbe and his teachings. Rabbi Carlebach promised he would repeat what he was told all over the world. Now you too have heard the story of the Peasetzner and his teaching, and not only that but also the hasid's story and Rabbi Carlebach's story. In the merit of the holy hunchback and his holy rebbe, the Peasetzner, and in the merit of all the holy martyrs who were swept away, and in the merit of all the holy tzaddikim throughout the generations, and in the merit of all the stories we tell about them, and all the good deeds and favors we are inspired to do from hearing the stories about them, may the Messiah come, soon and in our days. And may Justice, Compassion, and Peace reign throughout the world. Amen.

Afterword:
Applications for Today

THE NEXT STEPS

Just as storytelling once played a major role in reinvigorating Judaism, in Hasidism, it can do so again today and become a new, vibrant branch of popular religious activity. The current storytelling revival has involved relatively few tellers and many passive listeners. It has also been largely secular in nature, although religious stories are often told. Now we can take the next steps of making storytelling truly popular and fully integrating it into our religious lives. One of the reasons telling tales achieved such great popularity in hasidic life is that almost everyone could participate. The same can be true today. Storytelling can become an activity for everyone. A person does not have to be a Torah scholar to appreciate and tell a deep religious story. Sharing the profound spiritual wisdom of stories can become a regular part of our religious practice.

JUST BEGIN

Storytelling has a rich history in the hasidic community, with an accepted status and place. There are events, times, and circumstances when stories are supposed to be or can be told. An individual who is drawn to storytelling has scope for his activity. But how can those who are not hasidim, yet love hasidic and other religious stories, find an entrance to storytelling?

The answer is just to begin. Once a person realizes that he or she *can* tell the stories she loves, and that it is actually a *mitzvah* to do so, stories are more likely to come to mind at the right time. Circumstances will present themselves. They can also be created. Learn a story and tell it to every willing listener. Sometimes a good way to start is to occasionally read a favorite story to a family member or friend. When you begin to memorize and tell stories, start simply, with anecdotes and short tales. After telling a story, ask your listeners their thoughts about its meaning. If you have children, how wonderful to raise them on religious stories! You can question them also about the lesson of a tale. You can even teach them to tell, by asking them to repeat stories you've told and they've liked. There are many books available of religious stories appropriate for different ages. If you want to improve your telling, you can seek out a workshop on storytelling. Although there are techniques to learn, they should not be overemphasized, for the moment the telling becomes more important than the religious content of the stories, the whole exercise becomes spiritually empty and worthless. Not many hasidim ever consider the technique of storytelling, yet that doesn't stop them from enjoying telling. If you believe in the stories, what comes from the heart enters the heart. Books about storytelling and how to tell stories are also available. You can also improve your technique by listening to tapes of stories made by professional storytellers, which are sold in most Jewish bookstores.

SETTINGS AND OCCASIONS

Besides casual storytelling, it can also be rewarding to tell in a more formal setting. Perhaps you can arrange a monthly storytelling and discussion group at your synagogue or in your home. It's nice to light a few candles in a darkened room to provide some atmosphere. Everyone does not have to tell a story; some people may prefer to simply read a story and others to just listen and participate in a discussion.

Storytelling at Sabbath and festival meals does not have to be restricted to hasidim. It is a lovely custom to adopt, for example, to always tell a story at the third Sabbath meal, or to organize a *Melaveh Malkah* in your home for storytelling. Invite some friends over for light refreshments Saturday night and ask them to bring some good tales to share. You can begin a yearly custom of telling a certain favorite tale on a particular holiday. You can observe the *yahrzeits* of great rebbes.[1] One doesn't have to be a hasid to celebrate their lives. Many people feel a real soul-connection to certain rebbes they have read about. A person can light a *yahrzeit* candle for that rebbe, read about his life and teachings, and make it a point that day to tell friends a story about him and one of his teachings.

REPERTOIRE

Not all stories you tell have to be traditional. You can also tell religiously meaningful stories that have happened to you, your family, or to people you know. Part of the storyteller's "job" is not only telling tales, but collecting them, from books and from oral sources, even from acquaintances or people he meets. A good storyteller is also a good listener. He attracts stories because he yearns to hear them and knows how to elicit them from others. A compiler of favorite tales told by the Maggid of Jerusalem wrote about him:

> Possessed of a keen and retentive mind, always ready to listen to a good story, he elicits from his listeners their own stories, some poignant, some fascinating, which eventually find their way into his own repertoire. To Rabbi Sholom, a story is a jewel to be collected, treasured and polished—and to be displayed at the appropriate moment.[2]

A PRECIOUS PRACTICE

When people realize that sacred storytelling is as much a *mitzvah* as Torah study or prayer, they will be spurred to a greater involvement, particularly if appropriate settings and occasions are provided by synagogues and other religious institutions. Perhaps, if enough of us start telling and listening, we can make storytelling, which is such a precious spiritual practice, an integral part of Jewish religious life. May it become so.

Notes

CHAPTER 1:
WHAT MADE HASIDIC STORYTELLING DIFFERENT?

1. See, for example, Gunkel's *Legends of Genesis*, pp. 41, 96, 123.
2. *Maggidim & Hasidim: Their Wisdom*, p. xliii. However, compare "Maggid," *Encyclopaedia Judaica*, vol. 11, 698.

CHAPTER 2:
HASIDIC PRAISE OF STORIES AND STORYTELLING

1. *Shivhei ha-Baal Shem Tov*, p. 233, #160; *In Praise of the Baal Shem Tov*, p. 199, #194.
2. *Gan Hadasim*, part II of *Sifran Shel Tzaddikim*, published separately, p. 2b (3).
3. Ezekiel 1. See "Ezekiel," *Encyclopaedia Judaica*, vol. 6, 1081.
4. *Sukkah* 28a.
5. *Bereishit Rabbah* 47-6.
6. By equating story telling and listening to the most profound mystic Torah study, the Besht was following the lines of a Talmud teaching equating reciting Psalms to studying the most difficult parts of the Talmud. In each case a spiritual practice accessible to simple people is put on a par with the study of great scholars. Compare *Devash ha-Sadeh*, #77: "Perhaps Rav Aha's statement—that God prefers the conversation of the *Fathers'* (Patriarchs') *servants* to the Torah of their descendants—means that a conversation where stories of the *'fathers,'* the tzaddikim, who served the Creator, blessed be He, are told—is better than the Torah of their

descendants, that is, plain Torah, because these stories are considered the most exalted form of Torah study, as in the saying of the Baal Shem Tov."

7. *Sippurei Nifla'im*, Sefer Besorot Tovot, Preface; cf. Rabbi Nahman of Bratzlav's *Sefer ha-Middot*, Tzaddik, #147, and see the guide to text sources.

8. *Likkutei Eitzot*, Tzaddik, #91.

9. *Likkutei Moharan*, I, #248. Rabbi Yehiel Michal of Zlotchov told his hasidim to always share stories of the tzaddikim, because the letters of the story arouse the heavenly root of the miracles (as in the *Zohar*, Parshat Bo) (*Maaseh ha-Gedolim he-Hadash*, Preface, p. 4). The Zlotchover's teaching: "Telling miracle stories draws down the root of the miracles, and effects new miracles like the first, because the 'letters' of the stories contain the vitality and the power of the miracles, for everything is contained in the letters of the Torah" (*Yeshuot Malko*, p. 125).

10. Sometimes referred to as Rabbi Nathan of Breslov.

11. *Sihot ha-Ran*, #138; *Rabbi Nachman's Wisdom*, p. 268.

12. *Emet v'Emunah*, p. 111. Martin Buber paraphrases this as: "He told what he knew, and I heard what I needed" (*Tales of the Hasidim*, vol. 2, p. 270). Elie Wiesel paraphrases: "He would tell what he liked and what he knew, and I would remember what I needed" (*Souls on Fire*, p. 239).

13. *Toldot Adam*, by the Rabbi of Ostrova, Parshat Metzora, quoted in *Yesod ha-Olam*, p. 371.

14. *Noam Elimelech*, Parshat Shmot, p. 28b.

15. Unlike all the other rabbis quoted in this chapter, Rabbeinu Bahya (thirteenth century) was not a hasid.

16. Rabbeinu Bahya's commentary on the Five Books of Moses, beginning of Parshat Vayishlah.

17. *Baba Batra* 9a.

18. *Sippurei Tzaddikim he-Hadash*, Preface, p. 5. I've shortened the Rebbe of Lublin's words for the sake of clarity. This is the full text of what he said:

> Now I understand something that I've long found difficult about *Avot* 3:2, that "When two sit together and converse in Torah, the *Shechinah* comes to rest between them, as it is written: 'Then they that feared the Lord spake one with the other: and the Lord hearkened and heard, and a book of remembrance was written before Him, for them that feared the Lord, and that thought upon His name'" (Malachi 3:16). I've found many elements of this hard to understand: (1) Why is the Hebrew for "spake" in the passive tense, *nidbaru*, rather than *dibru* or *m'dabrim*? (2) Why is there the redundant "for them that feared the Lord, and that thought upon His name," since both parts seem to refer to the same people? It's even harder to understand Rashi and the Bartenuro, who interpret "one with the other" by saying: "There are two here." What's the point? Isn't that obvious?

But now that I've seen this [the light from the storytelling of the hasidim] everything is clear. *Yevamot* 96b helps to explain it. The sages say: "What is the meaning of David's words in the Psalm: 'I will dwell in Thy tents *forever* [*olamim*: literally, "worlds" or "two worlds"]'? Can a person live in two worlds? King David prayed that after his death people would repeat Torah teaching in his name, for then it is as if in the grave his lips were moving." The saying from *Avot* is about two who sit and engage in Torah study, that is, telling stories of tzaddikim. About this also it says that "the *Shechinah* comes to rest between them," and it causes the light of holiness to shine there. This is proved by the verse: "Then they that feared the Lord spake one with the other." "They that feared the Lord," that is, the tzaddikim; "one with the other," namely, those telling stories about the tzaddikim. *Nidbaru* is in the passive tense because "they that feared the Lord" are the tzaddikim who are being talked about between "one with the other." Then: "and the Lord hearkened and heard, and a book of remembrance was written before Him, for them that feared the Lord, and that thought upon His name," that is, both derive benefit from this: "for them that feared the Lord," the tzaddikim who are talked about, their lips move when they are in the grave; "and that thought upon His name," those who sit and converse, the *Shechinah* dwells between them and they cause the light of holiness to come to be revealed there. This makes Rashi and the Bartenuro interpretation sweet, because they interpret "one with the other"—"There are two here," that is, the activity of storytelling benefits two—the tzaddikim and those telling the stories.

This teaching is also found in the name of Rabbi Shalom of Belz in *Sippurei Hasidim*, Preface. Compare the similar teaching in the name of the Baal Shem Tov in Chapter 6, p. 45, this volume.

19. *Yesod ha-Olam*, p. 368, #531.

20. Rabbi Shlomo Carlebach, a contemporary storyteller of hasidic tales, has said that God created the world because He needed to tell stories. He needed to have listeners who would hear Him. "Hear O Israel . . ." is the Jew's primal command. Elie Wiesel wrote that God created man because He loves stories, meaning the many stories of men's lives (*The Gates of the Forest*, before the title page). A hasidic author cited the Kabbalah, which states that "God, blessed be He, created the world with the scroll, the scribe and the story," and said that the world could not exist without the story (*Nifla'ot ha-Tiferet Shlomo*, Yaffah Sihatan, p. 21, quoting *Sefer Yetzirah*).

21. *Beit Ruzhin*, p. 62.

22. Compare Psalm 135:1 and 113:1. The Rizhiner also intended to justify his preceding prayer with storytelling by pointing out that each phrase precedes the other without distinction in the Psalm verses.

23. *Knesset Yisrael*, p. 16b (32); *Ner Yisrael*, vol. 2, p. 167; *Beit Ruzhin*, p. 63. In the first two of these three versions the rebbe refers to Exodus 26:5 *makbilot ha-lulaot*, reading it as *makbilot hallaluot*—that the two *hallalu's* are equivalent. Lest anyone be misled, the Rizhiner was certainly not suggesting that storytelling could replace the daily prayers!

24. Literally, "fear of God," but in this context "devotion" is a better translation.

25. *Beit Aharon*, p. 8; *Beit Karlin-Stolin*, p. 208. See *Beit Aharon*, p. 46, for a similar teaching given, significantly, on the occasion of the *hillula* of the rebbe's father (see Chapter 4, this volume).

26. *Beit Karlin-Stolin*, p. 180.

CHAPTER 3:
THE FIRST HASIDIC STORYTELLER:
THE BAAL SHEM TOV

1. *Likkutei Dibburim*, vol. 3, p. 69.
2. *Likkutei Dibburim*, vol. 3, p. 236.
3. *Kovetz Sippurim* (5718-5719), p. 37, #36.
4. *Kovetz Sippurim* (5718-5719), p. 37, #36.
5. *The Baal Shem Tov*, p. 32; cf. *Rabbi Yisrael Baal Shem Tov* (*Sefer ha-Toldot*), vol. 1, p. 34.
6. The present Lubavitcher Rebbe, Rabbi Menachem Mendel Schneersohn, has said: "Stories naturally reach and penetrate wider circles in the population than do Torah teachings, whether esoteric teachings or even the revealed parts of the Torah" (*Kovetz Sippurim* 5713, Preface).
7. *Communicating the Infinite*, p. 27.
8. *Degel Mahaneh Ephraim*, Parshat Ki Tissa, p. 42a.
9. *Maasiyot u'Maamarim Yekarim* (in *Sippurei Nifla'im*), p. 7a (13); quoted from that source in *Kol Sippurei Baal Shem Tov*, vol. 4, p. 141; *Reshimot Devarim*, vol. 1, p. 7, #12.

CHAPTER 4:
THE BESHT'S STORIES

1. *Reshimot Devarim*, vol. 1, p. 7, #12.

CHAPTER 5:
THE BESHT'S USE OF SECULAR TALES

1. Much of the material in this chapter is derived from Y. Dan's *Ha-Sippur Ha-Hasidi*, pp. 40-49.
2. He introduces this story by saying that it "seems to him" that he heard it from his master.
3. *Sama* = poison, *el* = (of) God. Samael = the angel who is "God's poison."
4. *Sefer Baal Shem Tov*, vol. 2, p. 158, Parshat V'et'hanan.
5. *Ha-Sippur Ha-Hasidi*, p. 45, where the text is paraphrased.

6. *Keter Shem Tov*, #8, p. 3 (5).
7. *Mishmeret ha-Kodesh*, 5, p. 2a, quoted in *Ha-Sippur ha-Hasidi*, p. 46.
8. This is the view of Gershom Scholem (see *Ha-Sippur Ha-Hasidi*, p. 46).
9. *Degel Mahaneh Ephraim*, Parshat Vayeshev, p. 21b, quoted in *Ha-Sippur ha-Hasidi*, p. 47.

CHAPTER 6:
THE BAAL SHEM TOV'S STORYTELLER DISCIPLE

1. *Adat Tzaddikim*, p. 20. See also *Kol Sippurei Baal Shem Tov*, vol. 2, p. 58, #11, and *Ha-Baal Shem Tov u'Vnai Hechalo*, p. 211 (the source for both: *Adat Tzaddikim*); *The Storyteller*, pp. 230-242.
2. *B'Ohalei Tzaddikim*, p. 224 n. 86.
3. *The Maggid Speaks*, Introduction, p. 21.
4. *Rabbi Nachman's Stories*, p. 396, note.

CHAPTER 7:
STORYTELLING IN HASIDIC LIFE

1. Scattered throughout this section are bits and pieces of useful information taken from *Legends of the Hasidim* by Jerome Mintz, Introduction.
2. Rabbi Aaron (Arele) Roth, *Shomer Emunim*, Maamar Tzahali v'Roni, 11.
3. The term "tzaddik" generally means a very righteous, even holy, person or, more narrowly and specifically, a hasidic rebbe. Since in the Besht's time there were no hasidic rebbes, except himself, he told stories of the tzaddikim of earlier generations.
4. According to Lubavitch tradition, the Besht, during his lifetime, instructed his disciples to make it a practice to repeat among themselves the story of his "revelation": his transformation from a hidden to a revealed tzaddik.
5. *Kevutzat Yaakov*, p. 56a, quoted in *Ha-Sipporet ha-Hasidit*, p. 77 n. 100.
6. *Otzar Yisrael*, p. 131, #3.
7. *Or ha-Shabbat*, p. 217.
8. *Shivhei ha-Besht*, Preface of Kapust printer.
9. Rabbi H. Chitrik about his father, Rabbi A. Chitrik, both of Brooklyn, New York.
10. *Rebbe Rayatz (Sefer ha-Toldot)*, vols. 1 and 2, II, p. 138.
11. *Rebbe Rayatz (Sefer ha-Toldot)*, vols. 1 and 2, II, p. 139.
12. *Rebbe Rayatz (Sefer ha-Toldot)*, vols. 1 and 2, II, p. 139.
13. *Sippurim Nifla'im*, Preface.
14. *Tiferet Sh'B'Malchut*, p. 160.
15. *Sifran Shel Tzaddikim*, #40-14.

16. *Rabbeinu ha-Kodesh mi-Shinova*, vol. 1, p. 157 n. 23.
17. *Otzar Yisrael*, p. 265, #2.
18. *Ha-Sipporet ha-Hasidit*, p. 79 n. 116.
19. *Tiferet Sh'B'Malchut*, p. 237.
20. *Sefer, Sofer v'Sippur*, p. 440.
21. See *Divrei David*, p. 20a (39).
22. Some hasidic books of stories, such as *Mazkeret Shem ha-Gedolim* and *Otzar Yisrael*, include an appendix with the dates of the *yahrzeits* of all of the famous rebbes, so hasidim can honor them by telling stories about them.
23. *Otzar Yisrael*, p. 280.
24. *Yeshuot Yisrael*, p. 37.
25. "Thinking on God's name" might be an allusion to meditating on God's name (*In Praise of the Baal Shem Tov*, #228) or presence (*Keter Shem Tov* [Kehot edition], #169).
26. The text here cites *Midrash Rabbati*, Parshat Lech Lecha, 47 and *Zohar*, Parshat Pinhas, 252a.
27. Compare this of course to the teaching of the Baal Shem Tov quoted on p. 9, this volume.
28. *Sefer Baal Shem Tov*, vol. 1, p. 227, #9.
29. *Otzar Yisrael*, Preface, p. 4.
30. *B'Hetzer Pnimah*, vol. 2, p. 5.
31. *Otzar Yisrael*, Preface, p. 12.
32. See p. 11.
33. *Souls on Fire*, pp. 6-7.
34. *Ish ha-Pele*, p. 195.
35. See p. 51.
36. *Otzar Yisrael*, p. 163, #12.
37. *Beit Ruzhin*, p. 328.

CHAPTER 8:
AN ESTABLISHED PLACE IN HASIDISM:
THE *MITZVAH* OF STORYTELLING

1. *Otzar ha-Sippurim*, Part 10, Letter-Preface; cf. "It is an important *mitzvah* to tell stories praising tzaddikim" (The Hasam Sofer, *Sh'eilot v'Tshuvot Hasam Sofer*, quoted in *Yesod ha-Olam*, p. 363).
2. *Nifla'ot ha-Tiferet Shlomo*, Yaffah Sihatan, pp. 7-8.
3. Some examples: Rabbi Israel of Rizhin often asked people who knew other tzaddikim to tell him about them. Once he asked a man from Lublin, who had been a hasid of the Seer of Lublin and became a Rizhiner hasid after the Lubliner's death, to tell him about his previous rebbe (*Ner Yisrael*, vol. 4, p. 49, #3). Another time, when the Rizhiner visited a town where the Baal Shem Tov had lived, he

asked a very old gentile who had known the Baal Shem Tov to tell him about him (*Mazkeret Shem ha-Gedolim*, p. 93b). Another story tells how an old *shammos* at a *mikveh* in Tiberias, Israel, asked a visiting rebbe, Rabbi Hayim of Vishnitz, if he would like to hear a story and told him one about the Shinover Rebbe (*Rabbeinu ha-Kodesh mi-Shinova*, vol. 1, p. 147).

4. Rabbi Shneur Zalman, *Rabbeinu ha-Zaken* (*Sefer ha-Toldot*), vol. 3, p. 615. The final sentence of the first quote in this chapter ("And the more one tells stories praising the tzaddikim . . . the more praiseworthy it is") is an allusion to the Passover *Haggadah* and also implies that just as it is a *mitzvah* to tell the story of the Exodus, so is it a *mitzvah* to tell stories of the tzaddikim.

5. Rabbi Shneur Zalman, *Rabbeinu ha-Zaken* (*Sefer ha-Toldot*), vol. 3, p. 616.

6. *Sippurei Hasidim*, Preface, p. 4.

7. *Sippurei Tzaddikim he-Hadash*, #35.

8. The rabbis said that when times were bad, people especially wanted to hear *Aggadah*.

9. The following story, particularly its ending, clarifies the Tzemah Tzedek's remark about storytelling freeing a person from Egypt, from spiritual exile.

Every night after their Torah study, the regulars at the *Beit Midrash* of the Shpoler Zeideh (i.e., the men whose only "job" was to study Torah and pray, day and night) sat together, drank, talked about Hasidism, and told stories of the tzaddikim. One night the town's tailor happened to come in at that time, caught some of what they were saying, and sat down with them. He was thrilled at being privileged to sit with these holy men and listen to their praise of the tzaddikim. But when he feared that they were about to conclude their nightly session, he ran home, got a bottle of liquor, and resupplied them so they would be in good spirits and continue. This happened a number of times, and before they knew it, the whole night had passed this way. Since the Shpoler Zeideh prayed at sunrise, and they were his regular *minyan*, they decided not to go home but to take a quick nap in the *Beit Midrash* so they would have a little rest before he came in for morning prayers.

However, they did not get up on time and were embarrassed when he found them sleeping, stretched out all over the *Beit Midrash*. They told him that they had stayed awake the whole night in their session because the tailor kept bringing bottles of liquor. The rebbe asked for the tailor to be brought to him. The tailor came and was afraid the rebbe was angry at him for keeping the regulars awake so that they were not ready for the morning prayers. The rebbe was angry, but about something else altogether. He told the tailor: "You had the merit to help a group of Jews gather together in brotherly unity and good spirits, to forget for a brief time the oppression and suffering of the bitter exile and to taste true spiritual pleasure. When such a gathering takes place," he said, "the holy *Shechinah* also leaves her exile and is rasied from the dust. Why then didn't you invite me to be with you!" (*Ish ha-Pele*, p. 195).

10. Deuteronomy 30:20: "to cleave to Him."
11. *Nifla'ot ha-Tiferet Shlomo*, Yaffah Sihatan, p. 11.
12. *Sefer ha-Middot*, Tzaddik, #157.
13. *Nifla'ot ha-Tiferet Shlomo*, Yaffah Sihatan, p. 11.
14. *Besorot Tovot*, Preface (in *Sippurei Nifla'im*).
15. *Sippurei Tzaddikim he-Hadash*, II, p. 11a (21), #45.

CHAPTER 9:
DRAWING PEOPLE TO GOD
THROUGH STORYTELLING

1. *B'Hetzer Pnimah*, vol. 2, pp. 200-208. See pp. 188-199 for descriptions of the setting for the storytelling.

CHAPTER 10:
TRADITIONAL OPPOSITION TO STORYTELLING:
STORIES VERSUS TEACHING

1. Although it is my own judgment in evaluating the sources that some *misnagdim* disapproved of hasidic storytelling, academic scholarship corroborates that conclusion: "Both Yosef Dan and Mendel Piekarz contend that the Hasidim, certainly by 1780, had effected a radical change in the attitude toward the tale. Whereas the telling of tales had previously been frowned upon by Jewish authorities, it was regarded as a worthy pastime by Hasidic masters for a variety of reasons. . . ." (*The Tales of Rabbi Nachman*, p. 30).
2. *Keter Shem Tov*, II, #424.
3. Angels are God's Throne and Chariot, and studying about them is considered *Maaseh Merkavah*. That is what the Besht was teaching the Maggid. Yet the rabbis say that the tzaddikim are also God's Throne and Chariot and are even greater than the angels. If discussing angels is the Chariot, how much more so is telling stories of the tzaddikim. Rabbi Shlomo of Radomsk said that praising the angels is considered idolatry, while praising the tzaddikim is like praising God (*Nifla'ot ha-Tiferet Shlomo*, Yaffah Sihatan, p. 15, #45).
4. *Shivhei ha-Baal Shem Tov*, p. 233, #160; *In Praise of the Baal Shem Tov*, p. 199, #194.
5. *Ginzei Nistarot*, quoted in *Midrash Ribesh Tov*, p. 70; cf. *Be'er ha-Hasidut: Sefer ha-Besht*, p. 247, #13; *Me'orot ha-Gedolim*, p. 11; and *The Hasidic Anthology*, p. 345. Do not be misled by the element in the parable that the sons derived no special enjoyment from the rich food at the king's table: That element should not be interpreted. The point is not that the Besht's disciples did not like his teachings! but that they were so used to his exalted teachings they might overlook the homely illustrations provided by the parables and stories.

6. *Toldot Yitzhak*, Preface, quoted in *Sippurim Nehmadim*, p. 6 (in *Sippurei Nifla'im*).

7. Note the similar story about Rabbi Menahem Mendel of Rimanov on page 127, where it is evident that stories are intended.

8. See p. 10.

9. *Rabbi Shalom Dovber, the Rebbe Rashab* (*Sefer ha-Toldot*), p. 42.

10. *Sefer ha-Dorot he-Hadash*, p. 46.

11. *Sefer Maaseh Gedolim he-Hadash*, Preface, p. 4.

12. For example, see *Ohel Elimelech*, Preface; I recently saw in *Rebbe Rayatz* (*Sefer ha-Toldot*) hasidic stories referred to as the "pearls of hasidic teaching."

13. Personal communication.

14. From an early draft of *Shlomo's Stories: Selected Tales*.

15. *Kadosh Yisrael*, vol. 2, p. 323.

CHAPTER 11:
SCRIPTURAL SUPPORT FOR STORYTELLING

1. Not a court of law; hasidic rebbes have a "court," as does a king or nobleman, that includes the rebbe's residence and the people necessary for the court's functioning.

2. Lubavitch is in Lithuania.

3. The Bible and Talmud being revealed and exoteric, the Kabbalah concealed and esoteric.

4. *Yalkut Shimoni* 1:13, p. 4b.

5. Probably miracle stories are meant.

6. *Shmuot v'Sippurim*, vol. 3, Preface to the first edition.

7. *Yemei Moharnat*, Preface to Part One.

8. Samuel Dresner, quoting a comment heard from Rabbi Abraham Joshua Heschel, "Heschel and Halakhah: The Vital Center," *Conservative Judaism* 43:4 (Summer 1991):27.

9. *Bereishit Rabbah* 80:18.

10. I've given two examples in the text, from the Rizhiner and the Radomsker. See Chapter 2, n. 6, for another example.

11. *Beit Ruzhin*, p. 63.

12. *Nifla'ot ha-Tiferet Shlomo*, Yaffah Sihatan, p. 15, #45.

13. *Vayikra Rabbah* 13.

14. *Nahar Shalom*, p. 57a, quoted in *Gan Hadasim*, p. 2b(4). This text is not absolutely clear. My understanding of it is based on its context in *Gan Hadasim* and its similarity to the teaching of Rabbi Shlomo of Radomsk (which precedes it on page 80 in my text) and Rabbi Naftali of Ropshitz. A phrase in *Pirkei Avot* 2:1 says: "and all your deeds [*maasecha*] shall be recorded in a [heavenly] book," meaning that God holds a person accountable for his deeds. Understanding *maasecha*

as "stories," Rabbi Naftali interpreted this to mean: The Holy One, blessed be He, shall take all the stories we recount today about the tzaddikim and in the future make of them a complete book of the Torah (*Zera Kodesh*, quoted in *Rabbeinu ha-Kodesh mi-Shinova*, Preface, p. 9).

CHAPTER 12:
STORYTELLING AMONG THE *MISNAGDIM*
AND NON-HASIDIM

1. "Tzaddik" can mean specifically a hasidic rebbe, who is a leader of a sect, or more generally any exceptionally righteous and holy person. In the latter sense it applies to non-hasidic leaders also.

2. For a good discussion about *maggidim*, see *Maggidim & Hasidim: Their Wisdom*, Introduction.

3. See Chapter 1, n. 2.

4. The only professional storyteller I know of is the lone individual sent out by the Baal Shem Tov (see Chapter 6).

5. Adapted from *Maggidim & Hasidim: Their Wisdom*, p. 136; the original is from the collection of all the Dubner Maggid's parables.

6. Do not confuse the legendary thirty-six hidden tzaddikim, for whose sake the world exists, with the eighteenth-century Eastern European movement of hidden tzaddikim discussed in Chapter 3.

7. Honi "the Circle-drawer," was a first-century B.C.E. saint, who in the Talmud is recorded as having performed a similar act.

8. *Sha'al Avicha v'Yagedcha*, p. 347.

9. It is a practice with hoary Jewish antecedents for students hungering to learn from their teachers to secretly observe their private doings.

CHAPTER 13:
DERIVING LESSONS FROM STORIES

1. *Likkutei Sichot* (English), vol. 1, p. xiv and p. 194; *Likkutei Dibburim* (English), vol. 3, p. 276.

2. *Sh'al Avicha V'yagedcha*, p. 5.

3. *Kovetz Sippurim 5713*, Preface.

4. *Likkutei Dibburim* (English), vol. 3, p. 123; cf. Rabbi Nahman of Bratzlav: "Every Torah teaching has its story" (*Tzaddik*, p. 225; *Hayei Moharan*, 220 [94]).

5. *Shmuot v'Sippurim*, vol. 3, p. iii.

6. An article by Rabbi David Hollander in *The Jewish Press* of Sept. 1991 suggested this thought.

7. Note again the motif of people so engrossed in telling stories that they forget to pray.

8. *Divrei David*, p. 4b(8); *Tales of the Hasidim*, vol. 1, p. 102, divided into two stories: "Nearness" and "Effect."

9. *Kovetz Sippurim 5713*, Preface.

10. Both of these quotes are from *Kovetz Sippurim 5713*, Preface.

11. *Kovetz Sippurim 5713*, p. 5, #7.

12. This tale is part of a longer story in *Rabbi Yisrael Baal Shem Tov*, vol. 1, pp. 349-352, volume of *Sefer ha-Toldot*.

13. See *Vayikra Rabbah* 83:5.

14. It is best, however, for a storyteller to try to add small explanations at places in the story where difficult elements appear.

15. *Ha-Hozeh mi-Lublin*, p. 265; oral version heard from Rabbi Shlomo Carlebach, which I used particularly for the ending.

CHAPTER 14:
HOW TO TELL, HOW TO LISTEN

1. *Kovetz Sippurim 5713*, Preface.

2. *Shomer Emunim*, I, p. 29a.

3. *Shomer Emunim*, I, p. 29a.

4. *Otzar Yisrael*, Preface, p. 2.

5. *B'Hetzer Pnimah*, vol. 2, p. 5.

6. *B'Hetzer Pnimah*, vol. 1, p. 16.

7. *Bereishit Rabbah* 20.

8. *Rabbi Nachman's Stories*, Publisher's Preface, p. vii; *Likkutei Moharan*, #234.

9. See in Chapter 19, n. 15, Rabbi Nahman's concern about telling holy stories to unworthy people.

10. *Likkutei Moharan*, I, #234.

11. *Likkutei Eitzot*, Eretz Yisrael, #17.

12. *Megillat Polin—Ha-Admor Hanoch Henech mi-Alexander*, p. 85.

13. In fact, a common method of hasidic Torah interpretation is to use stories about the hasidic rebbes to help explain stories about Torah heroes. Something Moses did may be perplexing, but when you see that the Baal Shem Tov did something similar, and perhaps with the Besht the story is fuller and more understandable, you now are able to comprehend Moses's action.

14. *Sippurim u'Maamarim Yekarim*, p. 6a (11) in *Sippurei Nifla'im*.

15. *Likkutei Dibburim* (English), vol. 1, p. 276. Using the Hebrew version, which has *haya mesapair sippur*, I've changed the English from "related something" to "told a story," to make the meaning clearer. I've also changed the spelling from "chassidim" to "hasidim."

16. *Rebbe Rashab* (*Sefer ha-Toldot*), p. 42.

17. *Tzaddik*, p. 226; *Hayei Moharan*, 221 (95).

18. *Rebbe Rayatz* (*Sefer ha-Toldot*), II, p. 92.

19. *Souls on Fire*, p. 258.

20. *Rebbe Rayatz (Sefer ha-Toldot)* I, p. 51.
21. *Rebbe Rayatz (Sefer ha-Toldot)*, I, p. 7.
22. The Dubner Maggid was the most celebrated *maggid* of the eighteenth century, the Kelmer Maggid of the nineteenth century.
23. *The Maggid Speaks*, p. 133.
24. *Ramakrishna As We Saw Him*, p. 9.

CHAPTER 15:
HEARING THE HINTS IN STORIES

1. All of Rabbi Kalonymus Kalman's quoted teaching comes from *Ma'or v'Shemesh*, Parshat Devarim.
2. All of the teaching of Rabbi Kalonymus Kalman comes from *Ma'or v'Shemesh*, Parshat Devarim.
3. *Beit Ruzhin*, p. 120.
4. *Likkutei Moharan*, quoted in *Sihot Tzaddikim*, Introduction, p. 1, in *Sefarim Kedoshim mi-Talmidei Baal Shem Tov*, vol. 27.
5. Horses need real food, not the "bread of affliction," matzah. Similarly, the body needs real food to be fit to serve God and should not be deprived or subjected to fasting and other self-afflictions.
6. *Adat Tzaddikim*, p. 28; *Sippurei Hasidim*, vol. 1, #332; *Tales of the Hasidim*, vol. 1, p. 175.

CHAPTER 16:
MIRACLE STORIES: WHAT TO BELIEVE

1. See a good discussion of this issue in the Author's Introduction to Zevin's *A Treasury of Chassidic Tales*.
2. *Beit Avraham* (Rabbi Abraham of Slonim), p. 161, quoted in *Ha-Sipporet ha-Hasidit*, p. 71.
3. See p. 45.
4. *Toldot ha-Niflaot*, p. 44, quoted in *Ha-Sipporet ha-Hasidit*, p. 71.
5. *Ha-Sipporet ha-Hasidit*, p. 71.
6. *Degel Mahaneh Yehudah*, #23.
7. *Sippurei ha-Besht*, p. 53.
8. *Zichron l'Rishonim*, quoted in *Sefer Baal Shem Tov*, Preface, p. 22, #43.
9. Letter of the *gaon*, author of *Daat Torah*, quoted in *Sefer Baal Shem Tov*, Preface, p. 22, #45.
10. *Franz Rosenzweig: His Life and Thought*, p. 246.
11. This is, of course, another version of the saying quoted previously in the name of Rabbi Shlomo of Radomsk.

12. *Shlomo's Stories: Selected Tales*, preface.

13. *Souls on Fire*, p. 7.

14. Martin Buber said about the hasidic tale: "The legend is no chronicle, but it is truer than the chronicle for those who know how to read it" (quoted by Scholem in *The Messianic Idea in Judaism*, p. 234).

15. *Sippurei Hasidim*, vol. 1, #268.

16. Note that this is not the kind of miracle story that the Besht complained about. In this story the Besht's piety is miraculously "highlighted" by the supernatural light.

17. *Siftei Kodesh*, quoted in *Kol Sippurei Baal Shem Tov*, vol. 4, p. 146. This story is about Rabbi Jacob Joseph of Polnoye, but since I already used another, different, story about how he became a disciple of the Besht, I omitted his name so as not to confuse the reader.

CHAPTER 17:
DIFFERENT STORY VERSIONS:
ISSUES OF TRUTH AND FALSEHOOD

1. *Nifla'ot ha-Tiferet Shlomo*, Yaffah Sihatan, p. 24.

2. *Darkei Hayim*, Preface, p. 4.

3. *Yeshuot Yisrael*, Preface.

4. *Beit Ruzhin*, p. 365.

5. *Ner Yisrael*, vol. 3, p. 175.

6. *Nifla'ot ha-Tiferet Shlomo*, Yaffah Sihatan, p. 23, #69-73. This attitude and approach is obviously derived from a widespread hasidic view about miracle stories: that the miracle may not have actually occurred, but that it could have. (See my discussion of this in Chapter 16.) However, this author applies the concept generally, not only to miracle stories, as can be seen from his discussion of the story of Job.

7. Personal communication.

8. This does not contradict what was stated in Chapter 15 about miracle tales, for even when telling a story that contains a miracle the teller does not believe occurred, the teller presents the story's own claim to truth.

CHAPTER 18:
HOW REBBES USE STORIES

1. *From My Father's Shabbos Table*, Translator's Introduction, p. 10.

2. *Sefer ha-Middot*, Mashiah, #1. The guide to text sources notes the allusion to Psalm 104:2 about wearing light as a garment. Garments can be skin (of animal nature) or light (of spiritual nature). The Talmud says that it was written

in Rabbi Meir's copy of the Torah that the garments God made for Adam and Eve were of light (*aleph-vav-resh*), not skin (*ayin-vav-resh*). When the "garments" of thought, speech, and action are spiritually elevated, they are of "light." See Chapter 17, n. 2.

3. The reason a person merits clothes by telling stories is perhaps also because stories "clothe" holy teachings.

4. *Tiferet Yisrael*, p. 27, #87.

5. Perhaps it was not only his tears that ripped up the heavenly decree but also his storytelling. See Chapters 19 and 20 about how stories can save.

6. Rabbi Arye Leib of Shpola, the Shpoler Grandfather.

7. *Beit Ruzhin*, p. 265; *Ner Yisrael*, vol. 4, p. 369, #7.

8. *A Treasury of Chassidic Tales on the Festivals*, vol. 1, pp. 50-51; *Beit Ruzhin*, p. 264.

9. The *Kiddush* begins with Genesis 1:31b-2:3.

10. *Niddah* 31a.

11. *Avot* 2:8.

12. *Sukkah* 42a.

13. At the age of three, when a child begins studying Torah and learning the Hebrew alphabet, a feast is made and charity distributed. The child is wrapped in a tallis and given sweet cookies shaped in the letters of the alphabet.

14. A tzaddik might make a match with a wealthy man, so the boy would be supported, and able to study Torah and engage full-time in divine service, without the necessity of earning a living.

15. *Tiferet ha-Tzaddikim*, p. 9a (17); *Beit Ruzhin*, p. 266.

16. See the story about Rabbi Israel of Rizhin on p. 13 in this text.

17. *Likkutei Sichot*, vol. 4, p. 67, referring to *Zohar* II:107a.

CHAPTER 19:
AN EXCEPTIONAL CASE:
RABBI NAHMAN OF BRATZLAV

1. *Sippurei Maasiyot*, p. 7; *Rabbi Nachman's Stories*, p. 8.

2. *Sippurei Maasiyot*, p. 7; *Rabbi Nachman's Stories*, Introduction, p. 8.

3. *Rabbi Nachman's Stories*, Second Introduction, p. 16.

4. "We heard [the Rebbe] say explicitly that every word of these holy stories has tremendous meaning, and that anyone who changes even a single word of these stories from the way that they were told is taking away very much from the story" (*Rabbi Nachman's Stories*, Introduction, p. 5).

5. *Sihot ha-Ran*, #151; *Rabbi Nachman's Wisdom*, p. 292.

6. *Rabbi Nachmans' Stories*, Publisher's Preface, p. vii.

7. *Hayei Moharan*, p. 8b (16), #25.

8. *Rabbi Nachman's Stories*, p. 396.

9. *Degel Mahaneh Ephraim*, Parshat Vayeshev, p. 21b, quoted in *Ha-Sippur ha-Hasidi*, p. 47.

10. *Degel Mahaneh Ephraim*, Parshat Ki Tissa, p. 42a.

11. Although the Shpoler Zeideh at first accepted Rabbi Nahman and his storytelling and even thought his storytelling good enough to emulate (*Tiferet Maharal*, p. 27a [53] end of #9), he later became his greatest opponent and disparaged the fantasy stories (Ibid., p. 48a [95], #24; *Ish ha-Pele*, p. 96).

12. *Likkutei Moharan*, I, #60.

13. See *The Tormented Master*, p. 342.

14. See *Hayei Moharan*, Sippurim Hadashim, pp. 18b-26a.

15. Thus, Rabbi Nachman could, for example, take different true hasidic stories that portrayed characters of the pious simpleton and combine them into an archetypal "pious simpleton."

16. Similar to the traditional concern about unworthy students misunderstanding the provocative metaphors of the Kabbalah and being led astray, Rabbi Nahman expressed his concern about telling these especially deep and holy tales to unworthy people. He stated, however, that if a person tells the tales with the proper intention, God will protect him by causing unworthy listeners to forget what they heard. Although this sounds mysterious and miraculous, it may actually represent Rabbi Nahman's own experience in telling his tales— that "unworthy" people were uninterested (*Likkutei Moharan* I, #60).

17. See Chapter 20, about rebbes telling stories that mystically aid women who are unable to conceive or who are having problems in childbirth.

18. *Likkutei Moharan*, I, #60, p. 73a.

19. *Likkutei Tefillot*, I, #105.

20. Elsewhere, Rabbi Nahman said: "Praising the tzaddikim is like praising the Holy One, blessed be He" (*Sefer ha-Middot*, Tzaddik, #147).

21. This translation is taken from *Rabbi Nachman's Stories*, pp. 128-137, with minor alterations.

CHAPTER 20:
STORIES SAVE

1. *Likkutei Moharan*, I, #234.

2. Rabbi Nahman teaches: "When a person wants to purify his mind by means of stories about a tzaddik, what happens is that the *deed* [of the tzaddik] and the *speech* (of the story) become his *thought*. And certainly the tzaddik whom he is telling the story about must be on a higher level than he is, in order that the stories of that tzaddik will be on the level of his *thought*. Therefore, one has to know . . . who to tell a story about, and then his mind will be purified" (*Likkutei Moharan*, I, #234).

3. Just as talking and telling stories about tzaddikim elevate our minds, talk-

ing and telling stories—or reading news or novels or watching movies—about wicked people, if not in an appropriate context, can lower our minds. "Talking about wicked people can lead to evil thoughts, and draw bad and evil down to the world, God forbid. Therefore, talk and tell stories about the good traits of tzaddikim [for that will lead to good thoughts] and draw good down to the world" (*Darkei Tzedek*, ot mem).

4. Everything God does is for good. What seems "bad" is only good that comes to us in a painful and difficult form.

5. *Likkutei Moharan*, I, #234. See also the prayer of Rabbi Nathan, based on Rabbi Nahman's teaching on p. 165 in my text.

6. *Hayei Moharan*, p. 53, Sihot Moharan, #33; *Tzaddik*, p. 397, #479.

7. *Sefer ha-Middot*, Tzaddik, #186.

8. Perhaps the tzaddikim whom the stories are about themselves mention the storyteller's righteousness in heaven. Rabbi Shalom of Belz said: "When people speak about tzaddikim, the tzaddikim receive pleasure in the World of Truth [the next world]. And since they do not want to be shamed by receiving, without repaying their benefactors, they return a flow of *parnosseh* [livelihood], fear of heaven, and all kinds of salvation" (*Otzar Yisrael*, p. 24b). See the Baal Shem Tov's teaching about this on pp. 45–46.

9. *Bamidbar Rabbah*, Parshat Pinhas, on the verse, "And the name of the man of Israel who was smitten."

10. *Kovetz Eliyahu*, Preface.

11. For example, see *Ner Yisrael*, vol. 2, p. 167, for the same teaching in the name of the Rizhiner.

12. There is a hasidic concept that storytelling about different tzaddikim—or even mentioning their names—arouses different, specific potencies, depending on the specific qualities of the tzaddikim. However, various rebbes had diverse views about what these correspondences were. "The holy rabbi, Rabbi Abraham Jacob of Sadagora, said that speaking on *Motza'ei Shabbat Kodesh* about the Baal Shem Tov is potent for the soul; about Rabbi Moshe Leib of Sassov, for livelihood; about Rabbi Levi Yitzhak of Berditchev, to sweeten judgments. One does not even have to mention his name; merely mentioning the town Berditchev effects a sweetening of judgments" (*Or ha-Shabbat*, p. 217). "Rabbi Isaac Meir of Ger said that speaking about the Holy Jew [Rabbi Jacob Isaac of Pshis'ha] is potent for attaining fear of heaven" (*Tiferet ha-Yehudi*, Preface). Rabbi Shalom of Belz said: "Telling stories on *Motza'ei Shabbat* about the Baal Shem Tov is potent for livelihood, about Rabbi Elimelech [of Lizensk], for the fear of heaven, and so on" (*Otzar Yisrael*, p. 241). The teaching of the "three mistakes," that telling stories of any of the tzaddikim at any time brings benefits both spiritual and material, seems to suggest a disagreement with this tendency to "specify" the efficacy of stories about particular rebbes.

13. *Pe'er v'Kavod*, p. 26; *Ner Yisrael*, vol. 2, p. 167, in the name of Rabbi Israel of Rizhin; *From My Father's Shabbos Table*, Preface, p. 8, in the name of the present Lubavitcher Rebbe, Rabbi Menachem Mendel Schneersohn.

14. This biblical prophet, who was Elijah's teacher, was also the Besht's teacher and came to him in visions and instructed him.

15. *Yeshuot Yisrael*, p. 135.

16. Reb Arele Roth writes that in order to sweeten the judgments by telling a story it is necessary to have the *kavvanah*, intention, to arouse the merit and holiness of the tzaddik (*Shomer Emunim*, 1, p. 28b).

17. *Pe'er v'Kavod*, p. 37b; *Ha-Niggun v'ha-Rikud b'Hasidut*, p. 28.

18. *Ha-Sipporet ha-Hasidit*, p. 65; see n. 38 there for further instances of this thought in hasidic writings.

19. *Agra d'Kallah*, Parshat Ekev, quoted in *Ha-Sipporit ha-Hasidit*, p. 65; see n. 39 there for other sources of this quote.

20. The real name of the Bach, who was one of the greatest rabbis of his time (1561-1640), was Rabbi Joel Sirkes; he is known by the acronym of the title of his *magnum opus*, the *Bayit Hadash*.

21. Personal communication, January 10, 1993.

22. *Helkat Yehoshua*, first *maamar*, quoted in *Yesod ha-Olam*, p. 370, #535. An entire chapter in the biography of the Rebbe of Shinova is about how he performed miracles through storytelling (*Rabbeinu ha-Kodesh mi-Shinova*, Chapter 28).

23. *Pe'er v'Kavod*, p. 26b.

24. Numbers 11:2–"And Moses prayed unto the Lord, and the fire abated."

25. *Kovetz Eliyahu*, p. 60, #196; *Tales of the Hasidim*, vol. 2, p. 103.

26. *Pe'er v'Kavod*, p. 26b. The source does not say which of the Rebbes of Ziditchov.

27. The present Lubavitcher Rebbe once told a story that included three of his predecessors, commenting afterward that he told the story in order to mention their names. *Kovetz Sippurim 5713*, p. 3.

28. *Sippurei Maasiyot*, p. 7; *Rabbi Nachman's Stories*, p. 8.

29. *Shivhei ha-Besht*, p. 163, #86.

30. Not to be confused with the Baal Shem Tov's daughter Edel, Rabbi Nahman's grandmother, after whom he named his daughter.

31. The leader of the Bratzlaver hasidim after Rabbi Nathan of Nemirov, Rabbi Nahman's chief disciple.

32. *Avaneha Barzel*, p. 37, #53.

33. However, the continuation of the story tells how it was finally told by Rabbi Nahman of Tultchin, Rabbi Nahman's disciple. Perhaps after this incident of healing his daughter, Rabbi Nahman of Bratzlav applied this teaching generally, or perhaps his disciples were considered to have his merit as did his children.

34. *Knesset Yisrael*, p. 12a (23); quoted in *Kol Sippurei Baal Shem Tov*, vol. 3, p. 44. A version of this story in *Sofer, Sefer v'Sippur*, by the religious Israeli author Agnon, has an additional ending, in which Rabbi Israel of Rizhin himself cures a boy.

35. However, the merit of the teller is also important. Most people do not work miracles, and it is no accident that the storyteller is a rebbe.

36. Author's comment.

37. *Ohel Yehoshua*, p. 172, #6.

38. See Glossary: **Kabbalah**.
39. See Glossary: **Baal Shem**.

CHAPTER 21:
STORIES SAVE–CONTINUED

1. According to tradition the prayers of the morning, afternoon, and evening were ordained by Abraham, Isaac, and Jacob, respectively.
2. *Tiferet Maharal* (the Shpoler Zeideh), p. 110, #38; *Beit Ruzhin*, p. 65; *Tiferet ha-Tzaddikim*, p. 19 (10a).
3. *Ner Yisrael*, vol. 1, p. 226; *Mazkeret Shem ha-Gedolim*, p. 185 (93a).
4. *Hayei Moharan*, p. 8b [16], #25; *Tzaddik*, p. 151.
5. Why her husband would divorce her is unclear. Is it because he was a low person and suspected she had consented to adultery?
6. *Siah Sarfei Kodesh*, II, p. 124, #476.
7. Rabbi Noah of Lechovitz told a humorous folktale to miraculously help a woman having difficulty in childbirth (*Or Yesharim*, p. 21a [41]). In that tale, two men are arguing in a comic way about who is right regarding a particular issue and in essence yelling back and forth "go in!" versus "go out!" Then the announcement comes that the woman, who is elsewhere, has given birth. In this case it seems the rebbe mystically "participated" in the "argument" whether the baby would stay in or come out and hurried it to its conclusion.
8. Source unknown.
9. *Maaseh Gedolim he-Hadash*, #37. I did not want to use in my text the story Rabbi Israel tells because it involves a crude anti-Christian joke and might offend some people. The story is of a Christian woman who disguises herself as a man and becomes a priest and Pope. She then engages in sex and later, during a speech in front of an audience of priests, gives birth. At the end of this story the Rizhiner called out "*Mazal tov!*" and announced that the woman having trouble in childbirth had just delivered. This story has many similarities to the one his father told in similar circumstances. In each case a Jewish woman having difficulty in childbirth was asked to identify with a woman in a tale who is immersed totally in uncleanness and "miraculously" gives birth. The uncleanness here is not only that the woman is Christian–Christianity representing an anti-Semitic and unclean religion–but that she is a Pope, the head of that religion. Moreover, "he" is the leader of all celibate priests, who certainly cannot give birth! Yet, if despite all the implausibilities, the Pope gives birth, so can the Jewish woman. It must be remembered that when this story was told the Jews were despised, persecuted, and subjected to terrible pogroms instigated by the priests. Under such circumstances, it is not surprising, or to their discredit, that they considered Christianity unclean. But since times have changed and I am certain some readers would find this story painful, even if they appreciated the circumstances I have mentioned, I wanted to spare them by keeping this material out of the text itself.

In Chapter 11, we discussed the rabbinic comment on the Torah story about Eliezer's mission to get a wife for Isaac, that the conversation and storytelling of the Patriarchs' servants was superior to the Torah teaching of their descendants. Rabbi Israel sometimes referred to this, on one occasion saying that when Eliezer saw he could not extricate Rebecca from the house of the wicked Laban by the mystic power of Torah-teaching, prayer, or *mitzvot*, he realized that he had to do it by storytelling. Again, a woman held by evil and unclean forces was freed by the mystical effect of storytelling (*Beit Ruzhin*, p. 62). In the story in which Rabbi Israel used a tale to help a woman in childbirth, he also explained what he was doing by referring to the rabbinic teaching about Eliezer, but he did not mention Rebecca.

10. The story the Rizhiner told was not even about a Jew. See n. 7.

11. Versions of this story are found in *Kerem ha-Hasidut*, 3, pp. 164-166; *Heichal Bobov*, p. 81; *Legends of the Hasidim*, p. 285, #61.

12. *Rabbeinu ha-Kodesh mi-Shinova*, vol. 2, pp. 391-393.

13. In the text he is called "the Alter (Old) Rebbe," as he is known among Lubavitcher hasidim.

14. *Rabbi Dovber ha-Maggid mi-Mezritch (Sefer ha-Toldot)*, p. 107f.

CHAPTER 22:
MESSIAH

1. *Kovetz Eliyahu*, p. 29, #96; see the similar stories in the Preface of that book and in *Otzar Yisrael*, p. 22, #24.

2. *Besorot Tovot*, Preface, first page, in *Sippurei Nifla'im; Sefer, Sofer, v'Sippur*, vol. 1, p. 438.

3. *Ner Yisrael*, vol. 1, p. 53; see also *Sippurei Tzaddikim he-Hadash*, Preface, p. 6.

4. See p. 189.

5. *Sefer ha-Middot*, Mashiah, #1. Based on *Bereishit Rabbah* 1:6, where there are two interpretations of Daniel 2:23, "the light dwells with Him," one that this light is the stories of the deeds of the tzaddikim, and the other that it is the light of the Messiah.

6. Literally, "our righteous Messiah."

7. This book, containing Sabbath and holiday teachings of the Peasetzner Rebbe in the Warsaw ghetto, was published under the title *Eish Kodesh* (Holy Fire).

8. *Connections* 4:1 (1988):17.

AFTERWORD

1. See Chapter 7, n. 22, about dates of *yahrzeits*.

2. The *Maggid Speaks*, p. 24.

Glossary

Aggadah Those sections of Talmud and *Midrash* containing homiletic exposition of the Bible, stories, legends, folklore, parables, anecdotes, or maxims. In contradistinction to *halachah.*

Ari Rabbi Isaac Luria, the great kabbalist (1534-1572).

Baal Shem A Jewish folk healer in the Europe of earlier centuries, who used folk remedies and incantations. Sometimes the founder of the hasidic movement, the Baal Shem Tov, is called "the Baal Shem," for short. See **Baal Shem Tov.**

Baal Shem Tov Rabbi Israel, son of Eliezer, the founder of the modern hasidic movement. "*Baal shem,*" the "Master of the Name," was a title for faith healers who used divine names, a controversial practice in some disrepute. Therefore, with Rabbi Israel (who was a faith healer, as well as a tzaddik and Torah teacher) *baal shem* was combined with "*shem tov,*" a "good name," that is, someone of good reputation. So the "good" faith healer came to be called the "Baal Shem Tov," which is an epithet, not a name. *Baal Shem Tov* is often shortened to its acronym "Besht."

Badhan Jester, particularly at traditional Jewish weddings in Eastern Europe.

Bar Mitzvah Ceremony marking the initiation of a boy at the age of thirteen into the adult Jewish religious community.

Beit Midrash House of Torah Study, also often used as a synagogue for prayer.

Besht See **Baal Shem Tov.**

Bimah The elevated platform in the synagogue from which the Torah scroll is read.

Bris Ritual circumcision.

Davven (v.) To pray (in a Jewish manner); *davvening* (n.): Jewish prayer.

Days of Awe From Rosh HaShanah through Yom Kippur.

Erev Eve. Generally used for the daylight hours before a holy day, as for example: *erev Shabbat, erev Rosh HaShanah,* and so on.

Gaon   A title denoting exceptional rabbinic learning and genius.

Gartel   A twined silk belt worn by hasidic men during prayer.

Gemara   The commentary and discussion on the *Mishnah* (which is the earlier text), the two together making up the Talmud.

Gevalt   Yiddish: Oh!

Habad   Another name for the Lubavitcher hasidic sect. *HaBaD* is the acronym for *Hochmah* (Wisdom), *Binah* (Understanding), *Daat* (Knowledge).

Haggadah   Rabbinic text about the Exodus story, recited in the home on Passover eve at the *seder* table.

Halachah   Jewish religious law.

Hanukkah   Eight-day celebration commemorating the victory of the Maccabees over the Syrian Greeks and the subsequent rededication of the Temple in Jerusalem.

Hasid (pl. *Hasidim*; f. *Hasidah*, pl. *Hasidot*)   A pious person; specifically, a follower of a hasidic saint (*rebbe*, tzaddik) and a member of the hasidic movement of the Baal Shem Tov.

Hasidism   (1) Piety; (2) the pietistic movement founded by the Baal Shem Tov.

Havdalah   End-of-Sabbath ceremony that separates holy and profane time.

Hillula   A celebration of the anniversary of the death of a famous tzaddik.

Kabbalah   The main trend of Jewish mysticism or its texts. The Kabbalah is usually divided into two branches: one "theoretical," i.e., mystical and speculative; the other "practical," i.e., occult and magical, to produce miracles.

Kavvanah   The intention directed toward God while performing a religious act. Can also mean a particular intention (for a prayer, etc.); the plural in the latter usage is *kavvanot*.

Kiddush   The blessing over the wine made when ushering in a Sabbath or festival.

L'hayim   A Hebrew blessing and toast: "To life!"

Maariv   The daily evening prayer service.

Maaseh (pl. *Maasim*)   A "deed" or a "story"; *maasav*: "his deeds" or "stories."

Maaseh Merkavah   The mystic study of the Divine Chariot of the prophet Ezekiel's vision.

Maggid (pl. *Maggidim*)   Title for a preacher.

Mazal tov   Good Luck!

Melamed   A primary school teacher.

Melaveh Malkah   A feast immediately after the Sabbath to "accompany" it as it departs.

Midrash   Exposition or exegesis of the Scriptures, often including parables, sayings, and stories. The *Midrash* is the book or body of literature; a *midrash* is a particular teaching.

Mikveh   Ritual bath.

Minhah   The daily afternoon prayer service.

Minyan   Minimum prayer quorum of ten men.

Mishnah Ancient collection of legal decisions of the sages; the earliest part of the Talmud, it is the text to which the *Gemara*, the other part, is the commentary. With a lower case "m," a *mishnah* (pl. *mishnayot*) is one teaching from the *Mishnah*.

Mishnayos Ashkenazic pronunciation of *mishnayot*. See **Mishnah**.

Misnagid (pl. *Misnagdim*) An opponent of the hasidic movement of the Baal Shem Tov.

Mitzvah (pl. *Mitzvot*) A divine commandment.

Moshiah Messiah.

Motza'ei Shabbat The "departure of the Sabbath." The period following the end of the Sabbath, Saturday night.

Niggun A melody.

Parshah The weekly portion of the Five Books of Moses read on a Sabbath.

Rabban An ancient title of supreme distinction conferred on heads of the central academy or Sanhedrin.

Rabbeinu A title: "Our Rabbi."

Rashi The acronym for *R*abbi *Sh*lomo (ben) *Y*itzhak of Troyes, France (1040-1105), the great commentator of Bible and Talmud.

Rav A title for a rabbi, particularly one competent to rule on issues of Jewish law.

Reb A title of respect; Mister.

Rebbe A hasidic rabbi and sect leader of the movement of the Baal Shem Tov; often used as a title, sometimes together with Reb, for example, the Rebbe Reb Elimelech. Almost all rebbes were and are rabbis, but very few rabbis are rebbes.

Rebbetzin A rabbi's wife.

Rosh HaShanah The Jewish New Year and Day of Judgment.

Rosh Hodesh The Festival of the New Moon/Month.

Rosh Yeshivah The head of a *yeshivah*.

Segulah An object or act of mystical potency.

Selihot Early morning penitential prayers said during the days leading up to the High Holidays.

Shabbat Hebrew for Sabbath; in Yiddish: *Shabbos*.

Shaharit The daily morning prayer service.

Shammos Synagogue caretaker.

Shavuot The Festival of Weeks.

Shechinah The Divine Presence in this world; God as immanent.

Shemoneh Esreh The "Eighteen [Blessings]." The central prayer of the prayer service.

Sh'ma (Yisrael) The "Hear O Israel" prayer; the central faith declaration in Judaism: "The Lord is our God; the Lord is one."

Shofar The ram's horn, primarily blown in the synagogue on Rosh HaShanah.

Sholom aleichem Traditional Jewish greeting, "Peace be upon you"; answered by "*Aleichem sholom*," "Upon you be peace."

Shtibel   A small and intimate synagogue/*Beit Midrash* in a private home.

Succos   Ashkenazic pronunciation of Sukkot.

Sukkah   The booth used as a "temporary home" during the Festival of Sukkot.

Sukkot   The Festival of Booths (Tabernacles).

Tallis   Prayer shawl.

Talmud   The compendious series of volumes, which is, after the Bible, the most authoritative text in Judaism. It is comprised of the (earlier) *Mishnah* and the (later) discussion and commentary, based on the *Mishnah*, called the *Gemara*. The terms Talmud and *Gemara* are often used interchangeably.

Tefillin   Phylacteries. Worn on the head and the arm during the morning prayers.

Tikkun Hatzot   The midnight prayer service and vigil.

Torah   The revealed teachings of God. Can mean the Five Books of Moses, the whole Bible, or, more broadly, all Jewish religious writings throughout the ages; it can also refer to oral teaching given by a Torah teacher.

Tshuvah   Repentance; literally, "turning (back to God)."

Tzaddik (fem. *Tzaddeket*, pl. Tzaddikim)   (1) A righteous or holy person; (2) charismatic leader of a hasidic sect; a rebbe.

Unification (*Yihud*)   In a technical sense, usually a kabbalistic meditation on one of the letter configurations of the four-letter Name of God, or on configurations of such names with different vocalizations; also has a broader meaning of any meditative activity that unites the Holy One, blessed be He, with His *Shechinah*, the upper and lower worlds.

Yahrzeit   The anniversary of a death.

Yarmulke   Jewish skullcap.

Yeshivah   A higher Jewish religious school for the study of the Torah.

Yid   Yiddish for Jew. "*Hasidisher Yid*" is a hasidic Jew.

Yiddele   An affectionate diminutive for "Jew."

Yihud (pl. *Yihudim*)   See Unification.

Yom Kippur   The yearly Day of Atonement.

Zemirot   Devotional Sabbath table songs.

Zeideh   Yiddish for grandfather.

Bibliography

Adat Tzaddikim (1959). Jerusalem.

Avaneha Barzel (1972). Rabbi Abraham, the son of Rabbi Nahman of Tulchin. Jerusalem.

The Baal Shem Tov (1978). Z. A. Hilsenrad. Brooklyn: Kehot.

Beit Aharon (1972). Jerusalem.

Beit Karlin-Stolin (1981). Y. Yisraeli (Kula). Tel Aviv: Keren Yaakov v'Rahel (Peninah).

Beit Ruzhin (1987). Y. Klapholtz. Bnei Brak: Mishor.

Besorot Tovot (in *Sippurei Nifla'im*) (1927).

B'Hetzer Pnimah (1992). Y. Even. Edited by M. Moriah. Tel Aviv: Moriah.

B'Ohalei Tzaddikim (1990). C. S. Gluckman. Hillside, NJ: Mosad Zecher Naftali.

Butzina Kadisha (1957). Nathan Netta HaCohen. Jerusalem.

Communicating the Infinite (1990). N. Lowenthal. Chicago: University of Chicago Press.

Connections/Hakrev u'Shma (magazine). New York: The Inner Foundation.

Darkei Hayim (1968). R. Tzimetboim. Tel Aviv.

Darkei Tzedek (1965). Jerusalem.

Degel Mahaneh Ephraim (1986). Rabbi Moshe Hayim Ephraim of Sudilkov. Jerusalem: Hamol.

Degel Mahaneh Yehudah (1957). Rabbi E. Brandwein. Jerusalem.

Derech Emunah u'Maaseh Rav. Y. S. H. Lipshitz.

Devash ha-Sadeh (1972). Rabbi Dovberish (the shohet of Risha). Jerusalem.

A Dialogue with Hasidic Tales (1988). M. Friedman. New York: Human Sciences Press.

Divrei David (1863). Compiled by Y. Rapoport. Tchortkov.

Emet v'Emunah (1972). Rabbi Menahem Mendel of Kotzk. Compiled by Rabbi Y. Y. Orton. Jerusalem.

Encyclopaedia Judaica (1972). "Maggid." Haim Hillel Ben-Sasson. Jerusalem: Keter.

Franz Rosenzweig: His Life and Thought (1970). N. Glatzer. New York: Schocken.

From My Father's Shabbos Table (1991). Rabbi Y. Chitrik. Translated by Rabbi E. Touger. Jerusalem: Vagshal.

Gan Hadasim. Edited by Eleazar Dov, son of Rabbi Aaron of Koznitz.

The Gates of the Forest (1982). E. Wiesel. New York: Schocken.

The Hasidic Anthology (1968). L. Newman. New York: Schocken.

Hasidut Breslov (1972). M. Piekarz. Jerusalem: Bialik Institute.

Hayei Moharan (1962). Jerusalem.

Ha-Hozeh mi-Lublin (1985). Y. Klapholtz. Bnei Brak: Pe'er ha-Sefer.

Heichal Bobov (1986). A Surasky. Kiryat Bobov, Israel: Hesed l'Avraham.

In Praise of the Baal Shem Tov (1972). Edited and translated by D. Ben-Amos and J. Mintz. Bloomington, IN: Indiana University Press.

Ish ha-Pele (1987). M. Miller. Jerusalem: Machon Zecher Naftali.

Jewish Spiritual Practices (1990). Yitzhak Buxbaum. Northvale, NJ: Jason Aronson Inc.

Kadosh Yisrael, vol. II (1975). N. E. Roth. Bnei Brak: Machon l'Hotzat v'Hafatzat Sifrei Rabboteinu ha-Kedoshim.

Kerem ha-Hasidut, vol. III (1986). Jerusalem: Machon Zecher Naftali.

Keter Shem Tov (1968). Aaron of Apt. Jerusalem.

Knesset Yisrael (1976). Rabbi Israel of Rizhin. Edited by R. Ostila. Israel.

Kol Sippurei Baal Shem Tov (1976). Compiled and edited by Y. Klapholtz. Bnei Brak: Pe'er ha-Sefer.

Kovetz Eliyahu (1983). Rabbi H. E. Sternberg. Jerusalem.

Kovetz Sippurim 5713 (1992). Rabbi M. M. Schneersohn of Lubavitch. Brooklyn: Kehot.

Kovetz Sippurim 5718-5719 (1992). Rabbi M. M. Schneersohn of Lubavitch. Brooklyn: Kehot.

The Legends of Genesis (1964). H. Gunkel. New York: Schocken.

Legends of the Hasidim (1968). J. Mintz. Chicago: University of Chicago Press.

Likkutei Dibburim (1987). Rabbi Y. Y. Schneersohn of Lubavitch. 4 vols. Translated by U. Kaploun. New York: Kehot.

Likkutei Eitzot (1974). Rabbi Nahman of Bratzlav. Bnei Brak: Or Zorayah.

Likkutei Moharan (1976). Rabbi Nahman of Bratzlav. Jerusalem.

Likkutei Tefillot (1978). Rabbi Nathan of Breslov. Brooklyn: Hasidim of Bratzlav.

Maaseh ha-Gedolim he-Hadash (1925). M. Z. Sladovnik. Warsaw.

Maasiyot u'Maamarim Yekarim (in *Sippurei Nifla'im*) (1903). Y. W. Tzikernik. Zhitomir.

The Maggid Speaks (1987). Rabbi Sholom Schwadron. Edited by P. Krohn. New York: Mesorah.

Maggidim & Hasidim: Their Wisdom (1962). L. Newman. New York: Bloch.

Ma'or v'Shemesh (1986). Rabbi Kalonymus Kalman Epstein of Cracow. Jerusalem: Galim.

Mazkeret Shem ha-Gedolim (1967). Edited by E. H. Kleinman. Bnei Brak: Binah.

Megillat Polin: Ha-Admor Hanoch Henoch mi-Alexander (1969). Y. L. Levine. Jerusalem: Daat.

Me'orot ha-Gedolim. Compiled by A. Zeilingold. Reprint of Bilgoray edition.

The Messianic Idea in Judaism (1972). G. Scholem. New York: Schocken.

Midrash Ribesh Tov (1927). Rabbi Israel Baal Shem Tov. Edited by L. Abraham. Kecskemet, Hungary.

Ner Yisrael (1987). Edited by H. D. Stern. 4 vols. Bnei Brak.

Nifla'ot ha-Tiferet Shlomo (1975). Rabbi Abraham Samuel Tzvi Hirsh. Israel.

Ha-Niggun v'ha-Rikud b'Hasidut (1954). M. S. Geshuri. Tel Aviv: Netzah.

Noam Elimelech (1978). Rabbi Elimelech of Lizensk. Jerusalem.

Ohel Elimelech (1968). Edited by A. H. S. B. Michelzohn. Israel.

Ohel Yehoshua (1977). Rabbi Joshua of Belz. Jerusalem: Mahzikei Torah d'Hasidei Belz.

Or ha-Shabbat (1975). A. Y. Eisenbach. Jerusalem.

Or Yesharim (1967). Edited by M. H. Kleinman. Jerusalem.

Otzar ha-Sippurim. T. Moskowitz. Jerusalem.

Otzar Yisrael (1992). Rabbi Y. H. Rosenzweig. Compiled and edited by M. H. Bloom. Jerusalem.

Paamei Bat Melech (1984). Y. Elstein. Ramat Gan, Israel: Bar-Ilan University.

Pe'er v'Kavod (1970). B. Ehrman. Jerusalem.

Rabbeinu ha-Kodesh mi-Shinova (1992). E. S. Frankel. Bnei Brak: Mishor.

Rabbi Dovber ha-Maggid mi-Mezritch. Volume of *Sefer ha-Toldot* (1986). Rabbi A. H. Glitzenstein. Brooklyn: Kehot.

Rabbi Nachman's Stories (1983). Rabbi Nahman of Bratzlav, translated by Rabbi A. Kaplan. New York: The Breslov Research Institute.

Rabbi Nachman's Wisdom (1983). Rabbi Nathan of Breslov. Translated by Rabbi A. Kaplan, edited by Rabbi Z. A. Rosenfeld. New York.

Rabbi Shalom Dovber, the Rebbe Rashab. Volume of *Sefer ha-Toldot* (1987). Rabbi A. H. Glitzenstein. Brooklyn: Kehot.

Rabbi Shneur Zalman, Rabbeinu ha-Zaken, vol. 3. Volume of *Sefer ha-Toldot* (1986). Rabbi A. H. Glitzenstein. Brooklyn: Kehot.

Rabbi Yisrael Baal Shem Tov, vol. 1. Volume of *Sefer ha-Toldot* (1986). Rabbi A. H. Glitzenstein. Brooklyn: Kehot.

Ramakrishna As We Saw Him (1990). Ed. and trans. Swami Chetanananda. St. Louis, MO: Vedanta Society of St. Louis.

Rebbe Rashab. Volume of *Sefer ha-Toldot* (1987). Rabbi A. H. Glitzenstein. Brooklyn: Kehot.

Rebbe Rayatz. Volume of *Sefer ha-Toldot* (1987). Rabbi A. H. Glitzenstein. Brooklyn: Kehot.

Reshimot Devarim (1981). Yehudah Chitrik. Brooklyn.

Sefer Baal Shem Tov. Edited by Rabbi S. M. M. Gorvachov. Jerusalem.

Sefer ha-Besht. Volume of *Be'er ha-Hasidut.* E. Steinman. Israel: Machon l'Hotzat Sifrei Kabbalah, Mahshavah, Hasidut.

Sefer ha-Dorot he-Hadash (1965). Jerusalem.

Sefer ha-Middot (1978). Rabbi Nahman of Bratzlav. Jerusalem: Hasidim of Bratzlav.

Sh'al Avicha v'Yagedcha (1992). Rabbi S. Schwadron. Edited by I. Spiegel. Jerusalem: Machon Daat.

Shivhei ha-Baal Shem Tov (1990). Rabbi Dov Ber ben Samuel. Edited by Rabbi E. H. Carlebach. Jerusalem: Machon Zecher Naftali.

Shlomo's Stories: Selected Tales (1994). Shlomo Carlebach with Susan Yael Mesinai. Northvale, NJ: Jason Aronson Inc.

Shmuot v'Sippurim, vol. III (1990). Rabbi Rafael Nahman HaCohen. North Bergen, NJ.

Shomer Emunim (1978). Rabbi A. Roth. Jerusalem.

Siah Sarfei Kodesh. Y. K. K. Rokotz.

Sifran Shel Tzaddikim (1959). Edited by Eleazar Dov, son of Rabbi Aaron. Jerusalem.

Sihot ha-Ran (1961). Rabbi Nahman of Bratzlav. Jerusalem: Hasidei Breslov.

Sihot Tzaddikim (1985). Sefarim Kedoshim mi-Talmidei Baal Shem Tov ha-Kodesh, vol. 27. New York: Beit Hillel.

Ha-Sipporet ha-Hasidit (1981). G. Nigal. Jerusalem: Y. Marcus and Partners.

Ha-Sippur ha-Hasidi (1975). Y. Dan. Jerusalem: Keter.

Sippurei ha-Besht (1987). P. Sadeh. Jerusalem: Karta.

Sippurei Hasidim (1957) Compiled and edited by S. Y. Zevin. Jerusalem: Beit Hillel.

Sippurei Maasiyot (1976). Rabbi Nahman of Bratzlav. New York: Hasidei Breslov.

Sippurei Tzaddikim he-Hadash (1908). Rabbi A. Y. Zinkowitz. New York: Pardes.

Sippurim Nehmadim (in *Sippurei Nifla'im*) (1903). Y. W. Tzikernik. Zhitomir.

Sippurim Nifla'im (1976). H. Y. Malik. Jerusalem.

Sippurim u'Maamarim Yekarim (in *Sippurim Nifla'im*) (1903). Compiled by Y. W. Tzikernik. Warsaw.

Sofer, Sefer v'Sippur (1978). S. Agnon. Jerusalem: Schocken.

Souls on Fire (1972). E. Wiesel. New York: Random House.

The Storyteller (1981). N. Mindel. Brooklyn: Merkos l'Inyanei Chinuch.

Storytellers, Saints and Scoundrels (1989). K. Narayan. Philadelphia: University of Pennsylvania Press.

The Tales of Rabbi Nachman (1978). Edited by A. Band. New York: The Paulist Press.

Tales of the Hasidim (1973). Compiled, edited and translated by M. Buber. New York: Schocken.

Tiferet ha-Tzaddikim (No date). S. G. Rosenthal. Reprint of Warsaw edition.

Tiferet ha-Yehudi. Y. K. K. Rokotz.

Tiferet Maharal (1975). Y. Y. Rosenberg. New York: Ateret.

Tiferet Sh'B'Malchut (1986). Y. Alfasi. Israel: Ohel Moshe.

Tiferet Yisrael (1974). Yerahmiel Israel Isaac of Alexander. Bnei Brak: Machon l'Hotzat Sefarim v'Kitvei-yad d'Hasidei Alexander.

The Tormented Master (1978). A. Green. Tuscaloosa, AL: University of Alabama Press.

A Treasury of Chassidic Tales on the Festivals (1981). Vol. 1. Rabbi S. Y. Zevin. New York: ArtScroll/Mesorah.

Tzaddik (Chayey Moharan) (1987). Rabbi Nathan of Breslov. Translated by A. Greenbaum. Edited by M. Mykoff. New York: Breslov Research Institute.

Yemei Moharnat (1968). Rabbi Nathan of Breslov. New York.

Yeshuot Malko (1974). Jerusalem: Mosad ha-Rav Y. M. Levine.

Yeshuot Yisrael (1986). Rabbi Eliezer Hayim. Brooklyn.

Yesod ha-Olam (1990). Compiled and edited by M. Sharf and I. M. M. Brocher. Bnei Brak.

Credits

Every effort has been made to ascertain the owner of copyrights for the selections used in this volume and to obtain permission to reprint copyrighted passages. The author would like to express his gratitude to the parties listed below for their permission to use material from their publications. He will be pleased, in subsequent editions, to correct any inadvertent error or omission that is discovered.

Stories and Parables Index

Entries are listed according to the order in which they appear in the text.

General Index

Aaron Asher, Rabbi, 14
Aaron of Karlin, Rabbi, 14
Abraham, God appeared to, 99
Abraham, Isaac, and Jacob ordained
  three daily prayers, 187-188, 230
  n. 1
Abraham Jacob of Sadagora, Rabbi,
  59, 62, 228 n. 12
Aggadah, 17, 67, 68, 101, 103, 219
  n. 8
Agnon, 229 n. 34
Aha, Rav, 79, 80, 213 n. 6
Ahiyah, 176, 182
Alexanderer Rebbe, Old. See
  Hanoch Henech of Alexander,
  Rabbi
Allegory, 145-147, 150, 157, 194
Altshtader, Abraham, 59-64
Angels as God's Throne or Chariot,
  220 n. 3
Applications for storytelling today,
  209-211
Archetypes, fantasy tales as, 164
Arele, Reb. See Roth, Rabbi Aaron
Ari, 188
Av ha-Rahamim prayer, 180

Baal shem (faith healer, miracle
  worker), 132, 185
Baal Shem Tov, Rabbi Israel, 7, 9, 15,
  25, 27, 29-43, 59, 77, 100, 101-
  103, 108, 120-122, 147, 157,
  175-176, 188-189, 204, 214 n. 6,
  217 chap. 7 nn. 3, 4, 218 n. 3,
  220 n. 3, 223 chap. 14 n. 13, 228
  n. 12, 229 n. 14
  as baal shem, 132, 185, 189
  as hidden tzaddik, 17-23, 100, 131,
    217 chap. 7 n. 4
  as melamed, 18-19
  attracts crowds with storytelling,
    19-22, 100-101
  believe miracle stories about, 128
  parables and stories by, 21-22, 70,
    220 n. 5
  posthumous appearance, 71, 126,
    135, 182
  prays that storytelling about him
    saves, 176
  stories about and told by. See
    Stories and Parables Index
  storyteller disciple, 33-40, 222
    chap. 12 n. 4

ABOUT THE AUTHOR

Yitzhak Buxbaum is a *maggid*, an inspired and inspiring teacher and story-teller, who teaches at synagogues, Jewish community centers, and colleges. He graduated from Cornell University and has an advanced degree from the University of Michigan. The author of *Jewish Spiritual Practices* and *The Life and Teachings of Hillel*, he resides in New York City.